An illuminating look at a controversial icon,
the Playboy Bunny

The Bunny Years

"We were young women on the move, out there pushing a new frontier. We were like sisters learning together how to take charge of our own lives."

—Lauren Hutton, supermodel and actress

"When I look back at it, I'm glad I had the experience. . . . So much of life goes by with a sameness, but the experience of being a Bunny has a sharp, electric blue kind of color. The same color as my costume."

—Susan Sullivan, actress

"Being a Bunny involved a rare combination for a woman in the workplace—beauty, femininity, sexuality, and at the same time, ambition and intelligence. . . . Bunnies *were* the Playboy Club."

—Deborah Harry, musician

"I didn't have a lot of options when I started out. Nobody did. . . . Working at the Club gave me the opportunity to do something I had always dreamed of doing, which would probably not have happened otherwise."

—Barbara Bosson, actress

This title is also available as an eBook

THE Bunny YEARS

KATHRYN LEIGH SCOTT

GALLERY BOOKS

NEW YORK   LONDON   TORONTO   SYDNEY   NEW DELHI

G

Gallery Books
A Division of Simon & Schuster, Inc.
1230 Avenue of the Americas
New York, NY 10020

Originally published by Pomegranate Press, Ltd. book

First Gallery Books trade paperback edition October 2011

GALLERY BOOKS and colophon are registered trademarks of Simon & Schuster, Inc.

For information about special discounts for bulk purchases, please contact
Simon & Schuster Special Sales at 1-866-506-1949 or business@simonandschuster.com.

The Simon & Schuster Speakers Bureau can bring authors to your live event. For more
information or to book an event, contact the Simon & Schuster Speakers Bureau at
1-866-248-3049 or visit our website at www.simonspeakers.com.

Designer: *Cheryl Carrington*
Photography Editor: *Ben Martin*
Editors: *Smae Spaulding Davis, Rodger Claire*

Manufactured in the United States of America

10 9 8 7 6 5 4 3 2 1

Library of Congress Cataloging-in-Publication Data is available.

ISBN 978-1-4516-6327-3
ISBN 978-1-4516-6328-0 (ebook)

For Mother

and Geoff, with all my love.

Acknowledgments

hanks to a stimulating and rather nostalgic dinner conversation one evening with two close friends and former Bunnies, Susan Sullivan and B.J. Ward, and their mates, Connell Cowan and Gordon Hunt, and my husband, Geoff Miller, the notion of writing *The Bunny Years* was born. I thank them all for the inspiration, and even more for their steadfast encouragement during the four years it has taken to produce this book.

I also want to extend my gratitude to Hugh M. Hefner, who generously and graciously provided me with access to his personal library, and to the many people at Playboy Enterprises who helped me with the research and preparation of this book. I'm especially grateful to all of them for never once attempting to influence me in the telling of this story. My special thanks to Richard Rosenzweig and Jonathan Black for their wonderful support and assistance throughout this project, and to Steve Randall, Tom Staebler, Gary Cole, Gretchen Edgren, Tim Hawkins, Elizabeth Georgiou, Marcia Terrones, Barbara Hoffman, Cindy Rakowitz, Elizabeth Norris, Bill Farley and Diane Stefani, without whom I could not have completed this book. My warm appreciation to LeRoy Neiman for his beautiful illustrations, and to William Hamilton for providing me with my favorite Bunny cartoon.

I thank my mother, Hilda Kringstad, for, among many things, saving all the letters I wrote home, and for continuing to be such a loving and inspiring influence on my life. I also thank Kari Kringstad and my brothers Orlyn and David for their love and support. My gratitude to Duane Poole for always being there for me. My heartfelt appreciation to my publishing partner, Ben Martin, for photographing the former Bunnies profiled in this book, and for his adept production assistance throughout this project.

Among the many other people I want to acknowledge for their support and assistance are my publishing pals that I can always turn to for advice in times of need: Heather Cameron, Kimberly Cameron, Roy Carlisle, Patrice Connolly, Ginger Curwen, Laurie Fox, Jonathan Kirsch, Carol Judy Leslie and Lisa See. My thanks to the divine Smae Spaulding Davis (as always!), Rodger Claire and to designer Cheryl Carrington, who helped more than anyone to shape and pull this book together. Thanks also to Robert Sanders, Patrick DeBlasi, Jim Pierson, David Schwartz and Larry Worth for helping out in times of need. A special thank you to Sunnie Choi, Katie Hennig Bucklin and Shana Ting Lipton, three wonderful and talented young women who have assisted me over the years with research and office support.

Above all, my love and gratitude to the many former Bunnies who trusted me, confided in me and shared memories of their own Bunny years.

Foreword

I didn't meet Kathryn Leigh Scott when she worked as a Bunny in the New York Playboy Club in 1963. By then, we had Clubs in Chicago, New Orleans and Miami, and the array of young women who had donned the ears and cottontail numbered, in the roughest of estimates, at least 1,000. I pride myself on my ability to remember names and faces—female ones, at least—but even I could never hope to know all the Bunnies.

By the time Kathryn and I met in 1997, she was not just a former Bunny but also an accomplished actress and writer, and was well into her research for the labor of love that would become this book. I was hardly surprised to hear that a Bunny had gone on to do great things—you may already know that Lauren Hutton, Susan Sullivan and Deborah Harry (of the rock group Blondie) had been Bunnies. Kathryn had already interviewed more than 200 former Bunnies, including some of the original Chicago Bunnies, who had lived with me in the Mansion, and others who had worked as Jet Bunnies aboard my DC9-30, the Big Bunny. Among other former Bunnies, there were doctors, lawyers, teachers, entrepreneurs—and to a woman, they all saw their own Bunny years as crucial to their personal and professional development.

Was I surprised at the Bunnies' success? No. Was I proud of them? You bet.

I knew I had to give Kathryn access to my personal library of Playboyalia to continue her research, and I did. I don't do that for just anyone.

The result was *The Bunny Years*, Kathryn Leigh Scott's true, behind-the-scenes stories of life in the Club that embodied the sexual revolution, and the women who led the way. Donning the iconic Bunny costume meant not only appearing beautiful and desired; it also meant being confident and daring. For many Bunnies, working at the Playboy Club was the first step to financial independence—in a job where a girl fresh out of high school could earn as much as her father, while attending college or even starting a business of her own. Bunnies learned to handle their money and handle men. A Bunny was always a lady and never a plaything. In the following pages, you'll meet famous actresses, rock stars, restaurateurs and scientists, and you'll get an inside look at how working as a Playboy Bunny prepared hundreds of young women to enter a dramatically challenging world.

I am happy to say that the Playboy Clubs are still going today. After 25 years in hibernation, the Bunnies are back in a Playboy Club at the Palms Casino in Las Vegas. The Playboy Club is once again the hottest ticket in town. We've expanded our operations to Cancún, Macao and London (and along the way celebrated the Bunny's fiftieth anniversary) and everywhere we go people are as crazy about the Bunnies now as they were when they first appeared in the original club in Chicago on February 29, 1960. And just as Bunnies were featured in *Playboy After Dark*, the late-night television series I hosted in the 1960s, the Bunnies are back in an NBC prime-time series, *The Playboy Club*.

In a world where you can get just about any sort of thrill you want, whether in real life or online, it becomes ever more clear that a Bunny is more than just a desirable girl in a flattering outfit. Playboy has always stood for the very best, whether in food, fashion or music. Every man lucky enough to be a Playboy Club Keyholder knew that behind those doors was a world others only hoped to enter. Even today, the timeless glamour of the Playboy Club still sets the standards for sophisticated entertainment.

I hope you'll consider *The Bunny Years* your personal VIP invitation to sit back, enjoy a cocktail, and experience its irresistible allure for yourself.

Contents

Introduction

"Bunny Marie," 1963.

*Y*ou're . . ." said Gloria Steinem, with one of those give-me-a-second palms-up gestures.

"Oh, you won't remember me," I said.

It had been nearly 30 years since we worked together. I hadn't even expected to see her at the well-populated party launching a publisher's Fall List, which included Steinem's much-anticipated book, *The Revolution Within*. But as I threaded my way through the crowded room, Steinem had emerged from a group of booksellers right in front of me. When our eyes met, I thought I caught a vague flicker of recognition.

"I was Bunny Kay," I continued. "We worked together at the Playboy Club in New York."

"Oh, dear," she muttered. The sentence trailed off as she began backing away. To fill an awkward pause she added, "Are you doing anything now?"

"Yes," I answered. "I have my own publishing company."

As the gap between us widened, she ventured, "Oh, well, I guess there *is* life after Bunnydom."

"I never doubted it," I replied.

She was quickly inundated by a throng of admirers who had come to see America's foremost feminist. I turned away, astonished by the feelings the encounter provoked in me. Part of me wanted to reach out, catch her arm and say, "Wait a minute! Did you really think that the rest of us would stay on to work as Bunnies all our lives?" On the other hand, why hadn't I just congratulated her on the book and told her I couldn't wait to read it?

I was surprised to see how anxious she was to distance herself from even the slightest memory of the women like myself she had written about in her now-fabled piece, "A Bunny's Tale," for *Show* magazine in 1963 when she had secretly taken a job as a Playboy Bunny in order to do an exposé on the newly opened Club. Could it be a vestigial pang of guilt even now for deceiving her coworkers? Probably not. But I was just as surprised by my own reaction: As one of the Bunnies she had portrayed in the article, I still harbored after all these years a mild residue of resentment over what had seemed at the time a kind of betrayal.

Gloria Steinem and I had become Bunnies for very different reasons. Many of the girls, teenagers like myself, were aspiring actresses or models and college students. Some were single mothers. Most of us who stood in line and waited to fill out job applications wanted the job because of the convenient hours, the flexible schedules and the money, which was unheard-of at the time for women. The 1960s brought with them a dawn of change in America—economically, technologically, socially. It was the time of Camelot in the White House, of the optimism of youth, of a country and a culture emerging from a period when families concentrated primarily on just getting ahead, when hard work and education were the best means of forgetting the dark, stultifying cloud left in the wake of the Cold War and The Bomb. The country now boasted the Peace Corps, the Space Race, Hula Hoops—and The Pill. But the social revolution that engulfed the 1960s had yet to trickle down to women. For the first time, daughters were graduating in almost equal numbers from college with sons. But what was waiting in the real world was in reality not terribly different from what their mothers had faced. There was no clear-cut path from a four-year university to Wall Street or corporate America. Talk of the so-called glass ceiling was still a few years away. In 1962, there was just a ceiling, period.

Now, suddenly, there was this opportunity for many of us to earn more money than our fathers, in what was essentially an interim job, while exploring a range of options that would otherwise have been beyond our financial means. Here was an opportunity for a young woman to pay for a college education independently or stockpile funds to start a business, invest in real estate, travel the world or realize any number of other dreams. There were also those attracted by the showbizzy glamour of working in the daring new Club where men could experience firsthand the good life advertised and promulgated in the pages of Hugh Hefner's infamous men's magazine (which everyone, of course, claimed to read strictly for the articles and cartoons). Beautiful, scantily clad young women dressed up as Bunnies who personally served martinis and Manhattans in the dark, cushy confines of a sophisticated men's-only sanctuary was as close as many a man or woman would ever get to the fantasy world epitomized by the magazine. Talk about your New Frontier. Even President Kennedy was a *Playboy* fan.

But the odd Bunny out was undercover reporter Bunny Marie. That was the pseudonym Steinem, a 28-year-old fledgling journalist, used when she applied for her job as a Playboy Club Bunny at the just-opened and highly anticipated New York sister Club to the famous Chicago Club. Steinem knew a good story when she saw one. Other young female reporters had been unsuccessful in their attempts to get hired as Bunnies, but Steinem, attractive, leggy and exceedingly smart, succeeded. So "Marie Ochs" was fitted for a costume in January 1963, about six weeks after the New York Club opened. She began as a Door Bunny, greeting Keyholders in the entrance lobby of the seven-story Club. In quick succession, she graduated to Hatcheck Bunny and then to Table Bunny, serving cocktails and food.

None of us, her coworkers, ever singled "Bunny Marie" out as particularly unusual; there was a vast range of different types among the 150 or so women working as Bunnies at the time Gloria was hired. By law, only those women over the age of 21 could work at night, and among the older Bunnies there were many with college degrees and work experience that went beyond cocktail waitressing. Certainly no one I knew suspected that she was keeping a daily diary of the presumably hellish days and nights she worked at the Club with the intent of publishing these notes.

She struck me, personally, as someone I'd like to know better. We had met in Bunny training class and then worked together a few times. I was flattered when Bunny Marie sat down beside me at dinner one evening in the employees' lounge. She was older, more elegant and sophisticated. She told me she was a college graduate and had traveled in Europe. In fact, she was pretty much what I had wanted to be. When she asked me about myself, I eagerly told her that I'd come from Minnesota a few months earlier to study acting in New York and that I was a full-time scholarship student at the American Academy of Dramatic Arts. But Bunny Marie was gone before I ever had a chance to know her.

In fact, Steinem's career at the Club was virtually nonexistent. After about a week, she took a leave of absence on a trumped-up story of illness in the family. Less than a week later, she was back to clean out her locker and resign formally. Because the Club was short of Bunnies, she was persuaded to work the Playmate Bar for two more nights. Her agreement wasn't entirely altruistic. "Might I learn something new?" she wrote hopefully in her diary. For the truth was, as appealing as the job was made to sound, the reality was that it was like any job: hard work, long hours. In her diary she griped, Where was the "glamour" the recruitment ads had promised? The celebrities? The top money?

But for Steinem, nothing had changed. Same old grind. Bumptious customers. Crass jokes. Sore feet. Dumb Bunnies. One wonders what she had expected. Erudite discussions in the dressing room? New York's intelligentsia convening in the Playmate Bar?

After working a total of 11 days, she concluded there was nothing more to learn. She went off to fine-hone her article, which appeared as a two-parter in the May and June 1963 issues of *Show* magazine published by Huntington Hartford—perhaps not coincidentally, the liveliest rival of another Hefner venture, *Show Business Illustrated*.

The reaction of Steinem's coworkers at the Club to her exaggerated "insider" exposé was more or less "Good for her." After all, we couldn't quibble with her portrayal of the work as strenuous, the hours long and the costumes tight. But on a personal level, there was a feeling of betrayal, even hurt. How could Steinem, posing as a Bunny, talk to us, work among us, observe us and then profile us in such a condescending manner? A good many of her coworkers were every bit as ambitious as she was to get on with their careers. None of the women I knew anticipated collecting her first Social Security check upon mothballing her Bunny costume.

The characterization of Bunnies as naive, hapless victims who spent all their time complaining was not only clichéd and predictable, but also insultingly inaccurate. (In the course of time, Bunnies did, after all, negotiate benefits and effect a good many changes in working conditions.) I know that I, personally, felt ambivalent about the article. Working at the Club had been a job, both good and bad, like all jobs. Looking back on it, there was, if anything, the nostalgia of having been a part of an icon of the '60s. It had hardly been the kind of exploitative experience Steinem had managed to transform into a cornerstone of feminist folklore.

Our chance meeting at the publisher's party reminded me of the bad feelings I'd had at the time reading her article and the even more negative feelings I had in 1984 when "A Bunny's Tale" was made into a TV movie-of-the-week starring Kirstie Alley. Steinem was one of the producers of the movie, which was made a good *21 years* after she wrote the piece. Bunnies seemed to be stuck in some kind of Steinem time warp.

I began to wonder if maybe I had remembered only the good times at the Playboy Club, the quirky encounters with customers, the funny anecdotes? I rummaged through the cache of old diaries and scrapbooks I had stored away to see if memory had betrayed me. At the bottom of a hatbox, I discovered the long-forgotten pair of pink satin Bunny ears I had packed away. I slipped them over my head, to see if they still fit. I rifled through the weathered memorabilia and came across a snapshot of myself as a Bunny, taken in the service area of the Living Room soon after I had completed my Bunny training. I was wearing a beehive hairdo, of course.

Tucked in the back of a scrapbook was my Bunny Manual, still in the brown plastic folder, and stuck between its pages was the examination paper and my answers to the 61 questions. Sitting in my office 28 years later wearing my pink satin Bunny ears, I also found copies of *Show* with "A Bunny's Tale" by Steinem. I reread the article and yes, there I was, "the pretty brunette who never took off her coat." Steinem's description of me during the first afternoon of our Bunny training together reminded me that underneath my yellow polo coat, I was wearing decidedly unglamorous Academy school clothes. I was a student, after all, working to earn money for room and board.

And I remembered again our dinner together in the employees' lounge that night when she had confided her fear that friends or acquaintances might come to the Club and recognize her.

"What would they think of me?" she asked, almost terrified.

Her anxiety baffled me. An actor friend had just visited the Club to see me, bringing with him one of my acting teachers at the Academy. As it turned out, the two men were, if anything, in awe of the "bacchanalian" surroundings. I realized with some amusement that they looked upon me as a sort of demi-celebrity. It was a heady new feeling for me, a shy and, I thought, gawky kid from the Midwest. Even more, I realized with hindsight, it was deliciously empowering. Over time, other Bunnies proudly introduced me to boyfriends, parents and acquaintances who made their way into the Club. It never struck any of us as something to be ashamed of. If anything, though we were perhaps only vaguely aware of it on a conscious level, we were part of the novelty and publicity of a revolutionary sexual change in post-World War II society. But far more important than any such highfalutin concepts was the almost giddy realization that we had scored an unparalleled opportunity to earn great sums of money for what amounted to very basic waitressing work.

I had friends at the Academy working part-time as salesgirls, temporary secretaries, file clerks and waitresses who made only a fifth of what I was making. As easy as it is to exploit youth and inexperience, I was aware even then that I was better protected by a rigidly enforced code of behavior in my exotic waitress job than were many of my friends in their more traditional jobs that earned them only a minimum wage.

The fact was, Gloria Steinem couldn't identify with the rest of us and didn't care to. At that point in her life, she would never have considered working as a waitress, let alone a waitress with Bunny ears, except as research for an article. Her viewpoint was that of a journalist—or more to the point, a privileged professional.

Ironically, in some sense, she may have been the least liberated of all of us. Among the many young women there looking to become something different from Donna Reed—or even Madame Curie—Gloria was the least open to change, to experiencing the crazy, giddy, exhilarating age of experimentation when a woman, quite possibly, could do anything she damn well pleased. We flouted our beehive hairdos, padded our bosoms, wore false eyelashes, and defied convention in our daring satin outfits.

I remember something secretly divine about shedding the polo coat and loafers in the dressing room and stepping into the sexy satin Bunny costume and high-heeled shoes. In fact, a good number of us remember fellow Bunny-turned-actress Lauren Hutton, bawdy and always fun, arriving for work stark naked under her trench coat and wisecracking to us in the dressing room that it hardly made sense to put clothes on to come to the Club only to have to take them off again. It was the ultimate rush to leave the schoolgirl behind in the locker and strut around in a revealing costume for a few hours to the sounds of cool jazz and easy banter. For me, it was pure escape—as much from the altogether new pressures of adjusting to the big city as from my Midwestern background—and a brazen way of thumbing my nose at the establishment.

As for the men: Well, this *was* the early '60s. They wore suits, and most were businessmen who indulged in the then-proverbial three-martini lunch. We had our regular customers who confided in us, treated us like pals, teased us, yearned after us and talked with us. They were, on the whole, very pleasant. I blossomed from the attention. I gained confidence and authority. I learned how to handle myself in an adult world of easy intimacy and establish my own boundaries. I developed skills for deflecting unwanted attention, rather than becoming the victim of harassment. It was all part of the job. Part of the job that all the Bunnies accepted.

In a 1984 *New York Times* profile, Steinem referred to her brief stint at the Club. "It was a turning point," she said, "but not *the* turning point." Yet, for many of the young women at the Club, their brief stints as Bunnies did represent a real turning point in their lives. We were very much in the vanguard of the sexual revolution that presaged the women's lib era.

After rereading Steinem's *Show* magazine piece, I did the unthinkable. I called home and asked my mother if she really had saved all those letters I had written to her. "Yes," she said, "but you don't really want to read them, do you?" Memories had been stirred and I was unstoppable. "Send them," I said.

One of my brothers called to warn me: "Brace yourself. It can make your skin crawl to think you once wrote that stuff."

When I began to read the letters, I knew what he meant. The dreams. The idealism. The naive, unbridled curiosity . . . the convoluted syntax. How often I talked about "The World." I arrived in New York shortly before the Cuban Missile Crisis. President Kennedy was assassinated a little over a year later. A boy I went to school with and who played Billy in the senior class production of *Carousel* was killed in Vietnam. I was devastated to read in the newspaper that a girl from my hometown, someone I'd hero-worshiped in high school, had died of a drug overdose in New York just as her acting career was taking off. It was all in those letters.

I was a virgin. And then I wasn't. That was *not* in those letters.

I realized that the dates of my letters corresponded to the dates in Gloria Steinem's diary. We indeed had observed things from two radically different perspectives. My outlook reflected the bright-eyed, carefree teenager that I was then. To the general public, Gloria's bleaker viewpoint had become the Gospel of the Way Things Were.

On numerous occasions over the years, I had come across other women I had once worked with at the Playboy Club. No one ever bolted in embarrassment. I remembered, for example, seeing the reflection of a tall, striking brunette in the mirror during a strenuous jazz class in a Hollywood dance studio several years ago. After class, she tapped me on the shoulder. "Hi, Bunny Kay. Remember me?" "Oh, God! Jorjana! What're you doing out here?" I asked, thrilled to see her again. "I'm a film editor." Her hair was salt-and-pepper. She looked radiant. It had been 20 years since we'd worked at the New York Club together.

A year or so later my theatrical agent sent me to meet the producers of a television pilot. The casting director brought me into an office where several men and a woman were seated. I had barely settled into a chair facing them before the woman, who was vaguely familiar to me, grinned and said, "Hi, Bunny Kay." The co-creator and executive producer of the television pilot was Judith Allison, a stunning, 6-foot-tall former Bunny I'd worked with in the early days of the New York Club. My surprised reaction at seeing Judith after so many years was completely eclipsed by the stir she had caused among the men in the room, who were astonished by her revelation.

The fascination with Bunnies, even 25 years later, surprised me. Even more so because of that unmistakable flicker of surprise whenever a co-worker, a friend, a fellow member of the PTA would learn you had been a Playboy Bunny. There seemed to be that unspoken assumption even among the well-meaning that somehow Bunnies would just be Bunnies forever. So I began my own rabbit hunt, as it were, to find out just exactly what did happen to all those girls, poised on the dawn of an unexplored New Era, bedecked in satin ears and eager to explore.

What I found surprised even me. I began with the names and telephone numbers of two old friends from my Bunny years, who each passed along the names of other former Bunnies. Soon, I was calling complete strangers, but, happily, there was invariably an immediate bond, an assumption of shared sensibilities, when I introduced myself as a former Bunny.

Before I was finished, the list included such former Bunnies as actress, supermodel Lauren Hutton, who also designs her own line of eyeglasses; Teddy Howard, now Elaine Trebek Kares, an author, talk-show hostess and owner of a multimillion-dollar advertising agency specializing in fragrances; Jill Graves, now Linda Durham, owner of the Durham Art Gallery in Galisteo, New Mexico; rock singer and actress Deborah Harry; TV and film actress Susan Sullivan (*Dharma & Greg*, *My Best Friend's Wedding*); actress-producer Barbara Bosson (*Hill Street Blues*, *Murder One*); entrepreneur Monica Schaller Evans; former actress, congressional candidate and attorney Sabrina Scharf Schiller; and the National Institutes of Health's distinguished immunologist Dr. Polly Matzinger. In addition, there is a CEO of a New York Stock Exchange company, an architect, an opera singer, several attorneys, a book publisher, a restaurateur, a television director, a stock broker, a racehorse breeder, a real-estate tycoon, three psychologists, an award-winning hat designer, a nurse, several schoolteachers and a vast number of moms. I came across casualties, too, among our mutual friends—alcohol and drug problems, disastrous marriages, career meltdowns, ill health. This book in no way chronicles anyone's entire life story, my own included, but instead focuses on the lives of the women interviewed in terms of their experiences as Bunnies. Not surprisingly (at least to me), their stories mirror the struggle and enterprise of women throughout this tumultuous era.

Each had her own unique tale to tell, a piece of that long-ago forgotten Magic Time of the 1960s, when President John F. Kennedy was in the White House, the Moon was just a rocket shot away, and every woman had her dream that someday she could attain more than her mom, or even her dad, and still be sexy. Dumb Bunnies? Hardly. They were women with dreams, ideals and goals to achieve. Just like Gloria Steinem.

With Love, Bunny Kay

MY TALE

"Bunny Kay," 1963.

I arrived in New York City lugging a big suitcase full of clothes my mother had made for me and even bigger dreams of becoming an actress—the quintessential Small-Town Girl with Big-City dreams, straight off the turnip truck from Robbinsdale, Minnesota. Two months earlier, I had been doing summer stock associated with the liberal arts college I attended in Minnesota when one of the company's professional New York actors, Marty Davidson, told me about the American Academy of Dramatic Arts.

"If you wanna be an actress," the actor set me straight, "ya gotta go to New York."

I immediately sent off an application to the Academy. No more wasting time in the boondocks for me. I was accepted a month later as a full-time student and, on September 6, 1962, booked a seat on a red-eye to New York. Marty picked me up at Idlewild at dawn in the middle of a thunderstorm. I was turned out in the loving-hands-at-home red suit and the high heels I'd worn when I won the Minnesota State Declamation contest the year before. It was my good-luck outfit. Besides, I heard everyone in New York dressed up.

Marty drove me into the city and dropped me off at Ferguson House, a dormitory-style residence in a converted mansion on 68th Street near Madison Avenue on the Upper East Side. He informed me that we were four blocks from where *Breakfast at Tiffany's* was filmed and only two blocks from Paul Newman's home. The Ferguson was pure Old New York, complete with a grilled elevator, small window balconies and ornate fireplaces. The rent was $30 a week and included two meals a day, six days a week. Sundays you had to fend for yourself. With any luck, you were able to get a date.

"New York is so exciting" I wrote home that first week, after I had packed away my mother's homemade red wool suit.

It was as if I had gotten off the plane and walked on to the setting of *Stage Door*. My fellow Ferguson House residents included two girls attending a fashion design institute, an opera student, two ballet students, a Peruvian art student and another AADA student who came from Wyoming. As luck would have it, out of all the would-be models, dancers, actresses and singers, I was roomed with Madge, who sold greeting cards in a shop on Lexington Avenue. Madge had no show-business aspirations herself, but she loved the theatre and was a devotée of the latest Broadway gossip. I couldn't afford to attend plays with her, but I pored over the *Playbills* she brought home.

The first piece of business I had to attend to was money. Specifically, how to get it. I had to stretch every dollar I made to absurd lengths. I ate all my evening meals at Ferguson House. I walked everywhere, saving the few cents I would have had to lavish on a subway token. Cabs, of course, were out of the question.

Today, I wrote home, *I walked from 68th to 37th and back and stopped to eat at an Automat on the way—three nickels in a slot for a cheese sandwich on a plate. On Sunday I bought a hard roll and Danish soft cheese at Cushman's—20 cents for a whole meal and very European, I think.*

It was Madge who sent me to Bloomingdale's to find a part-time job. Bloomie's hired me at $1.40 an hour to work in the Customer Service Department of third-floor Better Dresses, Thursday nights and all day Saturdays. I made $21 a week. The best thing about the job was the employee cafeteria, which served incredibly cheap food. It was such a good deal that even on my days off, I ate there.

By then, I had started classes at the AADA. I went to school until 1 o'clock and then spent the afternoons and evenings rehearsing scenes and taking dance classes. In October, I moved out of the Ferguson to a five-floor walk-up in Yorktown near the East River on 81st Street with Sheila McGrath, an AADA classmate from Newfoundland.

It's so much cheaper than Ferguson House, even with the bus ride to the Academy, I wrote back to Minnesota.

Even with the Bloomie's job, I carefully rationed myself to one 23-cent can of tuna fish a day; I took the bus only if it was pouring outside. As the holidays approached, they gave me extra hours at the store selling gift certificates. I tried not to think about spending my first Christmas away from my family. Instead, I made an inedible Christmas dinner for Marty (discovering you should first remove the little plastic pouch containing the neck, heart, liver and God-Knows-What-Else before roasting a chicken) and faced the bleak days before New Year's buried in the Returns cubicle in third-floor Better Dresses.

Calamity struck when Bloomingdale's laid me off during the first sloppy days of January. Now how was I going to come up with the $55-a-month rent?

A few days later, I spotted an ad in the newspaper, announcing that the just-opened New York Playboy Club was auditioning for "Bunnies." Marty dared me to audition. What the heck, I thought.

But I knew what a Playboy Bunny was and how the ideal Bunny was meant to look. I had seen a photograph of the Perfect Bunny, Kelly Collins, a breathtaking brunette posed in the classic Bunny stance: come hither look over a bare shoulder, well-rounded left hip thrust out, full breasts spilling tantalizingly over the cups of the tight-fitting, strapless top.

Kelly Collins, the "Perfect Bunny."

13

I thought I could handle the over-the-shoulder look, even the thrust hip. But I had no hope of coming even close to fulfilling the upper-story requirements. I was a stick, with little hope of filling out on one can of tuna a day. A glamorous hitch as Miss Robbinsdale, Minnesota, the year before did not deceive me.

Until the age of 17, I was tall, skinny, with lank brown hair and crooked teeth. The one thing I had going for me was no pimples. But during the summer after I graduated from high school, some sort of miracle occurred and my body took on the beginnings of a shape. Not much, but enough to distinguish me from the neighborhood boys I'd spent most of my youth beating up.

That summer, it had turned out that the Junior Chamber of Commerce was one girl short for the Whizbang Days festivities. I was asked to fill in. When the mayor of Robbinsdale, Red Sahacki (who acted as the gym teacher in between banging his mayoral gavel), marched down the football field past 17 other girls—including former Robbinsdale High cheerleaders—and stopped in front of me, holding before him the coveted Whizbang Days rhinestone tiara, I thought he had made a mistake. To my shock, he placed it upon my head. I spent the next year fulfilling my obligations as Miss Robbinsdale, juggling freshman college classes with weekend stints perched upon the backs of various Chevy convertibles, waving and blowing kisses in one farmtown parade after another throughout Minnesota. But even during the big parade down the main street of Robbinsdale (population 15,000), never once did I entertain the slightest delusion that I was a great beauty on the ramp to fame and fortune. (I once told Marty I'd been a Miss Robbinsdale, but only on the sworn blood oath he would not tell anyone.)

It turned out that Marty never thought I would take him up on his dare. In fact, as he confessed at the last minute, he did not think I had an ice cube's chance in hell of making the Playboy cut. But from my perspective, the Playboy job would solve all my problems. I could work at night, so it would not interfere with my acting classes. The job had a fair amount of glitz, enough to pretend you were at least on the fringes of show business. And most importantly, it paid well, especially with the tips. Despite Marty's less-than-ringing vote of confidence, I accepted the dare.

At the appointed time, I showed up at the open-call audition at the Playboy Club on 59th Street—and so did 500 other girls. Wearing a dance leotard, I had my picture taken and sat for a short interview. My prospects did not look promising—but not, surprisingly enough, because I couldn't

measure up to the Bunny costume. The man who interviewed me seemed eager to hire me, but the sticking point
turned out to be the work schedule. Since I had classes
until 1 o'clock, I wasn't available to work the lunch shift,
and because I was under 21, I wouldn't be allowed to work
the evening shift. There seemed to be no solution. Dejected,
I headed for the elevator with another girl my age, Mary
Hutton, who apparently had been rejected for a similar
reason. A good-looking man joined us in the elevator and
on the ride down asked why we both looked so forlorn. We
told him our problems. He said he thought he might have
some pull and took us back upstairs.

Indeed, he wasn't exaggerating. He was Keith Hefner,
Hugh's brother, and he was in charge of Bunny hiring
and training. As a compromise, he arranged for me to be
a Cigarette Bunny. I would work in the afternoon as soon
as my classes ended, staying on the floor with my tray of
cigars and cigarettes until 5:30 p.m. Keith found a spot for
Mary Hutton working the king crab counter in the Playmate Bar. When she discovered there were already three
other Bunnies named Mary, she took the name Lauren.
She, too, was an aspiring actress, and the two of us became
friends. As appointments were made for us to be fitted for
costumes, we grinned at each other. We'd pulled it off! We
were Bunnies.

On January 11, 1963, I wrote an eight-page letter home
announcing my great news to my poor parents: *I've been
hired to work as a Bunny! I'm told that out of some 3,000
girls who have applied since last summer, I am one of
about 100 new girls selected. I'll be earning about $150
a week for four days' work—which sure beats Bloomingdale's! Bunnies also do guest appearances and promotional work, so that's good experience for me.*

Bunny Kay, 1963.

*I can't help but think about your reaction. You'll worry that I'm working
in a nightclub atmosphere—but don't. The place is elegant, clean, serves
good food and has excellent entertainment. The Club is located in the most
fashionable part of Manhattan. The girls wear bathing-suit-type satin outfits with black hose, high heels, white collars and cuffs, and cottontails. We*

work as waitresses and the tips are unbelievable. Incidentally, there's nothing cheap about being a Bunny. The girls are carefully screened and trained, and the Bunnies have an excellent reputation. I don't think the job has the same connotation in Minneapolis that it does in New York— I don't think Mrs. H would understand, for one. By the way, I checked with the school, and this job in no way breaks Academy regulations. I think the registrar was actually amused.

Because Bloomingdale's discharged me without notice, I'm a little short on money and I need to buy dyed-to-match satin shoes for the pink costume . . . Could you possibly send $25?

With love,
"Bunny Kay"

The response from my mother was immediate. She sent me a money order for $40 and wrote that if things didn't work out, I could always come home.

My miraculous transformation from schoolgirl beanpole to stacked Bunny was largely the work of Betty Dozier Tate, a one-time singer and dancer, who was the seamstress in charge of fitting Bunny costumes. Her sanctuary was a cramped space immediately to the right of the dressing-room entrance, and only 10 steps from the dreaded "Bunny Mother's" domain. Once the business of interviews and filling out applications was over, it was Betty's job to uncover that Bunny Image. (Later I would be sent to a fashionable hairdressing and beauty salon at Playboy's expense to have a facial, makeup instruction and hairstyling.)

I walked into Betty's costume department. Tiny and fierce-looking, sitting hunched over her sewing machine, she gave me the once-over and then asked me how the hell she was supposed to tell what I looked like with my coat on. Her husky, warm voice made me laugh. She was tart and sassy with a shrewd eye, and she looked like nobody I'd ever seen before. But my fate was now in her hands, and I figured she would take care of me. In fact, Betty left the impression that she would always be on your side no matter what. I stripped down to bikini panties and was zippered into a discarded Bunny costume in my approximate size to see if I had "it."

PLAYBOY CLUB of N.Y., Inc.	
5 East 59th Street	
New York 22, N. Y.	
Kay Kringstad	#64
EMPLOYEE NAME	EMPLOYEE NUMBER
5'5" 110 Brown Brown 999-99-9999	
HEIGHT WEIGHT COLOR EYES COLOR HAIR SOCIAL SECURITY NO.	
Bunny Barbara Conway	
DEPARTMENT AUTHORIZED BY	
EMPLOYEE IDENTIFICATION CARD	

The Woman Behind the Cottontail

L ook pretty." "Wear lipstick!" "Be a lady!" "You're a star!" Words of wisdom pasted to the bathroom walls of the New York Playboy Club by the unofficial spiritual head of the Bunnies, Elizabeth Dozier Tate, the longtime seamstress and wardrobe mistress for the Club. Known to one and all as Betty, she was the cheerleader behind those paste-on smiles that Bunnies, sometimes dragging a world full of problems behind them, were forced to assume for the Keyholders.

"Be a star!" she'd exhort. "You know, honey, I was once a star myself."

Indeed, she was. As "Chinkie" Grimes, a singer and show dancer, Betty knew and worked with all the big stars of her time: Dizzy Gillespie, Lena Horne, Count Basie, Art Tatum, Ella Fitzgerald and Louis Armstrong. She was born in Georgia, one of 12 children, and made her way to New York as a teenager. While working as a housekeeper and cook for actor Orson Welles and his family, Betty entered an amateur contest at Harlem's Apollo Theatre and sang "I'm Gonna Sit Right Down and Write Myself a Letter."

She won third prize and a job in the chorus. She started out as a singer and tap dancer. "My oriental cheekbones and eyes (my father had Japanese blood) attracted a lot of attention along with my dance, and I came to be known as 'Chinkie.'" She was featured on Broadway, appeared in the movie *Stormy Weather* with Lena Horne and Bill "Bojangles" Robinson, and while married to Tiny Grimes, guitarist with Art Tatum for many years, she toured the country.

"All this time I was designing and making costumes for myself and others," Betty recalls. In 1962, when the New York Club was opening, Betty's current husband, Robert Tate, was working for Playboy in key sales. "He heard they were having a hard time fitting the Bunny costumes, so I came in," Betty says, "and ended up spending the next 26 years there."

In fact, it lead to a guest spot on *What's My Line?* in 1964 ("I fit the Bunny costumes at the New York Playboy Club."). But that was not what Betty's job ultimately meant to her: "I do much more than just make and fit Bunny costumes. The Bunnies are my girls, and I love them all. I mother them. I've taught them how to sit, how to

Rosemary Costello and Elizabeth Dozier Tate.

walk and how to act like ladies." In 1994, she was honored at the National Tap Dance Day salute sponsored by the New York State Black Film Archives.

She let me know that it was only for me that she would go to so much trouble to find a ready-made costume that would make me look like the right stuff. I slipped on a red number and looked at myself in the long mirror. I was amazed. Even in stocking feet and without the transforming collars and cuffs, I thought I could make the grade. It was nothing short of a miracle.

"You're looking good, sugar. You tell 'em I said so," Betty growled.

I padded down to the Bunny Mother's office for an inspection. Claudia Burgess, a pretty blonde in her mid-20s and a former Bunny herself, told me to go ahead and get fitted. I would start work immediately as a Cigarette Bunny. I could take my Bunny training later.

I leaned against the counter with a blonde girl named Cheryl while I

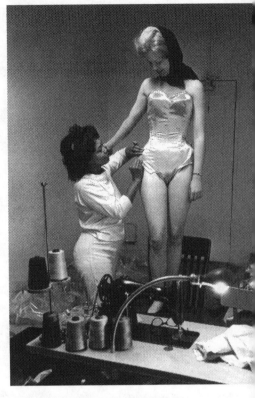

Betty fits a Bunny's costume, 1962.

waited for Lauren Hutton to be fitted in a blue costume. There were long steel poles hung with satin costumes in dry cleaning bags and stacks of new costume shells with muslin linings. As I stood there waiting, I watched the steady stream of girls hurrying in and out of the dressing room as Eva Shephard, Betty's cousin, handed out collars and cuffs and made sure the girls signed for the black mesh stockings. The $5 charge for hose would be deducted from their paychecks. The space was cramped, cluttered and intoxicating. Multicolored satin trims lay discarded on the floor. Bags of cottontails and satin ears rested in corners. High-pitched chatter, raucous laughter. It was "backstage." I was nervous and very excited.

Betty determined what color costume you got, based on what was available in your size from the stacks of prefabs and her determination to keep a rainbow of colors fairly balanced. I was told all the night-shift Bunnies wanted black costumes, "but only Bunny China refuses to wear anything but black." When I later met China Lee (who eventually married political satirist Mort Sahl), I discovered that her entire wardrobe—on and off the job—consisted of black or white clothing.

A pink costume was selected for me. (I eventually was given three costumes: red, gold and pink.) The prefab corset was shiny and stiff with raw edges and no side seams. I tucked my breasts into the cups and held the top in place while Betty pinned the sides together. Then swiftly, with a pinch here and there, the costume started to take shape. Not necessarily my shape, but I wasn't going to complain. Betty identified a hipbone and then snipped and tucked her way to my crotch.

"If I left it any wider, baby, the fabric would cut into you," she said.

"Yes, it would," I thought, and who's complaining? Grommets would be stamped in later to string the corset laces. Now my tummy was flat, my legs were looking longer than I believed possible and, for the first time in my life, I had hips. As my mother delicately put it while fitting me for a skirt, I hadn't quite "filled out" yet. In high school, I had once worn Bermuda shorts under a straight skirt to give the appearance of a figure. In those days I was even willing to settle for looking lumpy as long as I didn't look like a stick. I was indeed a late bloomer; I was still growing and would add another inch to my height before I turned 21.

The streamlined Bunny costume was clearly an improvement. The black mesh hose and the high-heeled shoes made even mediocre legs look better. The tail and ears were just plain silly. But something about the collar and cuffs actually made me feel like I was wearing a shirt. Still, there was the top problem. But Betty was not ready to raise the white flag. She bunched together a handful of plastic dry cleaning bags and told me to stuff them under my breasts.

"But don't use those all the time, baby; it'll make you sweat and you'll lose what you got," she added, hinting that I should look for more conventional help.

As it turned out, living up to the Kelly Collins ideal was a problem I shared with a lot of the girls, most of whom, it seemed, were content to stuff themselves with whatever came to hand, including gym socks and old Bunny tails.

While Betty finished my costume, I was sent back to the Bunny Mother for a hurried version of Bunny boot camp. As it turned out, I was to start immediately—with or without the dyed-to-match shoes. Miss Burgess was all business. She assigned me a locker and told me to leave nothing valuable in it. Girls pin their rings inside their costumes, I was told. Furthermore, she instructed, we weren't allowed to wear any personal jewelry, not even the tiny gold posts for pierced earrings that I was wearing. Just a white linen collar with a bow tie and cuffs with Bunny cuff links.

"And remember, the Bunnies have to be kissing," she warned. As I quickly learned, that meant that when you held your wrists together, the Bunny logos had to be facing each other—or you would be given demerits. There were also demerits for not keeping your Bunny tail white and fluffy. In fact, there were demerits for a wide variety of things. The Merit/Demerit System could have been a Parker Bros. board game. Demerits were what you got for absenteeism, tardiness, improper appearance, chewing gum or eating in front of customers. Accumulate 100 of those and you were out of a job. Merits canceled out demerits and could be earned by, among other things, working on your day off or doing unpaid promotional work for Playboy. At events where Bunnies were sent to promote Playboy, the girls wore remarkably chaste cheerleader-type outfits: black sweaters with a logo, white pleated skirts to the knee and black high-heeled shoes.

Miss Burgess informed me of the rules—and the dire consequences should they be broken—in a solemn, matter-of-fact tone. Of course, the ridiculous marine drill instructor façade was funny, even funnier delivered deadpan. But I was too afraid at the moment to laugh. I made a mental note to make sure my Bunnies would always be kissing. Miss Burgess then gave me a brown folder with a thick Bunny Manual to take home and study. I wouldn't take the Bunny training necessary to serve food and beverages for another week or more.

And so began the daily race from the Academy at 52nd Street and Broadway to the Club at 59th Street and Fifth. I flew down the stairs after class, jumped into a taxi, wriggled into the black stockings, glued on eyelashes, leapt out of the cab, ran up the stairs to the Bunny dressing room, grabbed my costume, changed clothes, hurled myself down to the gift shop to get my cigarette tray and began my parade through the Club by 1:30 p.m. As far as I was concerned, the Cigarette Bunny had the best job in the Club. Each pack of cigars and cigarettes was sold with a black-enamel lighter for $1.50. The lighter with the white Bunny logo and the cigar or cigarettes cost me 55 cents. I was allowed to keep the difference. Almost everyone bought cigarettes to get the lighter as a souvenir, and I was invariably asked to "keep the change" from $2 and, very often, from $5, $10 and $20 bills.

That first night after I returned home, my roommate, Sheila McGrath, sat with me at our kitchen table, smoothing out the crumpled dollar-bill tips I'd stuffed into my costume. After one day on the job, I'd earned $45 —more money than I made in two weeks of working at Bloomingdale's. Sheila, who eventually abandoned her theatrical aspirations for a 25-year career as executive administrator at *The New Yorker*, was amazed. That night, I peeled off my new and expensive false eyelashes and left them perched on the bathroom sink. Sheila awoke bright and early the next morning. Entering the bathroom, she mistook the eyelashes for cockroaches and slapped them down the drain. Clearly, the fast lane was going to take a little time getting used to.

I continued to write home several times a week, breezily informing my parents and two younger brothers of the worldly life I had been adopted into in New York. The letters must have struck them as news bulletins from Pluto.

I will need my birth certificate immediately for the cabaret license—it seems strange that I have to have a "performing artist" license to wait tables! Because I'm 19, state law prohibits me from working past 10 p.m. and I'll be off the floor before 7 p.m. Therefore, it will interfere less with school than Bloomingdale's did.

I won't really be a short-order girl. We have busboys who do most of the lifting and carrying. We pay them out of our tips. The training is excellent—we really will have classes on exotic and gourmet foods and wines. I was told that Bunnies are supposed to be as elegant and knowledgeable as a "garçon" in an expensive French restaurant.

As a Cigarette Bunny, I would wander throughout the Club, roaming into every room on every level. I walked to the beat of the music—an endless loop of jazz and easy listening. I lingered wherever I found a customer who caught my interest and wanted to talk. Whenever I sensed there was a business discussion or private meeting, I

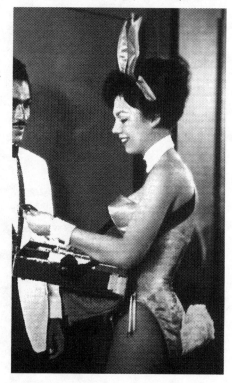

Cigarette Bunny Kay, 1963.

21

smiled and moved on. The best part was the anonymity. I could perch any-where, put a smile on my face and watch. Bunny Kay had no last name, if indeed that was her first name. I could have called myself Phôebe or Salomé. I could play any role I wanted to invent, or be myself. And it was all part of the job.

I made friends among the Bunnies, bartenders and busboys. Bunnies were free to stop and chat with anyone on a break. I soon discovered that the Club was full of young women just like me. We came from places like Baltimore, Seattle, Tampa, Laramie, Green Bay, Mason City, Newark and Butte. We all needed bread-and-butter jobs to tide us over until we finished school or figured out what else we wanted to do.

I confided in Lauren Hutton, who was stationed at the end of the Playmate Bar serving king crab, which was displayed on a bed of cracked ice. For $1.50, Bunny Lauren handed out a plate of king crab and was almost always told to "keep the change." Two 19-year-old acting students really did have the best jobs in the Club. The worst jobs, we figured, were Gift Shop Bunny (no tips) and Door Bunny (no tips and you had to stand in the draft). The job to be avoided at all costs was Hatcheck Bunny (drafty, boring, strenuous, no chance to sit or perch and you couldn't keep the tips). My one great fear was that someone would find out how much money I was making and take my job away from me. I didn't dare miss a day of work.

January 26, 1963, was my birthday. It was also the day that Gloria Steinem applied for a Bunny job, using the alias "Marie Ochs." As she

waited in the Playmate Bar, I roamed the Club with my ciga-rette tray. Despite another birthday, I was still too young to work later than 7 p.m. I didn't notice her; my thoughts were on the dinner Sheila and I were serving in our tiny apartment that night for 20 friends from the Academy.

Marty and his brother-in-law came in [to the Club]

Sheralee Conners, 1962.

yesterday to check me out, I wrote home. *I passed muster. They said I had a clean, wholesome, kid sister sort of look—well, I was hired, so they must want that image.*

Four days later, Gloria Steinem returned to the Club at 6:30 p.m. for her interview with Bunny Mother Claudia. It happened to be Claudia's last day on the job at the New York Club. With her was Sheralee Conners, a Bunny from the Chicago Club and a recent Playmate centerfold, who was replacing her. Sheralee had very long, very shiny chestnut-colored hair, porcelain skin, enormous clear brown eyes and looked more like a big sister than anybody's mother. She spoke in a rushed, little-girl voice, punctuating her speech with faces—happy, sad, perplexed and surprised.

Her face registered all four expressions when I raced into the dressing room to announce to her that a man who said he was an executive with Phillips Milk of Magnesia had given me a generous tip for a pack of cigarettes. Steinem would record the moment in her *Show* magazine article: "He gave me 30 bucks, and I only got him cigarettes . . ." At the time, Sheralee then frowned and told me I had better study my "Bunny Bible" for Bunny training, which would begin the following week.

I was now earning enough money at the Club to pay my expenses and even open a savings account. My first major discovery had been the welcome sight of an employee lounge that served what I thought was free food. Free food! Even better than at Bloomingdale's, where I had had to pay up to 50 cents for a bologna on white with lettuce and mayo. In the Club's employee lounge, I was overwhelmed by the choices on the steam table, usually some kind of fish and some kind of meat, and some kind of mélange with a red sauce. I loved the corned beef, long before I knew what it was. It was months, perhaps a year, before I realized the food in the employee lounge was rather ordinary cafeteria food. Even after I was issued a meal ticket and knew that the cost was deducted from my wages, I was still dazzled by the price.

I wrote home: *My expenses are few since I eat at the Club. My bus and cab fare account for only a dollar a day. Ten hours a week and perhaps an occasional weekend day as a substitute is all I need. I've even bought the Academy-required makeup kit, tickets to two plays and a couple of books I needed.*

On Monday afternoon, February 4, eight of us who were ready to become floor Bunnies, including "Bunny Marie," met in Sheralee's office in the dressing room for the Bunny Mother's lecture. Sheralee's office was tiny, and there weren't enough folding metal chairs. I perched on the edge of a filing cabinet and hoped we wouldn't be asked any questions. I hadn't studied my Bunny Manual at all.

Much of the meeting was devoted to Sheralee's admonition that we "not appear to" push drinks. However, since customers tipped us according to the amount of the bill, it was in our best interest (and certainly the Club's) to serve as many drinks as possible. Sheralee pointed out that customers would order more drinks if we gave good service. She impressed upon us that "pushing drinks wouldn't look nice" and that Bunnies were above doing that. Her explanation satisfied me; urging customers to drink up and have another did not appeal to me.

A Bunny sitting near me was more succinct. "They don't want us to look like B Girls hustling drinks." Right. We were not B Girls. The difference was clear to me, but the significance of Sheralee's comments had everything to do with the fact that the Club still had not been granted a cabaret license that permitted entertainment. New York City's license commissioner contended that our costumes were indecent and that the Bunnies might be mingling with the customers to increase liquor sales, in violation of the law.

In fact, the problems with the State Liquor Authority had made the New York Playboy Club unique. It was not allowed to operate as a private club. The general public had to be admitted. Customers entering without key-club membership were issued paper cutouts in the shape of keys and permitted to pay cash.

Almost everything discussed at the afternoon meeting had to do with discipline. All of the rules were strictly enforced to protect the Bunnies and to ensure that the Playboy Club would not only retain its liquor license but also acquire the permit for entertainment. At that time, there were three showrooms on the premises—and no entertainment. The Chicago, New Orleans and Miami Playboy Clubs, meanwhile, all had entertainment.

The rules for us were many. According to the Bunny Manual, they included:

520.2.3   Bunnies may not give out their last names, home addresses or phone numbers at any time in the Club for any reason.

520.2.4   Bunnies are forbidden to date employees of the Club, including managers, room directors, bartenders, musicians, performers and busboys.

520.2.5   Bunnies are not permitted to make dates with Keyholders, guests or any other person visiting the Club.

520.2.7   Bunnies are at all times forbidden to mingle or fraternize with patrons or their guests inside or outside of the club. Mingling, fraternizing, socializing, or any physical contact by any female employee with any patron or guest is not allowed and shall be cause for immediate dismissal.

We were instructed to meet husbands or boyfriends at least two blocks from the Club, and to do so discreetly. I envisioned groups of men skulking in doorways in a two-block radius. Mostly, I felt relieved hearing these rules. I didn't want to date Keyholders, room directors or busboys, and I wished it were always that easy to come up with a solid excuse to decline a date. At 19, the best I could come up with was, "I'm sorta going with someone back home."

There were exceptions, however. The "No. 1 Keyholders," those Very Important Playboys who were company executives, had the privilege of asking us out on a date. But they couldn't force us to go out with them if we didn't want to.

In case there were lapses, we were told that the Club had hired a detective agency called Wilmark to keep the Bunnies under surveillance. We never knew when these Wilmark detectives might appear in the Club, posing as customers trying to tempt us to meet for a date. Wilmark agents were also on the lookout for Bunny ears that didn't match, snags in the black hose, tails that needed fluffing and dirty fingernails. The former violation cost you your job; the latter transgressions resulted in demerits.

Counter to the custom at the other clubs, we would not be working for tips exclusively; New York State law required we be paid a minimum hourly wage. In turn, a portion of our charged tips would be withheld by the Club. We could keep all of our cash tips, but we were not allowed to state that preference to the customers. Again, Wilmark would be watching us. During the early days of the Club, there was a variety of changing rules regarding our earnings and charge-backs to the Club, but it was always clear to me that my real earnings would be the cash tips.

Sheralee wrapped up the Bunny Mother meeting by letting us know that we would be working in a very protected environment.

Then we got down to business. In one of the showrooms, we watched a film that Keith Hefner had prepared. A training guide to highly refined

Bunny Stance

Bunny Dip

Bunny Perch

and highly guarded Playboy Club esoterica, it revealed such signature moves as the "Bunny Stance," the "Bunny Dip," the "High Carry," the "Bunny Crouch" and the "Bunny Perch." The "Stance" was a model's pose with one foot behind the other and a hip slightly thrust out. The "Dip" was a graceful backward arch with knees together, employed while serving drinks to keep the girl's overstuffed, overextended breasts from popping out of the costume. The "High Carry," a tray full of drinks carried on the flat of the palm high over the head, made perfect sense when I saw the most naturally buxom in our group of trainees struggle not to topple the Tom Collins glasses on her tray. The "Crouch" was mandatory for taking drink orders during shows (should the Club ever have entertainment), preventing Bunnies from having to lean over a customer, exposing themselves while trying to hear an order. The "Perch" was designed to allow Bunnies to remain on display near their stations, when not serving drink orders, without giving the appearance of mingling. A Bunny could rest a hip on a banister or sit on the back of a chair—but not in it!

Throughout it all was the suave presence of Keith Hefner. A former high school teacher who also had trained at the Actor's Studio, Keith joined the fledgling Playboy Club fresh from a stint as Johnny Jellybean on a children's television show. At Playboy, he was put in charge of Bunny training. He worked with several of the original Chicago Bunnies in developing the stylized serving techniques, devising a training program to ensure that no Bunny would ever barge up to a table and slap down a drink. "What'll ya'll have" would not be in our vocabulary. Though in later years, a waiter ("server") introducing his or her first name before launching into the specials of the day would become *de rigueur*, in the early days of the Playboy Club it was a novelty.

Keith's presentation was a sublime blend of Lee Strasberg's method acting with the Reverend Norman Vincent Peale's Positive Thinking message. Bunnies in-training were asked to contrast the person who walked down the street and saw nothing but filth in the gutters with the person who looked up and saw the beauty in the landscape. To motivate a proper state of mind before starting a shift, we were told to take a moment and think of something happy, a positive thought, then enter the

STYLIZED SERVICE TABLE PROCEDURES

You are the reason that people come to the Playboy Club. Our Keyholders and their guests expect to receive the ultimate in efficient, friendly, personalized service.

The following is a step-by-step example of standard table procedures (as demonstrated by your Training Bunny):

1. The Bunny approaches the table with a warm, welcoming smile.
2. When she reaches the table, she pivots gracefully and "tails" the table. She should now be in her "Bunny Stance."
3. She then introduces herself and places down cocktail napkins (Logo facing the guest), doing her "Bunny Dip."
4. Then she will say "May I see the Playboy key, please?" She reads the name on the key and says "Thank you, Mr. Pochuchnik."
5. The lady's cocktail order is taken first. (If there are no ladies present—the gentleman to the right of the Keyholder). The Keyholder's order is taken last. She repeats each order as given.
6. When the cocktail order has been taken, the Bunny holds up her clean, empty mug, saying "Would anyone care to have his cocktail in a souvenir mug?"
7. She then asks if they will be dining with us. (She must know what is being served.)

8. When returning with the order, the first thing she will do is hand the key to the Keyholder saying "Here is your key, Mr. Pochuchnik."
9. The drinks are served in the order that they were taken—ladies first, Keyholder last—again repeating each drink as she places it down, doing her best "Bunny Dip." The drink is placed on the napkin to the side of the Logo. She serves the entire table from one spot, simply pivoting to reach each guest.
10. She makes sure to cap the ashtrays and checks to see that the table is clean and neat.

A Bunny NEVER:

✔ Places anything on, or removes anything from a table without doing her "Dip."
✔ Puts her tray down anywhere except in the service area.
✔ Eats, drinks or smokes in view of a customer.
✔ Carries anything in her mug.
✔ Says or does anything that is not representative of the feminine beauty and grace that is "Bunny Image."

room as though we were walking on stage.

"Make it special!" we were exhorted.

Even the serving tray had been reduced to an exact science. It measured 12 inches in diameter and was set up in a precise fashion with nine specific items: tax chart, Playboy lighter, tip tray, ashtrays, bar sponge, matches, napkins and bar checks. All of this essential equipment had to be in place before taking a drink order. Miraculously, there was still room to carry eight or more drinks at one time.

Bunnies were also required to commit to memory a precise order in which to call in drinks to the bartender in the service area. You had to set up your tray with the proper glasses in the proper sequence ("shots before cocktails"), slide the setups in front of the bartender, call out the order, garnish the drinks and make way for the next Bunny in line. Scotch, Canadian, bourbon, rye, Irish, gin, vodka (shots that corresponded to the sequence of bottles in the bartender's well) followed by rum, brandy, liqueurs, mixed-blended-creamed cocktails, beer, wine, mugs, Irish coffee.

I was overwhelmed at the prospect of remembering it all. And I couldn't really see any reason to learn it—a big mistake on my part, as I would soon learn within hours on "the floor" the following week.

In fact, I was so busy trying to commit to memory the bunny minutiae that I didn't take my first real notice of the other trainees—including "Bunny Marie"—until Tuesday, the day of our "Final Exam." There were eight of us, including another acting student, a slim redhead who confided that she hadn't studied for the exam. I confessed I hadn't, either. Little did I know, my lapse was about to make history. "Bunny Marie," who had sat side by side with me in the Penthouse during training, would later describe

THE PLAYBOY CLUB
BUNNY TRAINING QUIZ

1. List the dreaded "call-in sequence."
2. List Playboy "cash" keys.
3. List Playboy "charge" keys.
4. List acceptable major credit cards.
5. When you report to the floor, what information must you find out before beginning your shift?
6. When do you use the guest's name?
7. When do you do your "Bunny Dip"?
8. Do you ever:

   a) put down your tray?

   b) ask a guest if he wants his check?

   c) tell a guest his key is no good?

   d) tell a guest that you're tired and your feet are killing you and Bunny Peaches is living with your Uncle Fred and a monkey?

   e) smoke, drink or eat in view of a guest?

   f) smile and be charming in spite of #8d?
9. Why do you carry the following items:

   a) lighter?

   b) clean ashtrays?

   c) penlight?
10. When you want to take your break, what must you do?
11. If a guest remains seated for one hour after he has paid his check:

    a) Are you still responsible for his table?

    b) Do you remove his empty glass?

    c) Do you bring him 14 glasses of water if requested?

    d) Do you keep checking to see if he'd like anything?

    e) If he decides to have another drink, what do you do?
12. When you are very busy, do you:

    a) avoid eye contact, for fear someone will ask you for something?

    b) walk by a new party in your station because you can't pick him up at that moment?

    c) maintain your "stylized" service and your charm?

    d) say "sorry, this isn't my station"?
14. What phrase would you use if you are given:

    a) a "cash" key?

    b) a cash tip?

    c) a pinch?
15. What are the rules regarding your coming in to the Club?
16. Will you receive any phone calls or messages at the Club?
17. Will you ever be seen in the Club looking less than perfect?
18. Does the Bunny Mother love you?

Gloria's Gloria

"Yes, I remember studying the Bunny Manual," says Gloria Prince, the blonde Bunny Gloria Steinem wrote "had chewed her knuckle" during the Bunny training quiz. "I had to do well," Prince laughs. "It was the beginning of my career in show business.

"I was star struck. I'd grown up in rural New England, and I had wanted to be an actress—a movie star—from the time I was a child. I went to New York to study acting and, of course, I heard about the Playboy Club. For me, wondering if I was pretty enough to get hired and then getting the job after an 'audition' was the closest thing to show business that I had ever done. I soon discovered it was a cocktail waitress job, but in the beginning, to put on that costume, to be around all these glamorous girls, it was like being backstage in a theatrical production. I was incredibly naive at the age of 20. For me, it felt like the beginning of a life in showbiz, the next step being Hollywood.

"I had a little baby, so I always left for home immediately after working the lunch shift. I didn't really socialize with anyone at the Club, but I do remember working with Gloria Steinem and liking her very much. One day at lunch, a customer sitting at a table with several other people gestured toward Gloria, who was walking toward the kitchen area, and asked me if I knew her. I said, 'Oh, yes, that's Bunny Marie.' The customer said, in a very pointed way, 'Well, mark my words, one day she is going to be very famous.' I just interpreted that to mean 'famous actress and big star on Broadway.' I walked away perplexed, wondering why Marie had never told me she was in show business, too. With hindsight I realize they were probably people she worked with at *Show* magazine and they were referring to the article she was writing."

"Even now," recalls Gloria, a classical radio DJ, "when someone learns that I was once a Bunny, they'll say, 'You're kidding! I thought I knew you so well!' One friend looked at a picture of me as a Bunny and couldn't believe that was me with the little-girl face and the teased bubble of blond hair sprayed into place. If I'd shown her a picture of myself as a 19-year-old waitress serving ham and eggs in a diner it would have been entirely different. But somehow the sexy costume and the aura of showbiz glamour completely clouded the fact that we were really just well-paid servers." ∎

me in her article as the Bunny who only knew the names of Scotch whiskies. This was true, since the Scotch whiskies were listed first, and I hadn't committed most of the others to memory.

The quiz turned out to be a list of 61 short-answer questions, Steinem wrote. *Our class of eight scribbled seriously while Sheralee [the Bunny Mother] read the questions aloud. I could see the Texas model looking perplexed, her mouth slightly open, and the Bunny named Gloria was chewing her knuckle. I decided it wouldn't pay to be too smart, and wrote down six wrong answers. We scored one another's papers and read out the results. I was top of the class with nine wrong, the magician's assistant had 10, and everyone else missed 14 or more. Texas missed nearly 30. When the club says a Bunny is chosen for '1) Beauty, 2) Personality, and 3) Ability,' the order must be significant.*

Admittedly, there were no rocket scientists among us. There were also few among us with any real drinking experience. Steinem recorded that Sheralee told one trainee, who had never tasted champagne, that it was "like ginger ale only lots, lots more expensive." In truth, I, too, had been grateful for the explanation. As a teenager at the time, I'd never tasted champagne, either, and I wonder how many of us in Bunny training had. In fact, I had been well under the legal drinking age when I left Minnesota. A family jug of Manischewitz kosher wine inexplicably kept on hand as a sort of medicinal Lutheran toast on feast days such as Christmas and Easter constituted my working knowledge of liquor at home. (A thimbleful was tossed down in a single gulp to ward off something—no one in the family can recall the origins of this custom—and we moved on to our meat and potatoes.) Scotch was considered Republican. Champagne? Not in our kitchen cupboard.

But I passed the quiz, along with Steinem, and on Thursday, February 7, I began my table training with Bunny Jadee in the Playmate Bar. I worked from 2 o'clock until 6 o'clock. The Club was crowded even after lunch. To my amazement, I found I really could balance a tray, do a high carry, and call in my drink orders properly.

That Saturday, the Club was jammed with a long line of customers waiting in the street to get in. It really did feel like "show time." It was an exhilarating experience to be in charge of my own station, a narrow strip of tables near the balcony above the piano bar. And I soon discovered the need for the precise ranking of drink orders we called out to the bartenders

Bar Procedures

All Playboy procedures were designed to expedite service and to maintain constant quality. Your Bartender shares the responsibility for the appearance and proper proportion of each drink served. It is therefore vital that you work with him and always adhere to the following fundamentals:

1. Check each glass for cleanliness.
2. Glasses should be packed with ice.
3. Proper call-in sequence must be used.
4. Don't approach the bar until your paperwork is done and your glasses are set up in your tray in sequence, with appropriate ice, wash and garnish.

The correct level of wash, with full ice, is shown in the picture. It contains only 4 ounces of wash. When the 1 1/2-ounces of liquor is added, you are serving a 5 1/2-ounce drink, filling a 12-ounce glass and maintaining a healthy standard proportion of better than 4 to 1.

NOTE:

ALL cocktails, as well as beer, wines and sherries, specialty coffees, etc., are served in the 12-ounce Tulip Glass.

ALL beverages may be served in the Playboy Souvenir mug. The price is $1.45 over the cost of the drink. If a guest wishes to purchase just the Mug (without a cocktail), he may do so at the Gift Shop at $2.50 per mug.

over the packed and noisy bars. We had to move like dervishes. The bartenders had to produce drinks in seconds—and they hated it when a time-consuming creamed drink like a brandy Alexander was ordered before a lemon juice-based Scotch sour.

The more experienced Bunnies were ruthlessly professional and made no concessions for inept sister Bunnies. One did not dawdle or get in anyone's way. One did not "suddenly remember" a highball glass or "accidentally forget" a cherry garnish. You did things the right way. That first Saturday night, I saw one exasperated Bunny throw her tray at another Bunny, who was infuriatingly slow in assembling her drink order.

It was my first taste of working at night, although I had to be off the floor by 7 p.m. On my way out, I passed a petite blonde named "Bunny Irving," who turned out to be Playmate Lineé Ahlstrand, actually cutting up meat for one of her customers, an elderly gentleman. Omigod, the demerits! I thought. And she isn't even using the Bunny Dip . . .

I left the floor and headed to the dressing room. My feet ached and I was tired. Thank God I didn't have to work a full eight hours. As I finished my shift and turned in my costume, "Bunny Marie" was in the dressing room getting ready for her night shift as a trainee. I didn't envy her.

Playboy Club Memorabilia

By midmorning the following day, Sunday, I had to be back at the Club in costume for a photography session. The Club was closed and eerily quiet until someone figured out how to turn on the taped music. The girls straggled in, sleepy and yawning, carrying their ears, cuffs and bow ties. As we waited, I talked to another Bunny named Susan Sullivan, who told me she was a theatre arts major at Hofstra University. Together, we perched on tables in the Cartoon Corner of the Living Room and watched the session.

Outside the Club, it was a sleepy gray wintry Sunday. Inside, there was a bright pool of light on the staircase, where photographer Jerry Yulsman and his assistants were posing the Bunnies. As the session wore on and more girls showed up, everyone became more animated. The noise level rose, and groups of Bunnies were gathered, laughing and talking, throughout the Playmate Bar and Living Room areas. The girls in their jewel-colored satin costumes looked like flocks of rare and exotic birds.

In reality, they were birds of many feathers. There were the tall, slick former Vegas showgirls, who walked in a stately ripple. The long-legged dancers from the Copacabana nightclub around the corner, who worked at Playboy between engagements in the Copa line. The girls from Hunter College and NYU with long, straight hair, who wore Pappagallos and shetland sweaters and only worked weekends. The shaggier-looking acting students, who studied with Lee Strasberg and Sandy Meisner. The slim would-be models with long limbs and exquisite faces. The former secretaries, bank clerks and stewardesses, who wanted a change. The young girls newly out of high school, who worked the lunch shifts until they could figure out what to do with their lives. Newlyweds and working mothers with school-age children, who found the 11–3 o'clock day shift an ideal schedule. Single mothers, who left their children with grandma to work the night shift. Greenwich Village folk singers, fashion-design students, budding entrepreneurs who had their eyes on business ventures. And the magician's assistant.

In truth, there were girls with plain faces, exotic faces, plump to bony figures, big to virtually nonexistent breasts; there were waifs to heiresses to statuesque showgirls. And every ethnic combination under the sun. You would have to wait a couple of decades to see as much multiculturalism and ethnic diversity on a college campus as could be found in the Bunnies' locker room, circa 1963.

■ ■ ■ ■

Gloria Steinem at a
New York Party . . .

Two days later, on February 22, Gloria Steinem wrote that she turned in her costume for the last time, concluding that there was nothing more for her to learn. She packed up and went home. Two months later, *Show* magazine ran "A Bunny's Tale," and Steinem went on to a storied career, leaving us behind in her wake.

The article portrayed virtually all the Bunnies as hapless, malleable victims, and claimed that she, Gloria, working as a Bunny, felt less honest than a presumed hooker she passed on the street outside the Playboy Club: *As I walked the last block to my apartment, I passed a gray English car with the motor running. A woman was sitting in the driver's seat, smoking a cigarette and watching the street. Her hair was bright blonde and her coat bright red. She looked at me and smiled. I smiled back. She looked available—and was. Of the two of us, she seemed the more honest.*

I had worked at the Playboy Club at the same time as Gloria, and I could easily identify myself among the Bunnies she had specifically described and quoted in her article. I recalled the occasions in which she and I had crossed paths in the dressing room, talked during a meal in the employee lounge and sat next to each other in Bunny training. She certainly knew, then, why I was working at the Playboy Club because I had told her: I saw it as a good part-time job that didn't interfere with my acting classes at the Academy. It never occurred to me that delivering a drink order and collecting payment for it constituted anything remotely resembling prostitution.

And neither had it occurred to the other remarkably ambitious Bunnies I had befriended, all of whom took the work in stride. There was Lauren, of course, who delighted in mocking the job, but never the women who worked at Playboy. And Susan,

. . . three years *after* shedding the Bunny costume.

who, as a full-time university student, relished the campus notoriety she attained when it became known that she worked as a Bunny. And there was Sabrina, who set a rigid one-year time limit on her tenure at Playboy. Years later, after working as an actress, she became an attorney and ran for a congressional seat in California.

Sabrina has always been generous about offering shelter to strays. I remember staying with her for a short time before I moved into my apartment on 30th and Madison Avenue. She lived in a wonderfully eccentric, ramshackle building in a shabby backwater of the Village. The crooked old house had a fireplace, cozy thrift-shop furniture and sloping floors. Sabrina had painted the floorboards in a rainbow of colors.

Sabrina introduced me to Chumley's bar and the after-hours jazz joints in the East Village. I remember riding on the back of Sabrina's motorcycle, tearing down Park Avenue after work. Coming home late at night to her neighborhood was an adventure. The streets, as desolate and eerie as a moonscape, were deserted except for rats until the wholesale meat-packing plants opened in the early hours of the morning. Smoky, open fires burned in bins and oil drums until dawn. Finding a taxi was a chancy business. Most often, I was forced to walk through those bleak, shadowy streets to Eighth and Broadway to catch a subway.

On February 22, I wrote home: *I'm just working weekends at the Club now because we have exam plays at the Academy. I've also written a piece that's passed the first elimination—I may get to direct it. Thank God for meals at the Club, though—they had spareribs. Also, I'm able to put more money aside now—maybe I can afford some dental work. I really ought to get my teeth straightened. A Bunny with braces would be quite a novelty. I wonder if they'll let me.*

On April 3, I wrote home: *I'm thrilled! I've been cast in two exam plays, both to be directed by Max Fisher at the ANTA Theatre on Broadway. We rehearse from 2 until 6, so I will have to go back to the weekend schedule at the Club—and they are being really good about my work schedule. Thank you for sending my spring clothes—and guess what, I really did grow an inch.*

May 6, 1963: *Good news! Out of 87 girls at the Club, I'm rated #18—which is exceptionally good since they only see me 10 hours a week now. It also means that I'm considered a strong Bunny, capable of the more difficult, busy stations. We have seven different rooms and tips, of course, are better in the busier rooms.*

Two weeks later, I managed to land an interview with the New York Drama Guild for an Academy scholarship. I worried that telling the board members I was a Playboy Bunny would not enhance my chances of winning a scholarship.

May 20, 1963: *Last Thursday I went into Miss Fuller's office to meet the Drama Guild representatives. I was replaced at the Club at 3, dressed and grabbed a cab to get to the Academy by 4. I changed into my orange seersucker dress, combed my hair into a flip and wore glasses so I didn't look too much like a showgirl. Miss Fuller said I looked so fresh in my "gay little spring dress." So I guess I passed muster. Then Miss Fuller asked me if I worked and I mentioned that I was now working as a waitress. Miss Fuller asked where and I said, "Oh, a little supper club on the East Side," and she started to ask which one, but Mr. Letton jumped in and saved my hide by telling everyone about my performance in the final exam play.*

July 6, 1963: *Well, here's a bit of news—I'm "Bunny of the Week," chosen by the bartenders and room directors—isn't that nice? Also, I went to a film audition yesterday and I believe I've been cast in a comedy, which begins shooting in New York the latter part of July.*

By the end of July, I got the scholarship. After filming a small role in *The Troublemaker*, I took a leave of absence from the Club and flew home to visit my family in August. I returned to school in September and landed the part of Isabel in our production of *The Enchanted*. Even with the scholarship, I returned to work at the Club, doing 10-hour stints on weekends.

I wrote home: *I can always be a Bunny when I need money! Also, I've outgrown my clothes. Do you think you could make me another dress like the striped one—just use the same pattern, but make it a little broader in the shoulders and collarless? Enclosed is $10 for material—but don't do it if you are too busy.*

Increasingly, school was demanding more time. One day at the club, I ran into Keith Hefner. Apparently, there had been a Bunny meeting I hadn't attended. I reminded him I had acting school until 1 every day and, perhaps recalling his Actor's Studio days, he said, "Go, my child, you have my blessing—acting classes always come before work!" Soon after, I began training Bunnies on Saturday and Sunday nights, a $20 bonus each night besides tips and salary.

September 19, 1963: *Some wonderful news! Our play will be taken on tour to Buffalo and Albany after our opening October 17 at the AADA— a paying audience!*

September 27, 1963: *I'm moving! I found a 2 1/2-room rent-controlled apartment in a great building on Madison Avenue and 30th Street, across the street from the new American Academy building. The fireplace really works and the bathroom is big and old-fashioned. It'll cost me $110 a month, but I can manage.*

That fall, I got my first real on-camera job, a television commercial for a hair spray—and with it, a new name. The theatrical agent who sent me on the audition was an elderly woman and a bit hard of hearing. When I told her my name, Kathryn Kringstad, she couldn't grasp my last name. Since she was on the telephone with the casting director at the time, I kept mouthing my name and trying to spell it for her. She gave me a fierce look, clapped her hand over the mouthpiece and demanded to know what the hell kind of name that was! She looked down at the box of Lady Scott tissues on her desk and when she resumed speaking to the casting director, she said my name was Kathryn Scott. I got the job as Kathryn Scott, and I joined Screen Actors Guild as Kathryn Scott.

I then faced the terrible prospect of calling my parents to tell them I had changed my name. It didn't help matters that my family name was also the name of my father's birthplace in Norway.

"But why?" my mother asked when I called home with my latest bulletin from Pluto. I could hear my father breathing on the extension phone. I was sure my brothers were hovering in close proximity.

"Because, you know . . . I wouldn't ever want to embarrass the family name . . ." I mumbled in complete embarrassment.

Pause . . . alarm. My mother's quiet voice asked, "What are you thinking of doing that might embarrass us?"

"Oh, honestly, Mother, nothing! But, well, you know."

Of course, my parents didn't know. I didn't know. After another pause, my mother mumbled, "Don't be silly. I don't think anyone even knows our name out there."

For my part, I've always been grateful the hard-of-hearing agent didn't have a box of Kleenex on her desk. Imagine explaining that one.

I also slowly weaned myself off my mother's dressmaking.

October 7, 1963: *Today is the one-year anniversary of my arrival in New York—do hope you save my letters, because one day I know I will want to remind myself of my first year in New York.*

■ ■ ■ ■

The following summer, my parents and my kid brother drove from Minneapolis to spend a week with me in New York. I made special arrangements with the general manager so that my folks could visit the Club. I was working in the Playmate Bar when they strolled in. Luckily, I had a table free that gave them a good view. I brought them each a Tom Collins, "dipped" and showed off a bit. My mother scanned the wall of illuminated blowups of Playmates and idly asked if one particular picture was of me. Just as casually, I looked over my shoulder and asked, "that one, Mother?" I wanted to shout, "NO, MOTHER! THAT WOMAN IS COMPLETELY NAKED!!!"

She said, "Yes, that one with the pretty smile."

"No, Mother. That's Sheralee Conners. She was our Bunny Mother."

"Your Bunny Mother. Well, she's very pretty."

My father sat in abstracted silence. When I returned a few minutes later, my mother, still eyeing the naked lady in the picture, said, "No, I can see it's not you. Your hair was never that long."

■ ■ ■ ■

In January 1964, many of the Bunnies I had become closest to—among them Sabrina Scharf, Monica Schaller and Lauren Hutton—left the Club to work at a new resort casino in the Bahamas, one not owned by Playboy. Had I not been in my second year at the Academy, I would have been tempted to join the dozen or so Bunnies who signed on to work at the Lucayan Beach Hotel near Freeport.

While I missed my friends when they left, those early years in New York are marked by a sense of impermanence and wanderlust. Once I graduated from the Academy I knew I, too, would be leaving Playboy. I thrilled at the idea that a single audition or a screen test could change the course of my life. Aside from a wardrobe of suitable audition clothes, I lived with the barest essentials. Some books piled into homemade shelves, a teakettle, a bed and a thrift-shop couch, but no gracious, homey decor items to slow me down if I had to move fast. Once I could work nights at Playboy, my days were spent in classes and making the rounds of casting directors.

My 21st birthday coincided with the occasion of the American Academy of Dramatic Arts' Gala Tribute to Jason Robards (a former student) and his wife, Lauren Bacall, in the Grand Ballroom of the Hilton Hotel. I was among the six scholarship students (Sheila included) invited to serve as hosts at the event. I was still squeezing every nickel, but I had my eye on a red velvet dress hanging on a sale rack in Bergdorf Goodman. The saleswoman assured me the dress was due for another markdown before the Big Event, and I managed to take it home for $18. That Sunday night, January 26, Sheila watched in amazement as I managed to stand up in a taxi all the way to the Hilton so I wouldn't crush my dress. It was worth it. Adlai E. Stevenson, one of the many distinguished guests, handed me his homburg, and I gave him a program. I couldn't wait to tell my father, an ardent Democrat. Late that night, after the event and still dressed in my precious gown, I joined Academy friends at a tavern; I bumped into a friend there who took me to a walk-up shared by Faye Dunaway and her boyfriend, where I ate lobster and sang folk songs. Sometime close to dawn I wandered home, stopping in a deli for a cheese Danish and a carton of milk to breakfast on in front of Tiffany's, just across the street from where I had bought my red velvet gown and around the corner from the Playboy Club. It was a sensational birthday.

That summer, through auditions at the American Academy, I got a job at a summer theatre in Roanoke, Virginia. One of the room directors, Paul Goldenberg, was looking for an apartment, and I offered to sublet my place on Madison Avenue to him for three months. He moved in (with a dozen crates of books) the day I left for Roanoke. About five weeks later, I stood in a train station with a duffel bag at my feet stuffing quarters in a pay telephone trying to reach Paul in New York to tell him that the theatre had gone belly up and I was on my way home. He graciously invited me to sleep on the living room couch of my apartment. When I told him that I was traveling back with another young actress from the theatre, also homeless, he kindly offered to give up the bedroom with the twin beds and sleep on the couch himself. He also called the Club in advance of my arrival to get me back on schedule to work the following weekend. That was the beginning of a close, lasting friendship and the start of my tutelage with Paul Goldenberg—one of the most urbane, delightful and supportive men I have ever known.

Paul, the Cairo-born son of French parents, started his career working as a stage actor and a talent coordinator for the BBC in Egypt. Some years later, he moved to Northern California and managed the *hungry i* in San Francisco (advancing the careers of Tom Lehrer, Mike Nichols and Elaine May, Bob Newhart, Mort Sahl and a host of other young talents) before moving to New York and working at the Playboy Club. As we got to know each other, he became increasingly appalled at how much I didn't know and hadn't read. It was annoying to this man, who was widely read, well-educated and well-traveled, that I seemed to have a sound intelligence and an inquiring mind but scant knowledge. His solution was to give me a reading list and require verbal book reports. This remedy not only enhanced our *au passant* conversations in the kitchen, but also provided me with a treasured insight to a world of art and literature I would never otherwise have known. (As of this writing, incidentally, Paul is in his 22nd year as a manager of Manhattan's Carlyle Hotel, where he still oversees talent such as Bobby Short and Barbara Carroll.)

Another contributor to my *ad hoc* "finishing school" was Al Mandaro, a former Maitre d' at the El Morocco, who became the Party Room director at the Playboy Club after the celebrated nightclub went out of business. There isn't much that escapes the attention of a good Maitre d' and Al had wonderful vintage café society stories about everyone from boxers to debutantes, dowagers to movie stars and heiresses to gangsters. Eventually, Al asked me to join him for his customary Monday lunches when he checked out the new places and kept tabs on veteran establishments. I ate well and listened avidly, enthralled by his who-begat-who Genesis of New York society. "A society girl's breath is always sweet," he told me one day, "and they pay particular attention to their footwear." I also learned the proper way to order from a menu and eat things I'd never heard of before meeting Al Mandaro.

When the Academy term ended in the spring and I could sleep late, I was in for another education. I started to join the other Bunnies and some of the musicians at the after-hours jazz joints in mid-Manhattan, Greenwich Village and the lower East Side. I was a sponge. I absorbed it all: the music, the atmosphere, the language and lungs full of cigarette smoke. For a while, I would only smoke *Gauloise*.

■ ■ ■ ■

During my senior year at the Academy, the registrar, Bryn Morgan, called me out of class one Friday morning to offer me a job posing for fashion photographs that would appear in a *Time* magazine story. Bryn told me he often got calls asking for students to "model," but he'd vetted this job carefully and it was legitimate. If I was free to do the job after I got out of classes that day, I'd be paid $50. A fortune! I accepted immediately.

I arrived at the photographic studio bright-eyed and breathless with excitement. A skinny, tough-talking woman introduced herself as a fashion stylist and handed me a tiny package containing the outfit I was supposed to model. In the privacy of the dressing room, I pulled the garment out of its plastic wrapping and stared at the minuscule mound of black nylon in my hand. I learned later that it was the first stretch-lace body stocking in history (this was, after all, for a *Time* magazine *news* story), but I already knew I was in trouble. The good news was that I luckily had worn a black bra and black panties that day. Gamely, I stripped off my clothes and pulled on the body stocking, then stared at myself in the mirror. I looked like I'd been tattooed from neck to toes in black lace, not necessarily a pretty sight. At that moment, the stylist hollered at me to come out and get to work.

Ben Martin, the *Time* magazine photographer, had just arrived: 6 feet tall, suntanned and wearing a trench coat. A suntan in November! He took one look at me and said, "How come you're wearing your underwear?"

As I fled toward the dressing room I heard him say, "Wait a minute. Don't you have that thing on backward?"

I stayed in the dressing room a very long time, all the while overhearing the photographer talk about his flight back from Venezuela. From South American politics to pop fashion in 24 hours, and now he's stuck with some dumb kid who has never modeled before. For my part it seemed inconceivable that *Time* magazine would publish a photograph of a naked girl unless she was a member of a remote African tribe. I was sure, once they saw me naked under the black lace, they'd all come to their senses and send me home, maybe with $50 in my pocket for my time and trouble. No such luck. The hard-nosed stylist poked her head in to make sure the "backless" back was now in the front.

Mortified, I was pushed into the brightly lighted studio. "That's better," the photographer said when he saw me. I crept onto a roll of background paper and tried futilely to bunch up the little black lace flowers over my breasts and crotch. Reluctantly, I faced the camera and struck a number of poses, thinking, "I'm the first *Time* magazine Playmate!"

Afterward, the photographer invited me for dinner, but I had to tell him I was working that night "waiting tables." He offered to drop me off at work and I accepted. However, after my absurd display of modesty I could hardly tell him my regular job involved serving food and drink while *half-naked*. I climbed out of his car several blocks from the Club and walked to work in the cold drizzle. I had already begun to fall in love with him but was quite positive I never wanted to see him again.

Seamstress Betty Dozier Tate, surrounded by the Bunnies, who danced in the chorus line for the Sammy Davis Jr. Tribute at Carnegie Hall, 1964. Back row: Marcia Donen, Barbara Severn; middle row: Eva Nichols, Betty, Cathy Young, Carolyn Bridges, Joy Hayes and Cheryl Walters; front row: Jolly Young and Elaine Freeman.

The following week, one of the pictures from that shoot appeared in the magazine. *Time* had come to its senses; the photograph pictured me from the knees down to illustrate a story on textured stockings. Eventually, the photographer tracked me down through the Academy and we began to date.

■　■　■　■

At 7 a.m. the day of my graduation from the American Academy of Dramatic Arts, my doorbell rang. I sat up in bed and called out, "Who is it?"

The answer came back, "Surprise! It's your aunty Pat and Mom."

It did indeed come as a surprise, as I was sharing my bed at the moment with a fellow classmate who had appeared with me in our final senior production of *Pajama Game* the night before. As I scrambled to find a robe, my bleary-eyed friend had already joined the pigeons on the fire escape and was pulling on his blue jeans. I took a moment to appreciate the fact that he was every bit as cute as I'd thought he was, and then raced to the front door. I released the chain guard and peered out at the drawn but ever-alert faces of my aunt and mother.

"What took you so long? Aren't you going to let us in?"

"She's got a man in there, Hilda. Can't you tell?" my aunt sniffed.

My mother stared at me, eyes brimming. "This was supposed to be a surprise."

"Well, it is, mother. But I'm afraid aunty Pat's right. You see . . ."

I launched into a story so incredible that only a loving and completely daft mother could ever believe it. My mother believed it. My aunt, I could tell, did not. I persuaded them to go downstairs for breakfast at a coffee shop while I "straightened the place up." I retrieved my companion, now fully dressed, from the fire escape and sent him scrambling down the stairs. By the time my mother and aunt returned, I had showered and dressed. I had also dusted, vacuumed and even washed the telephone.

When my aunt was out of earshot, my mother confided that she'd had a similar experience in Minneapolis during the legendary *Syttende Mai* (17th of May, Norway's Independence Day) blizzard of 1938. She'd had to persuade my father, then her fiancé, to spend the night rather than brave the storm. Thank God for family precedent. I nodded, volumes left gratefully unspoken between us.

Second piece of news: I had decided to forgo the graduation ceremony (even though Robert Redford was the guest speaker) so I could work the lunch shift at the Playboy Club. I was saving every penny for a trip to Stratford, England, later that summer, so that I could be there for the 400th anniversary of Shakespeare's birth. In light of the morning's events, I decided it would be wise to call the Bunny Mother and explain my predicament. Once she stopped laughing, she agreed to arrange for a replacement so that I could attend my graduation. Needless to say, every male classmate I introduced to my mother and aunt that day was treated to a beady stare.

■ ■ ■ ■

In the spring of 1966, I got the so-called first "Big Break," when producer Dan Curtis hired me to play "Maggie Evans" in *Dark Shadows*, a new daytime television series. I was blissful. During the three years I'd worked as a Bunny, I'd graduated from the AADA, done some stage work off-off-Broadway, filmed a few television commercials and been cast by Worthington Miner to play a role in *The Contrast*, an early American play chosen to be staged at the first Eugene O'Neill Festival in Waterford, Connecticut. Now, with an offer of steady acting work, I had no need to work at the Playboy Club any longer. When I called my folks to tell them my news, my mother urged caution. It was a new show; I could be out of a job in no time, she told me. So, with her "one step at a time, don't burn your bridges" advice, I kept my Bunny job and worked weekends.

But soon after, on a Saturday night, a week after the first *Dark Shadows* episode aired on television, two female customers recognized me as "Maggie Evans." I talked with them for a few minutes and took their drink order. Back in the service area, I ran into Dina Kaplan, a Bunny who later would join the New York City police force.

"They want to know why Maggie Evans is working at the Playboy Club," I said. "And I don't have an answer."

I knew it would be my last night. It was time to cut the cord. For three years, the Club had been an integral part of my life. It had given me security, confidence, friends and an anchor in a confusing and sometimes scary city. And it had given me a living. A good living.

That weekend, I turned in my costume, but I kept my Bunny ears and bow tie.

I wish I'd kept the whole damn costume.

Chicago

Chicago

THREE MEN AND A BUNNY

Hugh Hefner and the Chicago Club Bunnies, 1960.

With a smiling Marilyn Monroe waving from the cover of the first issue, Hugh Marston Hefner began spinning the ultimate male fantasy on the pages of the men's magazine he dubbed *Playboy* in the summer of 1953. Intense, boyish, the 27-year-old Hefner conceived the magazine as a vision of his own wishful fantasies: a playful, urbane mix of articles, cartoons, fashion and fiction that would be an unashamed user's manual to the "good life" for young men like himself. The format struck an instant chord in the generation of men who came of age in the aftermath of World War II and the socially repressive 1950s. Thanks to the GI Bill and an expanding economy, many of *Playboy*'s readers were the first in their family ever to attend college and be introduced to a more sophisticated urban culture. They needed a roadmap. Like his contemporaries, Hefner found cherished role models like John Wayne or even Jimmy Stewart an ill fit for his generation, which no longer worried so much about how to "make it" as how to live it. Young American males were striving to be suave, hip and irresistible to women.

The appeal to upward mobility, along with the boldness of its liberated tone and graphics, set *Playboy* apart from its contemporary male market competitors, which assumed either an existing, inbred sophistication on the part of its readers, like *Esquire*, or, like *True* and *Argosy*, a primary interest in the outdoors. Even more importantly, that first issue delivered another all-American male dream come true: the pretty girl-next-door undraped. A nude pinup of Marilyn Monroe became *Playboy*'s first "Playmate." The surface sophistication, balanced (perhaps even unconsciously) by the almost wide-eyed innocence that then typified the American male, raised *Playboy* above the murky strata of any then-existent "nudie" magazines. In its own bizarre way, *Playboy* was as American as apple pie—if not exactly mom.

Playboy's first issue, December 1953.

The magazine became an immediate success—a 1950s phenomenon. Hefner, often working 36 hours at a stretch, still found time to play, often in the company of Victor Lownes III, the magazine's suave promotion director, whom Hefner had befriended in 1954. Far more than his boss, Lownes was a bona fide playboy, the embodiment of the carefree, pleasure-driven bachelor's lifestyle espoused in the pages of the magazine. By the late 1950s, both men had recently shed their wives and family ties, and Lownes introduced the workaholic Hefner to an after-hours nightlife. *La dolce vita*, Chicago-style, for the two newly sprung men-about-town centered around a handful of supper

Clubs: The Black Orchid, Chez Paree, The Cloisters. Cool jazz, hip young comedians and easy intimacy.

One night in 1958, Victor Lownes stopped by one of his regular haunts, the popular Near North Side nightclub The Cloisters, owned by Shelly Kasten and Skip Krask. There, he first encountered a local model and former Miss Chicago runner-up named Bonnie Jo Halpin. B.J., as her friends call her, remembers locking eyes immediately with the handsome, boyish 32-year-old Lownes.

"Victor just stood at the bottom of the stairs smoking and looking up at me. He made sure the party I was with got a good table. It was a great jazz joint—deep, dark and smoky—where you could hear the Ramsey Lewis Trio and see a new comedian, Lenny Bruce. When I went to the ladies' room, the woman who was with Victor followed me in and told me he wanted to meet me. I asked her how she felt about that and she said, 'If you say Yes, I get a raise. I work for him.'

"When I stopped by his table, he introduced himself as Victor Lownes III and asked if he could call me sometime. He also told me he worked for *Playboy*. I didn't know what that was. On my way home that night, I stopped and got a copy of the magazine. I thought, 'Oh, my God Almighty!'

"When Victor called me, I told him, 'I'm Catholic and I live at home with my mom and sister. I just can't do that.' He said, 'I wasn't going to ask you to do *that*. I was just going to ask you out to dinner.'

"The first night he took me out, I wore a polo coat, saddle shoes, a plaid skirt and a sweater because I didn't know where we were going. He took me to the Pump Room! I said, 'Victor, I'm not dressed properly for a place like this. Everybody's in low-cut dresses and gowns.' He said, 'You're just fine.' Artichokes! Oysters Rockefeller! Wow. When Victor asked me what I wanted to drink, I said, 'I'd love hot chocolate.' He said, without missing a beat, 'How do you want that, with a lot of milk? A lot of sugar?' I said, 'As rich as you can make it.' It came with lots of whipped cream."

Lownes swept Halpin off her feet. She was in love, but she couldn't "go all the way." She stopped seeing him, but five months later he called to take her out to dinner. "I told my mom I was staying with a girlfriend for the night and went to a dime store to buy a little nightgown. I just wanted to be with him. We went out to dinner and then went back to his apartment. Well, I stayed in the bathroom forever and then finally ran out and jumped into his bed. My heart was racing; no one had told me about sex.

Victor Lownes and Bonnie Jo Halpin, 1958.

It wasn't long before he screamed, 'Oh, my God, you're a virgin!' He figured I'd been around because I was a model. I was 18 years old.

"The next morning I remember getting on a bus thinking, 'Everybody knows I just had sex. I'm a woman.'"

Halpin moved in with Lownes soon after and became a part of the group that included Hefner. "I was expecting an older man, but he looked like Joe College," she recalled. "Hef was a recluse who wanted people to come to him. His secretary didn't wake him until 3 o'clock in the afternoon because he liked to work all night. Victor and Hef were very similar; both were intellectuals with very high IQs. The difference was that Victor came from a well-to-do family, while Hefner was more middle-class; his father was an accountant and his mother was a housewife."

■ ■ ■ ■

In 1959, *Playboy* ran a piece about the Gaslight Club, a Chicago nightspot established by ad executive Burton Browne in 1953. So-called "key clubs" were somewhat in vogue then, and the Gaslight charged its keyholders an initial fee of $25. But even more novel, the nightclub featured a music hall atmosphere with showgirl waitresses dressed in provocative Gay 90s-style corsets and fishnet tights. Lownes noticed at once the extraordinary response from *Playboy*'s readers. "We had more than 3,000 letters sent in by guys wanting to know how they could become members of Gaslight," recalled Lownes. "I saw that our readers were the best market in the world for such an attraction." The promotions director pitched the idea to Hefner: why not a Playboy Club sporting the ambiance of the sophisticated bachelor's pad created in the magazine? Intimate, urban, with gorgeous girls in provocative costumes as waitresses.

The need for such a place had been discussed in Hefner's after-hours circle. Part of that group was Shelly Kasten, co-owner of The Cloisters, who soon became one of Hefner's closest friends (and much later a regular at the

Wednesday night poker games at the Los Angeles Playboy Mansion). "Every single night around 1 o'clock, Hef would come in to The Cloisters when he finished work at the magazine," recalled Kasten. "I'd close up about 3:30 and we'd hang out the rest of the night doing something, like bowling or playing gin rummy. Hef used to say, 'Wouldn't it be nice if we had our own private little place to go to.' We wanted to have a private club seating about 80 people just for the guys to hang out in."

By 1960, with Lownes' urging, Hefner decided to launch his dream. Just as the magazine touted itself as "a pleasure primer for the sophisticated city-bred man," so, too, the Playboy Club was designed for "urban fellows who are less concerned with hunting, fishing and climbing mountains than with good food, drink, proper dress and the pleasure of female company."

Lownes turned to his friend Arnie Morton, the manager of a supper club called Walton Walk, and the scion of well-known Chicago restaurateur Morton C. Morton (as well as the father of the Hard Rock Café's Peter Morton) to develop the idea of a Playboy Club. The deal was made: 50 percent of the stock in Playboy Clubs, International, was assigned to H.M.H. Publishing, while the balance was split among Hefner, Lownes and Morton.

A savvy restaurateur, Morton knew location was crucial. He searched Chicago for a building that would be central, sophisticated—and not too expensive to lease. He found just the spot across the street from his own place, Morton's Walton Walk, at 116 E. Walton St., in the former Colony Club. The Colony Club property, which had already failed under four previous managements, was leased to Playboy at a minimal rent in exchange for a percentage of the Club's profits. In a matter of months, the Colony was stripped of its fusty continental decor and refurbished in the hipper, sleek leather-and-teak decor that would become the prototype of all Playboy Clubs to follow.

Morton trained the staff and handled the restaurant operations. But from the beginning, Morton's idea was to make the profit on the bar. The simple menu and standardized prices—$1.50 for food, drinks and a pack of cigarettes with the Playboy lighter—were designed to put even the most self-conscious young bachelor at ease on a date in the Club. "It was Arnie's idea to have everything priced at a buck-fifty," says Kasten. "There was no money in food—the steak and potato probably cost us $1.50—so we gave it away. In those days, $1.50 was a lot of money for a drink, so that's where we made the profit."

Next was the question of the waitress costume—a critical decision. Coming up with an alluring yet suitable outfit for the girls to wear was one of the biggest decisions to be made. For the Club's bachelor-pad look, it had been a simple matter to turn to the pages of *Playboy* for interior design and furnishing ideas. However, a scantily clad, real-live *Playboy* centerfold serving food and drink in a restaurant, precisely the male fantasy they strived to satisfy, had no precedent. At best, it seemed highly impractical. Hefner's first idea was to have "Playmates" dressed in short, frilly nighties, but as a serviceable waitress uniform, it was soon discarded.

Ilsa Taurins, an attractive blonde Latvian refugee Lownes was dating at the time, actually came up with the idea. Looking at the magazine's famous logo one day, she asked offhandedly, "Why not dress them as rabbits?"

Marle Renfro (the body double for Janet Leigh in *Psycho*) wearing the original costume.

As it turned out, Hefner had already considered the idea and rejected it. The rabbit in the logo, with its cocked ear and bow tie, was clearly male. But Lownes encouraged Taurins to work on a design, which her mother, a seamstress, fashioned out of a satin fabric. A few days later, Lownes, Morton and Hefner watched as Ilsa strode into the half-furnished Club, modeling the sample costume. To Lownes, it looked more like a one-piece bathing suit than a fetching outfit for a cocktail waitress. He was sure Hefner would discard the concept. But Hefner saw possibilities. He liked the fluffy tail and headband with ears, but thought the costume itself was cut too low on the leg. How would it look, he wondered, if Ilsa tucked up the sides of the garment?

The effect was astonishing, according to Lownes, who credits Hefner's uncanny eye for the transformation. By revealing more upper thigh, the length of Ilsa's legs had been dramatically extended, a trick schoolgirls in gym shorts had learned long ago. But the suits still seemed baggy. Eventually, the costume was cut even higher on the hip, and a new satin material replaced the original, along with added boning. The collar and cuffs had yet to be added.

The Bunny Costume

The signature Bunny costume, with its fluffy tail, white collar, cuffs, black bow tie and perky ears, can lay claim to the only patent ever granted a service uniform by the United States Patent Office (patent #762,884). But like any durable design, it was the product of much testing, tinkering and improvement over the years. The original costume was a strapless, one-piece rayon-satin garment constructed on a merry widow corset, accessorized with oversized satin ears and a tail, but without the collar and cuffs. The costume was available in 10 colors. In 1961, name tags on satin rosettes were pinned on the costume over the right hipbone.

Eventually, Paris-born Chicago dress designer Renée Blot was hired by Playboy to perfect the costume. She eliminated the seams under the bust, raised the cut high on the leg and supervised the production of the Bunny suit by Chicago corset maker Kabo. With the opening of the New York Club in 1962, Blot was sent to fit the novice Manhattan Club Bunnies and appoint a wardrobe mistress. Soon, Blot had Bunny costumes available in 12 shades and 12 sizes. Among the most popular colors were red, peacock blue and emerald green.

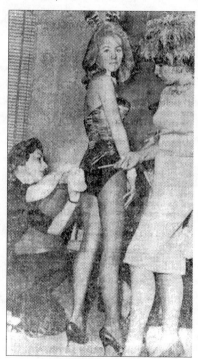

Danskin sheer black tights replaced the original black mesh dancers' tights in 1962. In 1964, a washable and highly durable one-piece boned foundation was adopted in a variety of colors, but only two cup sizes, a wishful 34D and 36D—requiring considerable padding for most Bunnies. In 1968, Playboy introduced sheer-to-the-waistband dancers' support tights. The original nylon yarn Bunny tails were replaced with white fake fur in July 1969. Throughout two-and-a-half decades, the dyed-to-match satin pump with a 3-inch heel remained the regulation shoe.

There were specialized bunny suits as well. When the VIP Room, serving "Very Important Playboys" a *prix fixe* three-course dinner, was inaugurated with the opening of the New York Club, an elegant blue velvet costume with silver trim was introduced for the mostly foreign-born Bunnies who worked the plush room. In the late 1960s, Emilio Pucci-influenced prints were introduced. Polka dots and psychedelic prints followed in the disco era. In July 1980, the lace-and-satin Bunny Cabaret costume was introduced, featuring mesh stockings, garters and dyed pumps.

Renée Blot with Bunny Mother
Alice Nichols and
Bunny Suzanne Clary.

As Playboy added casinos and resort hotels to its roster of Playboy Clubs, more variations on the Bunny costume theme were introduced. Barefoot Bunnies in bikinis with tails and ears served cocktails at the Jamaica Club. The original promotion costume that Bunnies wore to publicity events initially featured a white pleated skirt, black sweater with the Bunny logo, and black tights with pumps. In 1968, the redesigned miniskirt version was worn with white leather mod boots. The Jet Bunnies aboard the later DC9 Big Bunny were outfitted in sleek black wet-look costumes.

Only a few larcenous Bunnies out of the more than 15,000 women who wore the costume managed to leave Playboy with one as a keepsake. The vast majority turned their costumes in to the wardrobe mistress when their employment ended. On occasion, individual Bunnies found a novel use for the costume outside the Club. One Bunny wore her costume for her induction into the U.S. Air Force. Another walked down the aisle at her wedding in a white satin Bunny costume—complete with a veil and satin ears.

Not all Bunnies were created equal, however. In fact, according to designer Bolt, there were distinct regional differences. New York Bunnies, for example, boasted the largest bosoms among the four Playboy Clubs. The smallest Bunnies worked in Miami, with a B-8, measuring 34-22-34; New Orleans topped out at C-6, measuring 36-24-36; Chicago Bunnies tended to the bottom line with a C-3, measuring 34-24-37.

■ ■ ■ ■

"Beautiful, charming and refined young ladies, waitressing experience unnecessary," read the advertisement on January, 4, 1960, in *The Chicago Tribune*. The ad featured a photograph of winsome Bonnie Jo Halpin donning Bunny ears. Morton, Lownes and Hefner were looking for 30 young Bunnies. On a frigid Saturday afternoon, several hundred women showed up, bringing bathing suits to audition. Some of the first Bunnies hired were

Patti Reynolds, Virginia Hirschfield, Kitty Kavany and Ashlyn Martin, Chicago Club, 1960.

Joyce Nizzari and Hugh
Hefner, Chicago, 1960.
(Note original costume
without collar and cuffs.)

women who had appeared in the pages of *Playboy*—June Wilkinson, Kitty
Kavany and Kelly Collins, and Playmates Joyce Nizzari, Joni Mattis, Carrie
Radison, Teddi Smith (Delilah Henry) and Christa Speck. Several Bunnies
were lured from the Gaslight Club. Bunnies also were recruited from the
Chez Paree chorus line—including dancers Delores Wells, Nancy Downey,
Judy Roski, Marilyn Miller and Sandy Keto.

But there were strict rules. "From the beginning, we made it a rule the
waitresses couldn't date customers," recalls Kasten. "There were eight of
us—including Hefner, his brother Keith, Arnie, Lownes, general manager
Matt Metzger and myself—who had 'C1 Keys' and we were the only ones
that the girls could date. It made it very nice for us, but the rule was basically to keep guys from coming in just to pick up girls. We didn't want a B-
Girl place."

Finally, the Playboy Club opened on Leap Year, Monday, February 29,
1960. Aside from the black-and-silver rabbit emblem stamped on the over-
head canopy and on either side of the door, there was no indication outside the Walton Street building that this was the new Playboy Club—
except for the line of people around the block waiting to enter.

A member showed his key to the Door Bunny, his name was posted on
the directory board in the lobby, and he was free to roam throughout the
Club. A closed-circuit TV viewed on monitors throughout the building kept
tabs on members arriving and leaving the Club. High-tech "cutting-edge"
accouterments included an extravagant $25,000 hi-fi system. There were

three rooms to choose from, beginning with the wood-paneled Playmate Bar on the first level, featuring a wall of illuminated Playboy centerfolds and drinks touting a "full ounce-and-a-half!" measure. Next was the Living Room, the centerpiece of the makeshift bachelor pad, complete with cozy armchairs and coffee tables. Like any decent red-blooded American bachelor-pad fantasy, it also sported a piano bar, where small combos played and a liveried butler served roast beef at the buffet table. Framed cartoons from the pages of *Playboy* lined the walls of the Cartoon Corner. There was also the more sophisticated Library, which Lownes transformed into a cabaret, installing his favorite singer, Mabel Mercer. While Mercer—known for her smoky supper-club style—was ensconced in a roomy armchair, playboys and their dates sat on cushions at her feet. Later, the Playroom and Penthouse showrooms would be added as entertainment turned out to be a big draw for members.

All in all, Hefner had succeeded in creating an adult version of the very different make-believe world Walt Disney was busy expanding on the West Coast. Both fantasylands allowed guests to indulge their secret dreams, at least temporarily. At a time when it was hip to be cool and well-tailored, and female singers were still referred to as "songbirds" and "canaries," the Playboy Club became the most popular nightclub in town.

"The Chicago Playboy Club was the hippest Club there was," Kasten recalls. "It was exciting. Entertainment in the showrooms and cabaret acts in the Library. Billiards. Bunnies dancing on the piano."

By the end of the first month of operation, 16,800 Keyholders and their guests had visited the Club. The hours were extended during the day from 11 until 2 to accommodate businessmen who wanted to come in for lunch. "But it wasn't until the cocktail hour that the Club started to swing, and kept hopping until 4 in the morning," according to Kasten.

It was soon after the Chicago Club opened, with B.J. Halpin as virtually the first Bunny, that she began to experience the dark side of Lownes. "Victor had a short temper. He could be a screamer, and very abusive to his secretary and other people who worked for him. I used to tell him that, but he'd say, 'What can I do? They're incompetent.' Victor was such a perfectionist, and he had no patience with ignorance. Yet I'm sure I was the most ignorant, naive person he ever met and he loved me. He'd ask me, 'Why can't you get it? I got it.'"

Lownes showed B.J. how tough he could be. "He sat me down and said, 'I don't want to hurt you, Puddy.' We had lived together close to a year, but now he wanted to play around. I told him I didn't want anybody but him, but he said, 'No, Puddy, you deserve better.' I was heartbroken.

"They all played around. Victor didn't leave me for another woman—he left me for a *lot* of other women. Hefner and Victor each always had a special girl, but they went through a lot of women on the side and cheated like mad.

"It was more than a year before I started to date again. But the best way for me to get over Victor was to move away. Playboy always sent special Chicago girls to train Bunnies in the new Clubs. I opened the Miami and New Orleans Clubs and stayed in each city for about three months."

In July 1962, the Chicago Playboy Club hit its first rocky patch. A growing feud between Victor Lownes and Keith Hefner ultimately precipitated Lownes' abrupt departure from Playboy. The clash between the two men erupted over Keith's increased involvement in the operations of the growing empire, which Lownes felt encroached on his own area of management. One ongoing sore point was Keith's refusal to utilize the illuminated signs that Lownes installed in the lobby to indicate whether or not seating was available in the showrooms. Lownes wanted guests arriving at the Club to know they could still see a show; Keith Hefner thought the flashing lights were tacky. Ultimately, the personal dispute snowballed to involve personnel throughout the Club. Everyone took sides.

The seven-year business relationship between Hugh Hefner and

Bonnie Jo Halpin.

Victor Lownes III came to an end, at a five-hour conference—3 a.m. to 8 a.m.—at the Playboy Mansion. Lownes agreed to sell his 25 percent interest in the Playboy clubs. Kasten took over the management of the Chicago Club. But Lownes and Hugh Hefner did manage to remain friends. When Lownes moved to New York to open a public relations firm, his first account was the New York Playboy Club.

Meanwhile, the Club continued to fulfill fantasies of men everywhere, even though they had to travel to Chicago to experience them first-hand. New York record producer Bud Prager would recall the first time he walked into the Chicago Playboy Club and spotted his first Bunny, Bonnie Jo Halpin, at the door. "I was standing there like a guy from Kansas, just mesmerized. She was the most beautiful girl I had ever seen in my life," recalls Prager. "Guys were scared to death of the reality—and here was the ultimate fantasy come to life."

Bonnie Jo Halpin

"All the priests said 'No, no, no' to everything," recalls B.J. Halpin, who grew up so poor that she, her sister and two brothers had to live in an orphanage. "I was a skinny kid with these big boobs, and the priests told me I could never wear a sleeveless blouse or a sweater because I was too busty and there were boys attending the school."

She was chosen high school homecoming queen and, following graduation, moved back home to live with her mother and older sister. B.J. was working in the advertising department of Standard Oil in Chicago during the week and modeling bathing suits on the weekends for a neighborhood shop owner. He entered her in the Miss Chicago contest and B.J. won runner-up. The publicity led to a job modeling bridal fashions and evening wear on live television commercials for a local store.

After B.J. met and started dating Victor Lownes, Hugh Hefner asked her to pose for the magazine's centerfold. Halpin demurred, but it was not the end of her Playboy career. As the two men made plans to open the first Playboy Club in 1960, Hefner came up with the idea to use Halpin as the quintessential Bunny to run with the employment ads. *If You Are As Pretty As Bonnie Jo Halpin, You Too Can Be . . .* ran the first ad copy.

Arnie Morton hired Halpin as the Door Bunny, and she was the hostess who greeted customers on Opening Night, February 29, 1960. "So I was the First Bunny," says

Halpin. It was a whole new world to the Catholic girl, who recalls, "I would travel all over the country with Victor to talk to girls on college campuses and tell them, 'You can work your way through school as a Playboy Bunny.'

"Working at the Club was wild and crazy, and in the beginning we could barely accommodate the crowds. The girls were terrific, and we had so much fun together. We looked after one another, like a sorority."

Halpin and several other Chicago Bunnies were eventually recruited to help open the New York Club. She and another Bunny, Linda Wickstrom, drove cross-country to New York through a blizzard,

Above: B.J. at the New York Club, 1963.
Left: B.J. and Digby, 1998.
These days, B.J. runs marathons, attends Mass every morning at a neighborhood church and continues her longtime schedule of hospital volunteer and animal shelter work.

with all of their belongings in the trunk of the car. "By the time we got to New York in that weather, I was sick. There was also a newspaper strike and the Club was fighting for its liquor license. Kelly Collins, who was dating Keith Hefner, and Kitty Kavany had both come out from Chicago, too, to train new Bunnies.

61

"I worked at the New York Club for about seven months. Gloria Steinem worked with me as a Door Bunny for a while. Although I'm now a fan of hers, at the time I thought the article she wrote about the Playboy Club was a terrible put-down. I'm not college educated, and I'm not someone who wanted a career. When she asked me how I liked working at the Club, I told her that when I worked at Standard Oil in Chicago, I made very little money. At Playboy I earned $45 a night, plus tips, working as a Door Bunny—that was a lot of dough in those days! And Playboy changed my life. Later, when neither of us worked for Playboy and I would run into Gloria at parties, I'm not even sure she remembered who I was.

"In the summer of 1963, I left Playboy. I wanted to see the world and try everything. After a few romances, I fell in love with a wonderful man, and we've been together for 35 years. I still have so many friends from my days at Playboy—even Victor. I adore his wife, Marilyn Cole, and I've stayed with them in Aspen." ∎

Nancy Downey Caddick

One night, Hef took me to a spot on Walton Street and showed me where he wanted to open a Playboy Club. He told me what he had in mind, but I just couldn't envision it.

"At the time I was dancing in the Chez Paree Adorables chorus line. The nightclub was just around the corner from the original *Playboy* offices, and Hef would come in after work to see the show and have a drink. I'd also been a guest on his television show, *Playboy After Dark*.

"When the Chez Paree closed in 1960, I headed for New York to try out for the Copacabana dance line. I was still a naive kid and I didn't last long in New York. As soon as I got back to Chicago, I called Hef to see if there was a job for me at the Playboy Club, which I knew had opened a few months earlier. I was hired as a Photo Bunny, and later worked as a Bumper Pool Bunny and Door Bunny. I often worked both the lunch and night shift, going home at 3 or 4 in the morning. I lived at home the entire time I worked at Playboy. I was one of seven children, and my father died when we were all quite young. A lot of my Bunny earnings went to my mother, who earned considerably less than I did even though she had worked for one company over many years. It was an extraordinary opportunity for me.

"I may have been somewhat naive, but I was not easily dazzled. The glamorous night-club atmosphere could go to your head, and some women were more impressionable than others. While some Bunnies wanted to party, others were raising their kids, going to school themselves or supporting husbands through school. For me, it was a juncture, a way station while I figured out what I should do next.

"In 1961, I left Playboy to try my luck in Holly-wood and was accepted into an actor's program at Columbia Studios. I played small roles in *77 Sunset Strip*, *Route 66*, a beach movie with Tommy Sands and a few other things, including a commercial for Lestoil with Zsa Zsa Gabor. She was very funny. After we finished filming, she offered me a job as her sec-retary! I declined. I remained in California for a year, but missed my family so much I decided to return to Chicago. Again, I wasn't sophisticated or shrewd enough to deal with the real world of Hollywood.

"I returned to the Chicago Playboy Club, where I eventually met my first husband. We weren't sup-posed to date customers, of course, but I made an ex-ception in his case, and left Playboy to marry him in 1963. At that time in my life, marriage and a family were what I wanted.

Dr. Nancy Caddick, a clinical social worker with the AIDS-HIV hospice at Chicago's Northwestern Memorial Hospital.

"Many years after I'd worked at Playboy, and the youngest of my three sons started school, I applied for a job at Chicago's Northwestern Memorial Hospital. I sent in my appli-cation, waited and heard nothing. Finally, I went to the hospital and personally handed in my résumé on which I had included my work as a Bunny. The secretary who looked over my application was amused—working at the Playboy Club seemed such an unexpected thing for someone in my line of work to have done. She set up an appointment for an inter-view, and I got the job as an office manager for their respiratory therapy department. That job enabled me to go back to college and complete my bachelor's and master's degrees in social work. I was then able to change jobs within Northwestern from the business to the medical side, and began working with terminally ill patients in the hospice program. A few doctors who know I once worked as a Playboy Bunny still tease me about it. Well, I *loved* the job. Dancing, acting and working as a Bunny were great life experiences that really add a dimension to who I am today and my understanding of people.

"In 1985, I began working with my first AIDS/HIV patients, and 10 years later got my doctorate in clinical social work. Now I'm looking ahead to teaching and doing some writing." ∎

Delilah Henry

I was the first girl to be invited to live in Hef's Mansion in Chicago. It was one of the magical things that happened to me as a result of posing for the *Playboy* centerfold in 1960. That summer, shortly after my Playmate photographs appeared in the July issue, I moved into the Mansion and started working as a Bunny in the Chicago Playboy Club. When it was discovered that I was only 17 years old, too young to work legally in the Club, I became Hef's receptionist at *Playboy* and traveled the country doing Playmate promotions. A few years later, after working as a Bunny in Chicago and New Orleans, I got a job in *Playboy*'s photo department.

"The Bunny job and promotional work helped me learn how to deal with people—and hang on to my sense of humor. My photography work at the magazine engendered the idea that I could actually have a career in design and also gave me a sense of how to handle myself in the corporate world.

"For more than 15 years, I've had my own New York-based interior design firm. I've come to realize that my career was motivated equally by the Playboy years and by my early environment. As a teenager living at the Mansion, I was introduced to antiques: fine furniture, paintings and other works of art. From my childhood came indelible memories of the light and color of changing seasons and spatial proportions of the giant redwoods surrounding our small log cabin.

"I was born in Hastings, Nebraska, but when I was still a baby my parents became migrants, traveling from Northern California to Oregon, stopping wherever they could find work. My father, who had been a featherweight Golden Gloves boxer and aspiring actor, looked for carpentry jobs. We finally settled in Grant's Pass, Oregon, where we built a log cabin. There was a lot of creative stimulation in those rustic surroundings, but I was not good in school. Many years later, I was diagnosed as having all the classic symptoms of dyslexia. In those days I was just regarded as 'backward' and a slow learner. My parents' only hope was that I would get enough schooling to be able to find work. I left school at 16 without finishing seventh grade. By that time, we were living in Los Angeles.

"My father knew he had a very pretty daughter who might become a model or actress. A photographer friend of my parents took some stills of me, fully clothed, and sent a few to *Playboy*. Ultimately, it was photographer Bill Graham and his wife Shirley who did the centerfold story and photographs. They befriended me and became surrogate aunt and uncle to me.

"In 1960, it was considered very prestigious to be a Playmate. At the time I was still a 16-year-old kid, and far from the prettiest girl chosen to be a centerfold. I think I was also the only fully dressed Playmate. I met Hef for the first time in Los Angeles after my centerfold pictures had already been shot, and his first words to me were, 'My God, if I had seen you before we went to press, I would have brought you to Chicago for a re-shoot.' I have a feeling if I'd done a reshoot, the pictures would have been less modest.

"One Sunday in July 1960, the Grahams invited me for brunch. Shirley said to me, 'Delilah, nothing is going to happen with your life here in Van Nuys. Why don't you go to Chicago and work as a Bunny?' Sometime later I leaned that my mother wrote Hefner a letter asking him to 'take care of my little girl.' But I think my parents felt instinctively that I had good sense and could handle this opportunity. As a teenager, I was fairly inde-pendent. I spent most of my time around adults, listening. I didn't want to hang out with other kids my age, doing silly things.

"At the time the Playboy Mansion became my home, Hef didn't own the entire building. As individual leases expired, he would acquire the space. Hef knew that girls were coming to Chicago from all over the country to become Bunnies or Playmates, and they had no place to stay. As more apartments became available, they were refitted to become part of a dorm, known as the Bunny Hutch. The Mansion's kitchen was open 24 hours a day so the girls always had food available, even if they worked at the Club till 3 a.m.

"A small one-bedroom apartment on the very top floor was available when I moved in. I shared a connecting bath with the apartment where [writer] Shel Silverstein and [artist] LeRoy Neiman stayed. Both of my 'roommates' were great guys, and we had loads of fun. I told Shel one day that 'the girls are going to find you more desirable if I creme-rinse your fuzzy beard'—and he let me do it. LeRoy Neiman loved fine wines and the best of everything. In those days, Hef had nothing but

The Playboy Mansion, Chicago.

Baccarat crystal, exquisite china and the finest napery. One night while LeRoy and I were drinking an incredibly good wine, he said 'Why don't we see Chicago by helicopter?' We had the cook make us a picnic hamper, grabbed a bottle of the wine and the Baccarat glasses and flew over Chicago in a rented helicoptor just to see the sights. It was like a fairy-tale world in those days.

"Bonnie Jo Halpin was one of the first girls I met when I arrived in Chicago. She just opened her arms and told me, 'I'll be your friend.' She was dating Victor Lownes at the time and said, 'I can tell you everything that's going on around here.' A few weeks after I moved in, Bonnie Jo was staying overnight with me. It was the night Hef was throwing a bachelor party for Sammy Davis Jr., who would marry Mai Britt the following day. Hef came to my apartment and told us he was going to lock the door from the outside and that, 'under no circumstances do you two come out!' Bonnie said, 'That's interesting. I guess they're going to have an orgy.'

'Oh, lots of food and things.' I was thinking 'banquet.'

'My dear,' Bonnie said, 'there is more to an orgy than just a whole lot of food.'

"Bonnie and I became great friends. Joyce Nizzari, a very elegant, feminine girl who was both a Bunny and a Playmate, was my roommate for a while. Later, two other centerfold Bunnies, Terre Tucker and Carrie Radisson, roomed with me.

"The Playboy Mansion was a bachelor's fantasy. Hef would give parties that went on until 4 or 5 o'clock in the morning. People who worked until 3 a.m. were still revved up and loved having a place to unwind. He served them sumptuous buffet breakfasts. It was a fast world, and boy, everybody wanted to go to the Chicago Playboy Mansion parties. Intellectuals, movie stars, politicians, sports figures—really interesting people of every sort, including celebrities: the Shah of Iran, Elizabeth Taylor and Lenny Bruce.

"Hef was into hypnosis and very good at it. At smaller gatherings of 10 or 12 close friends, he was at his best. Under hypnosis, a subject's body language and voice would change to that of a 6-year-old, and Hef would ask questions. 'Where are you now?' 'What do you see?' Unfortunately, he had a problem bringing people out if it. On one occasion I watched him hypnotize Joni Mattis, a Playmate and Bunny whom he was dating. While she was under, he told her that after he brought her out she would revert to a hypnotic state whenever she saw him with a bottle of Pepsi-Cola. Well, he drank Pepsi all the time! In the middle of a party she saw him with a Pepsi in his hand. Bam! She was under.

"Although the opportunity was there, all around me in Chicago, I never strayed into the fast lane. I never got mixed up with 'wise guys.' Partly, I'm sure, because I lived at the Mansion and Hef kept an eye on me. Also, when I became Hef's receptionist at *Playboy*, I was exposed to a different world. I was attracted to people on the magazine—the editors, photographers and the entire creative staff—and enjoyed the intellectual stimulation. I did a minimum of talking, a lot of listening and learned a great deal. When

I turned 18, I started working as a Bunny again and went to New Orleans for the opening of that Club.

"I've always had an eye for design. A small contribution to improving the look of the Bunny costume was my suggestion of using a cat brush to fluff up the Bunny tails and then attach them higher on the fanny to give the girls a prettier line. My next idea was to use the soft cottontails as bra push-ups. It became a running joke that we all had three tails. I worked with the wardrobe mistress to fit the costume higher on the hip to make the legs look longer and give more definition to the waist.

"From the outset, Hef and I had very good rapport and he always listened to me. I went into a rage one day at the Club because of the way one of the managers was treating a Bunny. When I told the man that I was going to speak to Hef about it, he fired me. 'I don't think so,' I said. On that particular day, Hef was in the Club being interviewed for a Canadian television documentary. That didn't stop

Delilah and "Maxie" the cat at home in her Manhattan penthouse.

me. I marched up to him. 'There's something you have to hear. It's very important.' Without knowing what my complaint was about or what I would say, Hef told the camera crew to keep rolling and invited me to sit down. 'Let's talk,' he said. 'Tell me what's going on.'

"In 1964, I began working full-time in the photo department at *Playboy* and no longer worked as a Bunny. From the beginning I admired Hefner's great respect for professional women. He took pains to advance their careers, promoting women who had started as secretaries to executive positions. I had no idea I had creative talents that could lead to a career until I was given an opportunity at *Playboy* to do setups for various pictorials on food, stereo equipment and clothing items. I traveled to Europe to work on various shoots, helping to select the women and the locations.

"In 1967 I fell in love with Enrico Sarsini, a New York-based *Life* magazine photographer, who came to Chicago to shoot a cover for *Playboy*. I was chosen to be the model photographed behind a shower door tracing the Playboy rabbit in the steam. After the shoot, we commuted back and forth and talked endlessly by telephone. Eventually, he asked me to move to New York. We lived together in his West Side apartment for a year before we broke up. He became a Vietnam War photographer, while I remained on my own in New York modeling and doing television commercials.

"Later, after we had split up and I had traveled the world, my interior-design career sort of found me. Friends asked me to redecorate their apartments because they liked my eclectic style and the way I handled the chronic New York problems of limited space and light. A textile manufacturer approached me about designing his new showroom to feature his art collection. By the time I started my interior-design business, I was into the next chapter of my life and no longer mentioned my background with Playboy. No one, I thought, was going to hand over a half-million dollars to a 'Playboy Bunny' to do a design project. Above all, I had to avoid being mistaken for 'someone's cute girlfriend who's redoing the place.'

"Also, I had personally become more conservative while I saw *Playboy* magazine becoming more risqué. As a businesswoman running my own firm, I didn't want to be associated with that image. Up until a year ago, I didn't even want to be identified as 'Teddi Smith,' my pseudonym as a Playmate, and avoided giving any interviews for *Playboy*. Hef, who remains a good friend, has respected that decision over the years. But after I finished a major design project for a Fortune 500 company earlier this year, I had a change of heart about my Playboy experience. It had to do with feeling more secure about my professional standing and less concerned about giving up some of my privacy. I was very pleased to appear in the 1996 *Playmate* book.

"I've also renewed my long-standing relationship with Hef. Today his home in Los Angeles is architecturally beautiful, but almost casual in decor compared with the Chicago Playboy mansion I remember in the '60s. But, you know, these days he has a family life with kids and dogs, so it's a different lifestyle. Times are changing for women, and Hef has always been receptive to evolving social attitudes. I've talked to him about including older women, and not just older celebrity women, in *Playboy*'s pictorials. Hef was warm to the idea and said that he was moving in that direction.

"I love my work. I love scouting through warehouses for vintage architectural pieces I can rehabilitate and mix with modern design. I love the engineering work involved in creating sculpture out of unexpected materials. It's magical. It's interesting to me how much the influences of my youth still shape my life. My parents were always helping their neighbors build a house, cut down a tree, fix something broken. Maybe it's just called survival, but that 'helping out' was always a part of our everyday life and it's ingrained in me. One thing I would like to participate in now is setting up a charitable program among the Playmates and former Bunnies to assist women who need help making a transition or getting back on their feet. Financially, psychologically and emotionally, we can offer a helping hand to those who just need a boost so they can once again support themselves." ∎

Alice Nichols

R ecently divorced, Alice Nichols needed a job that would allow her to be with her young son during the day. She found work as a cocktail waitress in one of the "bust-out" joints, as they were called, on Rush Street.

"I didn't know anything about those places. but I learned quickly enough that hookers worked out of there. Those girls were very protective of me. They made sure I got good tips and that customers didn't come on to me, but I still felt uneasy working there. Then I heard about the Playboy Club opening.

"Arnie Morton was running the Club. If he hadn't been such a 'leg and behind' man, I would never have gotten the job! The Bunnies who were hired in the beginning all had big breasts. The girls with the really humongous breasts were usually assigned to the '26' table playing dice with the customers. I guess the theory was that guys would be mesmerized by voluptuous girls and wouldn't pay attention to how much they were betting.

"In those days, you had to buy your own merry widow corset at Schwartz's on Rush Street. The Bunny costume was then built around it using a thick, satiny material. Later, we added a satin shell that came in a variety of sizes that could be adjusted. The tails were also fabricated from a different material because customers were always trying to light them—they had to be made out of something fire-retardant. The satin ears were attached to very tight plastic hair bands, which caused agonizing headaches and were a source of contention between the Bunnies and Victor Lownes. On opening night, when a good number of Bunnies took the ears off, Victor flew into a rage and ordered the women to put them back on.

"I was the first Bunny trainer, and I kind of stumbled into the job. On one of my first evenings in the Playmate Bar, I went up to a customer and said 'I'm your Bunny Alice. May I see the member's key, please?' The man told me his name was Hugh Hefner. But I insisted upon seeing a key before I served him a drink.

"He said, 'You don't understand, I'm Hugh Hefner.' And I said, 'You don't understand. You don't get a drink until I see your key.' At that time, all I knew was that Arnie Morton ran the Club. The bartender quickly put me straight. 'Why didn't somebody show me a picture of this guy?' I asked.

Bunny Alice, 1960.

"When I came back to the table where Mr. Hefner was sitting, I spilled my drink tray all over him and his guest, one of the comedians performing at the Club. It was a disaster.

"There was no training program at that time, only a few loose rules for taking and serving a drink order. After that accident with Mr. Hefner, I proposed a training program and worked with Keith Hefner and Arnie Morton to develop it. Later, I worked as a Bunny Mother, training Bunnies for the Club openings in Miami, New Orleans, New York and Los Angeles. All of the Clubs were different and, of course, labor laws and policies varied from city to city. In New York, girls under 21 couldn't work past a certain hour. Scheduling around school hours was a factor in almost all of the Clubs because Playboy wanted to promote that image of the college girl. We didn't want Bunnies to be thought of as nothing more than empty-headed pretty girls. Ideally, each girl had to be someone with intelligence and good conversational skills. And a sense of humor was a *major* asset.

"The newly hired Bunnies generally started out in the Playmate Bar and worked their way up to the Showrooms. I preferred working in the Showrooms. So many entertainers performed on the Playboy Club circuit: Red Foxx, Bill Cosby, Peter Allen, Jackie Gayle, Dick Gregory, Lainie Kazan and George Carlin, to name just a few.

"It was a hard job because you were on your feet the whole time, walking in high heels and carrying a heavy tray. A tray of drinks for four people weighed at least 10 pounds by the time you had your shots and the glasses of ice with water or soda on the side.

"On one occasion, I was serving a party of about a dozen men, who all worked in the same office. The key member, who was not the boss, got everybody into the Club, but it was his boss who became drunk and obnoxious. All the other men were uncomfortable, particularly the Keyholder because he knew it was Club

Chardonnay, B.C.

Bunnies from coast to coast learned how to garnish 20 cocktail variations (sours, slings, collins, martinis, Manhattans, sidecars, gimlets, etc.). They were also required to identify 143 bottles brands of liquor, including 31 Scotches, 16 bourbons and 30 liqueurs.

policy that if you got out of line, your key was confiscated. Once you lost your membership, you couldn't come back. I was carrying a trayful of drinks and doing the Bunny Dip when the drunken man grabbed my crotch and said, 'How do you like that?'

"Everyone else at the table was mortified. But I was mad. I had my tray on my left hand so I smacked him on the nose with my right hand—without spilling a drink. As his eyes started to water, I said, 'How do you like that?'

"I was sure I'd lost my job and I really didn't care because I didn't want to put up with that kind of behavior. Instead, everyone, including the management, took my side. The Keyholder gave me my first hundred-dollar tip.

Alice Nichols, Los Angeles, 1965.

"We developed a secret means of dealing with unruly customers. One of our favorite Bunnies was Vera. Her parents didn't approve of her job as a Bunny but finally agreed to visit the Club. Everyone was sure that once they saw her working in a nice, protected environment they'd be pleased. But that night, a guy in Vera's station seemed to be giving her a hard time—and here Vera had told her parents it was such a safe place to work. So her friend, Bunny Denise, followed our standard procedure: she ordered a *Pousse café*—a drink with layers of sweet, heavy cordials that the bartenders hated to make—and proceeded to dump it on the offender, making it look like an accident so Vera's tip wouldn't be affected. Denise, looking very smug, thinking she'd done Vera a favor, said, 'I took care of him!' But Vera had this terrible look on her face. 'That's my father,' she said.

"We developed a Merit/Demerit Program to reward Bunnies who adhered to the rules and penalize those who ignored them. Something had to be done to keep things fair. Most of the demerits came from poor grooming and tardiness. If your Bunny tail wasn't fluffy and you were late for work, you could count on demerits. Initially, each demerit cost a dollar, and the money went into a kitty to reward the Bunny of the Month who had earned the most merits for helping out with promotions, working as a replacement or selling the most drinks in souvenir Playboy mugs.

"As a Bunny Mother, I had to fire girls for two primary reasons: tardiness and noshows. There were others who chronically disobeyed the rules, and some who couldn't physically do the work. Those were the worst dismissals, firing a girl who desperately wanted to be a Bunny but just couldn't carry the tray or endure standing on her feet in high heels for any length of time.

"When the Clubs started, 4-inch high heels were the fashion for women. The Vargas girls in *Playboy* magazine were considered appealing and sensuous and high-heeled shoes were part of that image. But New York was so fashion-conscious and sophisticated that women in the 1960s never thought of wearing anything other than high heels. Somehow, women managed to walk all over town in dressy shoes, whatever the weather.

"But the New York Club was where the Bunnies wanted to change everything, including having the option of wearing lower-heeled shoes with the Bunny costume. The New York Bunnies also wanted to unionize, and that meant the beginning of seniority and the automatic 15 percent tip. Bunnies thought it was wrong to pay bar fees, that it should be illegal to make an employee 'pay' to work. But that money went straight to the busboys who also deserved tips. If it hadn't been for the hardworking busboys clearing tables quickly, the Bunnies would lose money on turnover.

"I worked 11 years for Playboy, moving from one Club to another until late 1970. I was working as Bunny Mother in the Los Angeles Club when I decided it was time to

Alice at home in Phoenix.

move on and find another career. I became a vice president with Merle Norman Cosmetics, and later worked for Marriott Hotels. I'm now retired and live in Phoenix.

"I had one dull job while I was still in high school, and I swore I'd never have another boring job. I never have." ∎

Joyce Nizzari

It was absolutely true that when you visited a Playboy Club you saw Playmates from the pages of the magazine greeting you at the door. I had already appeared as a *Playboy* centerfold when I worked as a Door Bunny for the opening of the Chicago Club (February 1960), Miami Club (May 1961) and the New Orleans Club (October 1961).

"Hef was the first romance in my life, my first real love. Bunny Yeager, who had photographed me in swimsuits on the beach, introduced me to Hef at a party when he visited Miami in February 1958. I was 17, and he was a very boyish 33. There was an immediate attraction, but

I really fell in love with him when we stood on the dock that evening and kissed.

"The first time I visited Hef, we stayed in a sparsely furnished apartment he kept in the same building as Victor Lownes. We would often double-date with Victor and Bonnie Jo Halpin, and we all celebrated New Year's Eve together at The Cloisters in 1959. Late at night, the guys would toss ideas back and forth about the kind of Club they wanted to start. At one time, they thought that the Bunnies should be cats— and tried to come up with ideas for the costume.

"I posed for a *Playboy* cover photograph on my first trip to Chicago. The picture that appeared on the July 1958 issue is still one of my favorites. After that I think Hef just assumed that I would be open to becoming a Playmate, and we didn't really talk about it. I had done only cheesecake photos before— never anything nude—but I did the centerfold for December 1959 because I knew it would please him. That's how women were in those days when so much between the sexes was taken for granted.

Joyce Nizzari at home in Los Angeles.

"At about the time of the first Playboy Jazz Festival, I discovered that Hef had other women in his life. He had invited Betty Zuziak, who worked at the magazine, to the festival instead of me. I was heartbroken, simply devastated to think that I wasn't enough for him. I had grown up with parents who had me believing that happily-ever-after happened once you found someone you loved.

"It was a terrible time, made worse because I kept thinking things would change. I moved back to Miami, but in January 1960, he invited me to join him in Washington D.C., to attend John F. Kennedy's inauguration. That was our last time together.

"In the early 1960s I moved to Los Angeles. While working as a dancer and actress, I fell in love with my landlord and next door neighbor in Laurel Canyon, Bob Hogan, who was then doing the TV series *Combat* with Vic Morrow.

"I've stayed in touch with Hef over the years. Bob and I were living in Florida for a brief period in the early '70s. Hef, who was then dating Barbi Benton, invited us to join them for the opening-night gala of Playboy's Miami Plaza Hotel in December 1970. I had recently given birth to my son and I was so tired. I was thinking, 'I'm only 30 years old—is this all there is?' A night out at an exciting, glamorous event lifted my spirits and made me think things would get better—and they did.

"I now live in Los Angeles close to both my son and my daughter, and run my own business doing medical transcribing. Age matters little to me. I'm always taking classes, looking for new things to do. Lately I've been working on a children's story based on a Hawaiian tale, 'The Rabbit in the Moon.' " ∎

Barbara Grant DeNoux

Eighteen-year-old Barbara Grant, a Sandra Dee look-alike, was working at the Gaslight Club in 1960 and dating Matt Metzger, the newly hired general manager of the Playboy Club. "Matt was a friend of Hugh Hefner and Shelley Kasten," Barbara recalls, "and one night they all came into the Gaslight on Walton Street. Hefner asked if I would like to be a Bunny at the Playboy Club, which hadn't yet opened. I liked the singing and dancing, which was part of the job at the Gaslight, but I wanted to give the new Playboy Club a try. I became one of the first Bunnies hired to open the Chicago Club. Working the lunch shift and occasionally filling in at night as a Door Bunny or a Table Bunny in one of the Showrooms, I could easily earn between $300–$500 a week. I shopped on Michigan Avenue and spent money on cocktail dresses and dry cleaning. I don't know where else it went!"

"Some of our customers—wealthy, older men—felt free to come on to us. One middle-aged man asked me how much it would take to get me in bed with him that night. I was about 18 years old at the time. I looked him in the eyes and asked if he had a daughter. He did. I asked him how he'd feel if some man approached his daughter like that. He said, 'I wouldn't like it and I'm really sorry I said it.' From that day on, I knew I could handle myself.

"Going out with a customer after work was forbidden, but I didn't want to do that anyway. You have to wake up in the morning and look at yourself

Shelly Kasten

"The bookkeeper came to me one day and said that a lot of the Bunnies weren't cashing their payroll checks. I couldn't believe it, but some of the girls were making so much cash in the beginning that those checks would just lie in their dresser drawers for weeks and months."

in the mirror. No thanks. I liked my job. I was so fortunate to be independent and earning so much money. When I look back, I wish I'd had the common sense to invest that money! But I also think about the common sense I did have at 18—working in that Rush Street club environment and not getting pulled into drugs or prostitution.

"In those days we drank Scotch—hard liquor—and we played as hard as we worked. It was easy for a girl to OD on speed and booze. After work she'd party, sleep a few hours and pop a Dexedrine to go back to work, not realizing that the pills would hit the liquor still in her body. There were several girls working at various clubs on Rush Street who did OD.

"But Playboy couldn't do enough for you if you conducted yourself like a 'lady' and did your job well. There were girls who were trying to raise kids on their own, or break out of a marriage or start a career—and the management worked with you. I was always in love, always having a problem with the man I imagined myself in love with. I think the management at Playboy realized it was dealing with very young, very pretty girls who were going to be a handful.

"We were Playboy Bunnies at a good time. I never looked back later and thought I was out of my mind to have worked as a Bunny. In 1961, I left Playboy to launch an acting career in Los Angeles. Later, after I married and

One Bunny who did OD on booze and pills was Connie Petrie, a pretty brunette with a lively personality, who had grown up in Chicago. Connie had been married for three years when she gave birth to a baby, who lived only 13 days. Her marriage failed and Connie took a job as a cocktail waitress at Mister Kelly's, a hot jazz club on Rush Street. She went to work at the Playboy Club in December 1961, and was soon one of the most popular Bunnies in the Penthouse, earning up to $300 a week. She lived with her boyfriend, a bartender, in a plush apartment and enjoyed the high life. A doctor told Connie to cut out the drinking or her kidneys wouldn't make it. But booze and pills fueled the nightlife on Rush Street and she didn't stop.

In late July, six months after Connie had started work at Playboy, Victor Lownes called the 26-year-old into his office to ask her about rumors that she was using marijuana. Connie flatly denied the accusation. Lownes asked her if she would be willing to take a lie detector test. Connie refused. It certainly wasn't an indication that she was guilty, but Lownes felt obligated to protect the Club's reputation. He fired her. Connie, reportedly devastated at losing her job, had a fight with her boyfriend, who managed to prevent her from jumping out an 11th-floor window. Hours later, her boyfriend awoke to find her sprawled on the bed, with four empty prescription bottles on the floor near her cold, outstretched hand. The newspapers reported that Connie Petrie had committed suicide because she had been fired from her Bunny job.

Barbara Grant DeNoux owns
six clothing boutiques in
Palm Desert, California.

my daughter was born, I worked briefly as a Bunny Mother. All in all, it was a great experience. I've explained to my daughter that you can become a very strong, independent person when you know you can support yourself and not have to depend upon anyone else to take care of you." ■

Judy VandER HeydEN DeSerio

Hugh Hefner and Victor Lownes used to come into The Cloisters, where I was working as a cocktail hostess, and tell me I ought to be a Bunny. I told them they were crazy. I was too skinny and the costume was too risqué. My roommate, Barbara Grant, kept urging me to 'just come in and try on a costume.' One day I did, and the costume looked fine on me. It pushed everything in the right places.

"The girls in those costumes were what set Playboy apart. People came because they thought they would see the Playmates from the magazine—very often they would—and what they did see never disappointed them.

"Eyeglasses were forbidden, but I couldn't get used to contact lenses. I had a pair of glasses on my tray that I used only to check a member's key and take the drink orders. In 1962, an item appeared in a newspaper column: 'Cute Bunny Judy, wearing tortoise-shell-frame glasses, looks very unique . . .' After that, I became the first Bunny officially allowed to wear eyeglasses.

"The vocabulary in the Bunny Room was tough, rude and ballsy. We cut loose in the dressing

76

room: full of ourselves, tired and letting off steam. When some girls unzipped their costumes, their backs were bloody from the stays. Some Bunnies tried to line the inside of the costume with tissue paper or napkins to keep the boning from pressing into their skin. The fishnet stockings that we wore in the early days bit into your feet and caused them to bleed. You'd go home feeling pretty tired and miserable, but with a lot of money in your pocket.

"One night, Lenny Bruce, who played at The Cloisters and was often a guest at the Playboy Mansion, showed up very late outside my apartment throwing pebbles at my window. He wanted me to make him breakfast. He was carrying a big bag of groceries—everything I needed to make breakfast—and a bottle of perfume for me.

Judy at Chicago's Trattoria Roma, which she co-owns with her daughter and son-in-law.

"None of us wanted to work on weekends. On Friday and Saturday nights we, too, wanted to be out having a good time, going to clubs like Chez Paree and The Cloisters. If you needed a replacement, you could always count on Sue Gin, a Bunny who worked one shift after another. She lived on Rush Street, very near the Club, and sometimes wore her costume home to take a nap between lunch and dinner. She always invested her money.

"Barbara and I still kid each other, saying that between us we should own about five or six brownstones each.

"After I married and left Playboy to have a baby, a friend persuaded me to work a few days a week at The Cloisters. Victor Lownes came in and asked, 'What are you doing here? Aren't you coming back to Playboy?' They made it so easy for me, offering to let me choose shifts that would work around my husband's schedule. Frankly, I felt spoiled.

"Eventually I was fired because of Bunny Image. I looked too old. I wasn't told in so many words, but that was generally the reason you were let go. However, that wasn't the end of my career at Playboy. After I took training in cosmetology, Tony Roma hired me as a makeup consultant to the Bunnies, and I assisted the Bunny Mother with the 'Bunny Hunts' for new recruits." ∎

SUE LING GIN

I went to Chicago when I was 17 to attend DePaul University. I stayed three semesters, then ran out of money and figured it might be better just to work really hard and save some money. I'd started buying real estate when I was 17, living in Aurora, Illinois. (I still have the property.) When I began making money as a Bunny in 1960, I looked around and saw all these properties available—and they were really cheap. I bought my first property with Bunny earnings in the Lincoln Park area of Chicago. It was a 27-unit building, three stories. I had two other partners, and I think my total mortgage was $175 a month. Today the building is worth a million dollars. I still have that, too.

"I lived just off Rush Street and worked at the Club as many hours as I could. After the lunch shift, I would train Bunnies for a couple of hours in the afternoon and then work the night shift. It was like found money. As I recall, according to a national survey done at the time, Bunnies' earnings were in the top 2 percent to 5 percent of the female population in our age group. I used to get very large paychecks. In fact, Arnie Morton once said to me, 'Your paycheck is larger than mine!'

"Adrienne Foote, one of the Bunny Mothers, became a friend, and a kind of mentor as well as a boss. The girls that worked there had a great deal in common—and we had a lot of fun together. I think that we were, as a group, typical of our age. I started a Bunny sorority, Pi Beta Sigma, and we did charity events. We raised money for the needy, visited the county jail and hospitals, supported causes—it was our community outreach effort. The Bunnies were very popular, so we raised a fair amount in donations.

"We decided to do a promotion with the Chicago Bears, but none of us knew how to play football. We managed to get Dave Condon, the No. 1

Chicago Bunnies Marge, Judy and Dana, members of Bunny sorority Pi Beta Sigma, visit with two youngsters in the Cook County Hospital. Proceeds from their cookie sale bought thousands of diapers for the hospital's charity children.

sports writer at the time, to serve as our coach. It wasn't easy for him—none of us weighed more than 110 pounds, and we all wore long fingernails and eyelashes—and the game is rough even if you play it nicely. Dave decided we should play the Bears pound for pound; three Bunnies against one 300-pound Bear.

"There was a social revolution going on throughout the nation in the early '60s, and the whole concept of Playboy was very timely. I don't necessarily think that that operation would work today, but when you look at where we came from in the '50s, it was an edgy, progressive concept for its time.

"After reading Gloria Steinem's article in *Show* magazine and commenting on it at the Club, someone

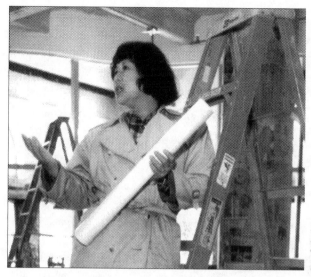

Real-estate tycoon Sue Gin, who is often described as Chicago's most prominent self-made businesswoman, bought her first piece of property at the age of 17. In 1983, she launched Flying Food Fare, a catering company servicing three-dozen domestic and international airlines, Amtrak passenger railway and a Chicago-based grocery chain. She is the widow of William McGowan, founder of MCI, the long-distance telephone company.

asked me if I would debate her on a television interview program. I agreed to give it a try, but I was very nervous getting ready to fly to New York for the interview because I wasn't sure that I could be as articulate as I wanted to be against someone of her stature. Then, for some reason, the plans for the debate didn't mature, which was a disappointment to me. She had taken such a negative approach, and I was ready to defend the job because I truly believed I was reaping benefits; the job was financially rewarding, and I learned a lot about business. I later started a food service company [Flying Food Fare], so I don't think that I spent four years at Playboy not learning anything. But there is no question I was also having a lot of fun, laughing and goofing it up, like you do at that age. Today, Gloria Steinem is one of my heroes, but at that time we had a difference of opinion. I didn't see things the way she did at the Club, but then I didn't go to Playboy to do an investigative piece. When you are on the cutting edge, like we at Playboy were, it's 'open season'—you have to expect those kinds of potshots.

"I worked at Playboy for four years. I had continued to buy property the entire time I was a Bunny. On Saturday afternoons, I'd go out and buy a piece of property, then go back to work again at the Club. But I wanted to broaden my horizons, and I talked to Playboy about management positions. I was told quite frankly that any management position I would get probably wouldn't pay the kind of money I was used to making as a Bunny. It would have been a difficult transition for me, so I left to go into the insurance business, and shortly thereafter into real estate.

"I still stay in touch with some of the women I worked with. I spent a great many hours in the club; the result is that I probably spent more time with those girls than I spent with any other group of people in my entire life." ∎

Pearl Bey Price

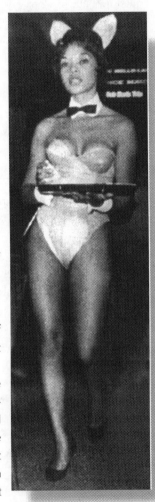

It was Opening Night and my costume wasn't ready! There I was, a 24-year-old single mother with a year-old daughter at home with a baby-sitter while a Japanese seamstress named Mrs. Doi was still fitting my Bunny costume. I thought I wouldn't make it, but at the last minute, Mrs. Doi finished and her son drove me to work. There were crowds lined up outside the Club when I arrived. It was a madhouse. I could barely push through, but once I got inside the door I said, 'I work here, I think,' and opened my coat to show them I was wearing my costume.

"When I applied to be a Bunny, I had been asked if I had any waitress experience. I told them I'd worked in my aunt's restaurant when I was in school, serving short-order food and 3.2 beer. On my first night at Playboy, a man told me he wanted a Heineken. I'd never heard of it—in fact, it sounded kind of suggestive. I told him to get serious and I'd be back to take his order.

"Before I became a Playboy Bunny, I'd been in the army for two years. That's how I made it out of the Northern California farming area where I grew up. You could work for the phone company or be a cashier in a movie theater, but there weren't many choices if you hadn't found a husband by the time you graduated from high school. I thought there had to be something more. It didn't occur to me that just anybody could go to college.

"While I was still in the service, I met and married my first husband, who died of cancer a month and three

Bunny Pearl, 1960.
Now a portrait artist and
a trader on the Chicago
Mercantile Exchange.

days before the birth of my daughter. By October 1959, I was living in a small apartment in Chicago with my baby, and dating a professor at Northwestern University. I had an office job, but it was hard to make ends meet. When I heard the Playboy Club was opening, I applied.

"Victor Lownes was my nemesis, always pressuring me to go out with him. I turned him down because he went out with so many women and I didn't want to be one of the pack. But he had such a temper. He fired me again and again, but each time, Arnie Morton would ask me to come back, promising that he'd speak to Victor about leaving me alone. I was always rehired not because I was gorgeous or charming, for I was neither, but because I was one of their best waitresses. But one night I was so fed up with Lownes that I went to the dressing room, changed out of my Bunny costume and went back on the floor to find him. Victor was talking with a group of people. I threw my costume in his face and said, 'You're always trying to get in my pants. Here's your chance. Have a ball!' That's when I quit for good.

"Years later, I ran into Victor in London and he asked me, 'Do you remember the last time I saw you?' I said No, to be polite, and then he related the story to me almost exactly as I remembered it. He was with a young woman who said, 'Victor has told me all about you.' I said, 'All?'

"During the years I worked at the Club at night, I had a day job so I could keep up my clerical skills. After I left Playboy in 1965, I became office manager of a commodity clearing firm. I started watching what the guys were doing, and it began to make sense. I then started keeping charts and trading pork bellies and live cattle on the Chicago Mercantile Exchange. I wanted to be on my own. In 1983, I bought the first IOM [International Options Market] seat that went on sale to the public, thereby becoming one of the first women with a seat on the Exchange. I got a bloody nose in the bargain—literally! It gets very physical on the floor, and some guy inadvertently swiped me right off my feet.

"I still have my seat on the Exchange, but for the past several years I've devoted most of my time to painting. I've now been married for more than 25 years to a bail bondsman I had first met when I was working as a Bunny." ∎

DANA MONTANA

I was a sponge, soaking up every ounce of knowledge I could about the service end of running the Playboy Club, and saved every penny I earned there. At the age of 23, I opened my own nightclub, the Sugar Shack, in Lake Geneva, Wisconsin, about an hour out of Chicago. I would never have been able to do what I did for myself if it hadn't been for the three years I spent as a Bunny. But the ultimate twist is that I reversed the roles and made men the sex objects.

"I absolutely adored working at the Playboy Club. I was hooked from the moment I walked in and got hired. The service was impeccable; there was glamour and a sense of occasion about the Club.

"God, we had fun! The big dance was the Twist, and the Playroom had Twist parties that went on until 4 a.m. Everyone hated working them and having to dance, but I'd stay on to the end. There was a man named Bob who always came in, a big, fat guy who wore a trench coat and always had a lot of money to spend. I'd dance with him and he'd give me a hundred-buck tip. So I started introducing him to the other girls, and suddenly everyone wanted to stay on and Twist with this guy. He'd drop over a thousand dollars a night for about three months. One night, after work, I went into the dressing room and Lucy, the woman who did wardrobe, had the *Sun-Times* open to a story with the headline, 'Embezzler Caught!' And there was a picture of Bob, who worked in a bank and had stolen money so he could Twist with the Bunnies. For months we'd been asking him, 'So, Bob, how do you make a living?'

"The bottom fell out when Playboy fired me. Seventeen Bunnies were let go in one swoop. It was a big story in Chicago, but I couldn't talk to the press. I was sick. I kept thinking, I can't lose this. Even though I was saving my money and preparing for the day when I would leave and open my own place, I didn't want that cord to be cut. Hollywood may not be your dream, but there's a time in your life when anything's possible, stardom or whatever you've set your heart on, and that's what I felt as a Playboy Bunny. I was a star in my own little corner of the

Chicago Bunnies doing the Twist.

world. It gave me a sense of importance, that I counted for something and could really make it in life. Nothing compares to that youthful moment when the world is yours.

"I was an outsider all through parochial school, a kid from the wrong side of the tracks. I was raised by my grandmother. My mother was a professional tap dancer; my dad was a Las Vegas character. I was no beauty, but Playboy hired me any-way. All I had was my personality and resilience. I always con-sidered myself the 'black swan' among all the white swans, but

Dana Montana at her nightclub, The Sugar Shack.

I just put myself out there. Jesus, I sold cases of those damn Playboy souvenir mugs—I'd serve martinis in them! When the bartenders saw that I was on the schedule, they'd haul in cases of mugs from the storeroom.

"I tried to re-create everything I loved about Playboy in my own club. The Sugar Shack was literally a derelict shack when I bought it over 30 years ago. I made a down payment with my Playboy savings and parlayed that investment into a huge success when I came up with the idea of hiring the first male strippers. We had buses pulling up with women from all over the world who just *had* to see these male dancers.

"I can't imagine what would have become of me if I hadn't worked at Playboy. It opened my eyes to a style of life and an aura of beauty and sophistication that I wanted around me the rest of my life. To this day, I use the Playboy Bunny Manual as my train-ing guide. I'm a fanatic about 'capping' ashtrays and calling out a drink order properly at the bar. The Bunny Dip is still the best way to serve a drink because if you tip your tray, everything dumps on the floor, not the customer.

"I'm a grandmother, but I'm still referred to as the 'former Playboy Bunny who . . .' whenever there's a newspaper article about me and The Sugar Shack or my Arabian horse farm. And that's fine with me. " ∎

Marilyn Miller

In 1960, I was captain of the chorus line at the Chez Paree in Chicago when the Playboy guys came in and hired all my girls. One night, I got a note backstage that Victor Lownes III wanted to meet me between shows. I said, 'Who's Victor Lownes III?' Someone said he looked like the 'Before' in the Wildroot hair cream ad. I went out to meet him and, sure enough, here's this guy with a big head of hair. He was seeing

Dance master "Killer Joe" Piro and Skitch Henderson with New York Bunnies
(left to right): Patti Burns, Pam Marty, Marilyn Miller and Judy Cortner
doing the Mouse for the *Tonight Show.*

a Bunny named Sue Gin at the time. Victor said, 'Why don't you come to Playboy, too—
you'll make a lot of money.'

"So off I went. Playboy was such a family thing in the beginning, just a little Club
off Rush Street for Hef's friends. Sandy Keto, a dancer who had been on tour with me in
Brazil, came along. We were only going to stay for two weeks, but we couldn't believe
the money we were making. You know what it's like being a dancer: living out of a suit-
case, making only enough to get by. We ended up staying—and staying. I was with
Playboy seven years. Sandy worked as a Bunny for 14 years.

"People always confused Bunnies with Playmates, but few of the girls ever posed for
the centerfold. Pompeo Posar, who photographed a lot of the Playmates, called me at
home one day and asked if I could meet him at the Playboy Mansion. He was checking
out the lighting around the swimming pool and needed a model. I said 'sure.' So I stood
here and there while he snapped pictures. When he asked me to drop a strap, I did.
While he was telling me he loved the color of my hair, he had me reach up for something and the entire top of my bathing suit dropped. I got home and reported to my
roommate, Sandy Keto, that I'd posed for Posar without my top on.

" 'No!' she said. 'You didn't!'

"I told her, 'You don't understand. The way he works, my top just came off.'

" '*Well,*' she said, 'he'd never get me to do that.'

"Two weeks later, Pompeo wondered if Sandy could help him out, and she did. In no
time at all she was stark naked. Several of the photographs appeared in *VIP* magazine. I

was too embarrassed to let them print the pictures of me, even though nothing showed because my arm was across my chest.

"It was an innocent, fun time. I get defensive even now if someone puts down Playboy Bunnies. I loved being a Bunny. We could work as hard as we wanted, save up some money, go off to travel and do whatever we wanted. That was the lure.

"I'd moved to New York to become a singer by the time Playboy opened the Manhattan Club. In July 1963, after a season spent as a magician's assistant being sawed in half at the World's Fair, I went back to being a Bunny.

"In 1967, I had a severe case of pneumonia and when I got out of hospital, I just wasn't strong enough to work as a Bunny. I became a room director, a job usually held by men wearing tuxes. I told Playboy I couldn't wear a Bunny costume as a room director—I'd get no respect from the girls!—so I was allowed to wear a skirt and blazer.

"One day I saw a customer getting fresh with a Bunny, and I went over to take care of it. Another customer watched me handle the incident and afterward introduced himself as an executive with Clairol. He said he liked the way I'd dealt with the situation and wondered if I would be interested in a job with the company in Arizona. I jumped at the chance. My doctor had been urging me to get out of New York and recuperate in a better

climate. The day after I arrived in Arizona, I met the man I later married. We had two sons together.

"Years later, when I was getting a divorce and needed a job, Tony Roma, who had been general manager of the New York Playboy Club, hired me to work in his rib place on 57th Street in New York. We had to wear these little costumes with ruffles on our panties and the other waitresses, all much younger than me, thought this was awful. In 1981, Women's Lib was a big thing, and it was considered so exploitative to wear a uniform like that. Worse, we had to be inspected by Tony,

Marilyn Miller, pastry chef and author of *Cookie Time* (Abrams, 1992), is a consultant for New York's Ferrara's Bakery (established in 1892 and still family-owned). Marilyn will soon launch a bed-and-breakfast in the Brittany region of France.

and if two ruffles weren't showing below the hem of the skirt, he'd reach out and mark your skirt where it had to be shortened. You should have heard the other women—'Disgusting! Panties showing!' I wondered what all these feminists would have thought if they'd seen me in my Bunny costume. So when my turn came to be inspected by Tony Roma, I did a dance step and swung my ruffles right into his face. The girls all burst out laughing.

"I've always loved to cook and bake. During the five years I worked at Tony Roma's, I started baking in earnest, selling cheesecakes to a local pastry shop. Eventually, in 1987, I opened my own bakery, ChocoRem Patisserie. Some of my cookies found their way to an editor at Harry Abrams, and I was signed to do *Cookie Time*, a book of recipes to accompany photographs of Andy Warhol's collection of vintage cookie jars.

"Today, I'm still in touch with so many of the girls from my Playboy days, but we never talk about being Bunnies anymore. It was a long time ago, and we've all been through so much else together. Some of the women have lost husbands and children. Others have had to deal with serious health problems, but we always support one another unconditionally." ∎

Marika Lukacs

I will always remember my first day as a Bunny, November 23, 1963. As I walked down the staircase wearing my new costume, I was told that President Kennedy had been shot. Two hours later, when it had been confirmed that he was dead, the Club was closed and we were all sent home. How could I ever forget such a terrible day.

"I left Hungary with my mother in 1954, arriving on the last boat to Ellis Island. I went back to Europe in 1957 to finish my schooling, but returned two years later when my mother died tragically in California, a crime victim. That was a sad time for me, and I appreciated the laughter and fun I found working with the Bunnies at the Chicago Club.

"I loved working as the Bumper Pool Bunny, and became known as the 'Annie Fanny' of the Club. I didn't mind at all playing the 'Dumb Blonde' because I enjoyed being funny and making people laugh. I loved to be liked.

Marika Lukacs in her kitchen.

After a while, when you played every night, you got to know the table so well you could shoot with your eyes closed. The Keyholders played at a dollar a game, but it was free if they won. I would always give them their money's worth, but when it came down to the last ball, I would make sure to win.

"I lived in the Bunny Dorm at the Playboy Mansion with 28 other Bunnies, ranging in height from 4'11" to 5'11", all of us between the ages of 18–23. Mr. Hefner didn't just open the doors of the dorm to any Bunny; we had the privilege of voting in new Bunnies. We all got along terribly well, and for me, the girls became my family during the three years I worked at the Club.

"Now I live next door to Patti Reynolds, a good friend from my Bunny days. We are both 'sidewalk therapists,' and rely on each other's advice. I run a small catering company in Chicago specializing in low-fat, healthy cooking . . . but of course I can always prepare Hungarian dishes." ■

Olivia Richards

London-born Olivia Richards lived in Peru as a child, immigrated to California with her family at the age of 9 and moved to Chicago to work as a Bunny in 1964. "During the year I worked at the Club, I lived in the Bunny Dorm for $50 a month," Olivia recalls, "and even after I married, I continued living there for another four months until my husband and I could afford a place of our own.

"The rules were strict: No men, no pets in the Bunny Dorm. On a dare, I sneaked my hairdresser into the Mansion and he spent the night in the dorm with seven Bunnies. However, I never managed to sneak my husband in." ■

Patti Reynolds

I've always been a prankster and game for anything. When I was 17, I heard that Burton Brown's Chicago Gaslight Club was hiring. I took my older sister's ID and went to audition as 'Bonnie' Patricia Reynolds. A woman named Roxanne took one look at me and asked, 'How old are you?'

"I was a scraggly little thing with wild hair, and looked like a troll. I said, 'I need the job. I'm old enough.' I put on a costume, and after she stuffed the bra and did my make-up, I was introduced to a gentleman named Capt. George Murphy, the retired Chicago police force captain who had connections in everything and was running the club for Burton Brown. Capt. Murphy said, 'I don't know, she looks so young.' Roxanne said, 'She's different. You want someone different, don't you?' They hired me.

"I learned how to swing my pearls, do the Charleston and sing songs like 'A Good Man is Hard to Find'—only we would spice up the lyrics and sing, 'and a hard man is a good find.' Everybody in the speakeasy would scream, throw peanuts on the floor and fill up our trays with dollar bills.

"One day, Capt. Murphy called me off the floor and said, 'Don't come back here until you're of age.' I went straight to Playboy with the same ID and got hired. I was still 17—at least for a few more weeks.

"I was invited to live at the Mansion, but I didn't want to move into the Bunny Dorm with seven other women. I was raised in a Catholic boarding school from the time I was 5 years old; like the army, we slept in bunks. When I saw the dormitory I said, 'No way. Not again. Let me out, I've suffered enough.' I talked to Hef about it and learned there was one studio apartment available because a Playmate, Terre Tucker, was moving out. However, Hef had rules: No pets, no boyfriends. Well, my studio was a tiny room, but I moved in my dog, two cats, a parakeet and an aquarium. And I was a slob. I didn't pick up anything. I'd bring my boyfriend, an Italian guy, into the Mansion and walk right up the stairs with him to my room. A couple of times, we ran into Hef walking down the stairs in his silk pajamas and smoking jacket, carrying his pipe. I said 'Hi, Hef,' as we walked by. He never said a word to me about my friend.

"Hef had a Saint Bernard named Humphrey. My little Pekinese would jump up and bite Humphrey's lip, then hang on, his feet off the ground, as Humphrey walked around with him dangling. That's how these two very different-sized dogs would play together.

"I had a horse stabled just three blocks from the Mansion, and in the early mornings I would ride through the gates, tie my horse up near the door and go in for breakfast. My horse, of course, would make a mess, and the butler would go out and sweep it up. One day I rode up and the gates were locked; I took the hint and didn't bring him back.

"During the two years I lived at the Mansion, I reveled in every sort of mischief. On one occasion when Hef was entertaining, and there were a good many celebrities invited, Marika Lukacs and I got a huge inflatable naked doll and tied her to the railings of the little balcony outside my window. The police came as soon as the neighbors reported seeing a naked Playmate about to jump off a balcony. I don't think Hef thought it was very funny.

"I wanted to be a Playmate and I thought Hef would never notice me with all those gorgeous girls around—but he did. One morning, I pulled on a little shift with an elastic top to run downstairs to get a coffee. I was wearing nothing under the shift. Hef and the usual movie star and celebrity guests were in the breakfast nook as I pranced in. I saw a bowl of giant Delicious apples, grabbed two and put them in my pockets—and with that, the entire shift slipped to my ankles. I was totally naked. Then I had to bend over to pull up my shift, with the butler standing behind me. Needless to say, Hef noticed me.

"Later that morning I ran through the living room in a suntan and white bikini, my bra stuffed to perfection, as Hef stood talking with Tony Bennett. As I streaked past on my way to the pool, I heard Tony Bennett say, '*Who* is *that*?' The next thing I knew, things started rolling and I was asked to be a Playmate.

"I worked as a Bunny for three years, and I loved it. I love people, and the Club was a place where I could just joke and have fun. Another Playmate, Mickey Winters, [September 1962] and I got demerits the minute we walked on the floor: mismatched shoes, no lipstick, messy hair. Finally, we both got fired. We looked at each other and laughed. It was the middle of winter, we were both Playmates—

Entrepreneur Patti Reynolds, with her invention, The Bird Guardian™, which protects nesting birds from predators.

we knew they would take us back. We went to Florida for a two-week vacation and came back to our Bunny jobs.

"After I left Playboy in 1966, it was my love for animals that led me to my career as an entrepreneur. I became the only female naturalist with the Cook County Forest Reserve Conservation Department—and wore my uniform with skintight, butt-grabbing jeans. I would do nature walks with kids, give lectures and do rescue work with birds. One day, I saw a bluejay poking its head in a birdhouse, pulling out baby birds and eating them. I got so upset, I went to a hardware store and bought some materials to fashion a screen to keep the predator birds from entering the birdhouse. My little invention worked so well, and there was nothing like it available commercially, so I decided to patent it. I now market the Bird Guardian nationally, and have several other patents pending for various birdhouse accessories." ■

Kelly Collins

I think I was the one who came up with the Bunny Dip," says Kelly Collins, whose perfect Bunny Image adorned the cover of the Bunny Manual throughout the 25-year history of the Playboy clubs. "I'm tall—5'8"—and with 4-inch heels I topped 6 feet. Bending over in a Bunny costume to serve a cocktail was unattractive from all angles, so I came up with the idea of bending at the knees. It was easier, more graceful, and gave a nicer line to the body. Besides, we were always tugging the costume down in back and pulling it up in front, so this stylized service helped keep everything in place."

Kelly, who was born in Colorado, was modeling in Chicago when she saw a newspaper ad about the new Playboy Club opening. She met her future roommate, Bonnie Jo Halpin, at the Bunny auditions, and the two worked as Door Bunnies opening night, February 29, 1960. "I remember the two of us looking at each other that first night with the crush of people at the door and wondering, 'What's going to happen to us now?' It was such a new experience, and I felt like a fish out of water in the beginning.

"There were no rules or guidelines when I first started as a Bunny, but over time I started to pass along my ideas and comments to Keith Hefner, who took charge of Bunny training." Kelly, who dated Keith for three years, traveled with him training new Bunnies for Club openings in Miami, New Orleans, New York, St. Louis, Detroit and Cincinnati.

"Few of us had any idea what the ingredients were in a particular cocktail, or how to garnish a drink, so it was necessary to come up with a training program. The notorious call-in sequence for the drink orders was designed to make things easier and faster for Bunnies and bartenders alike.

"I loved the Club openings, but I always had First-Night jitters. Everything had to go perfectly, and I took pride in being a big part of making those events come off smoothly. It was a great opportunity for me to travel and to be at the center of something that was very special. While working as a Bunny, I continued to do a lot of modeling in Chicago, Miami and Los Angeles, and did ads for *Playboy* magazine. I didn't do a centerfold because, in those days, models couldn't even do lingerie ads without harming their careers.

"Bonnie and I lived together in a small apartment in a women's-only residence in Bellevue Place, a half-block from Lake Michigan and four blocks from Playboy. Those were wonderful times, and terribly exciting. I loved feeling like I was part of a team."

In 1966, Kelly left Playboy to marry Ron Alexander, one of the room directors at the Club. She's been divorced since 1980, and lives outside Chicago with a horse, two dogs and three cats. "When

Kelly Collins with "Sonny."

you don't have children of your own, you find a way to nurture that 'mothering' thing." For the past 10 years, she's worked as a "headhunter" for office management positions, "because I like people and this is a way of helping others." ∎

Miami

Miami

A BUNNY HOP TO MIAMI

Bonnie Jo on the Miami-bound Champagne Flight, 1961.

he truth was, the huge and immediate success of the Chicago Club caught Hugh Hefner by surprise. The mounting circulation numbers of *Playboy* magazine proved that Hef's philosophy of Post-50s Male as Sophisticate was certainly not limited by state boundaries; so, too, there was no reason to believe his Playboy Club would not be equally successful throughout the country—perhaps, one day, throughout the world.

But Hefner was not prepared to bankroll a national chain of clubs. Plans were already on the drawing board for a New York Club, which would cost millions to open. Instead, Hefner opted to franchise the idea, a kind of sexy, upscale twist on Ray Kroc's new

McDonald's venture that suddenly was exploding across the country, all based on the original fast-food burger counter in California. Hefner franchised six Playboy Clubs in 1961; among them were the Miami and New Orleans clubs, which would be the second and third Playboy clubs to build on the Chicago success.

On Friday, May 19, 1961, Bonnie Jo Halpin and five other Bunnies flew out of Chicago's Midway Airport at 6:30 aboard the Bunny Hop Champagne Flight to open the new Miami Playboy Club the next day. Halpin and a contingent of veteran Chicago Club Bunnies, including Kelly Collins and Alice Nichols, were responsible for training the new Bunnies and ensuring that Playboy's strict quality and rules of behavior were observed at the new franchises. The women would spend three months in Miami and then New Orleans training the Bunnies.

SIENNA WONG INMAN

In 1961, I was in my senior year at a Catholic women's college when one of my favorite Miami restaurants, the China Doll, closed. The space was covered by a tarp while construction was going on—all very mysterious—but I heard that Playboy had taken it over to build a club. One day when I walked by, I saw that interviews were being held for Bunny jobs. I thought it would be fun to see what it was all about. I filled out an application, spoke with a woman named Kitty and was hired then and there. For a while, I kept my job a secret from everyone except my family. I also kept secret that I wanted to pursue an acting career. Working as a Bunny was not what the nuns expected of an English and philosophy major.

"The Miami Playboy Club immediately became the elite place to go. Even though it opened in May, in the 'off-season,' 2,000 people jammed Biscayne Boulevard trying to get into the Club.

"Even though I had five brothers, I got quite a different image of males while working at Playboy. You would see men you recognized as 'pillars of the community' coming on to the Bunnies. Of course, it was an onstage performance for the Bunnies, and the better you played your role, the more money you made. The exposure to that nightclub scene and knowing I could handle it gave me confidence to pursue my dreams of being an actress.

"When I heard a New York Club would be opening, I jumped at the chance to transfer. I'd wanted to go to New York anyway, and having a good-paying job waiting there was certainly the way to go. The calibre of Bunnies working in the New York Club was impressive, including a variety of foreign women and an array of models and actresses. Kitty Kavany, a tall, sophisticated model from Chicago, was dating English actor Peter Cook, who used to stop by to visit.

"On one of my first nights in the Penthouse, Warren Beatty came in with William Holden and Delores Hawkins, who was a top model at the time. Warren asked me out. I told him, 'No, I'm sorry, a Bunny can't date the customers.' But he was pretty insistent. He started following me around the Penthouse, insisting I go out with him, but I refused. Years went by and I thought, 'Boy, I was really stupid!' At the time, I thought obeying the rules of the Club was more important.

"David Susskind came in one night with a beautiful blonde wearing a royal blue dress and a matching turban. The two of them sat under a spotlight at a table next to the

Private dock at the Miami Club.

stage and were the perfect picture of Manhattan nightlife. There was a sense that everyone in the Club was part of a big party. The Club was tastefully decorated, the lighting glamorous, and it was a place where people could have a good time and feel safe to let their hair down. It worked. The steak was a dollar fifty and the drinks were straight—you couldn't beat it.

"There were always parties. You could go to them after work, but there were many of us who were smart enough to know what kind of guys hang out after 2 or 3 o'clock in the morning. After working in high heels all night, you want to home and rest up for the next day. Besides, I had a steady boyfriend and a career to pursue.

"I found a theatrical agent in New York and started to go on auditions while working at the Club. I did several TV spots, including the Arthur Godfrey show as a spokeswoman for La Choy Chow Mein. I worked quite a lot as an actress, then got married and started having babies—six altogether—beginning in 1964. It was hard to continue a career and, of course, each time I got pregnant it seemed I was flooded with offers

Sienna Inman, a proud grandmother, works a few days a week as executive assistant to the chairman of the board of mutual funds at Paine Webber, and is also the East Coast sales director for *Pacifica*, the inflight magazine for Continental-Micronesia airlines.

of acting jobs. My husband, a producer-director, and I formed a production company in 1978. We sold department stores on the idea of using in-store video screens with interviews of authors as a selling tool for new book releases. I've done so many things over the years, one career after another involving film production, real estate, advertising. I even became the managing editor of a wine magazine called *Wine Now*." ■

JudiTH CuRRy AllisoN

O n my first night on the floor of the Miami Playboy Club, I realized that the high-cut Bunny costume exposed the tan line from my bathing suit. I had white hips and brown legs, and I was kind of embarrassed about that. Then the first customers I laid eyes on in the Playmate Bar were the parents of one of the pupils I'd taught in parochial school. I was absolutely beside myself and felt completely nude!

Television producer-writer Judith Allison in her Hollywood offices.

"My parents didn't tell anyone what I was doing, because in those days it was like being a stripper. But personally I never had any problem with being a Bunny.

"When my mother became ill, I went home to New Jersey and took a job at the New York Club. It was February 1963 and the Club was very new; people used to stand out front pressing their faces against the glass, trying to look in.

"Working as a Bunny was hard work, but the financial rewards were very good for a woman at the time. We were glorified waitresses, but I never, ever for one moment felt demeaned by it. The majority of the women I met at Playboy were independent, focused on who they were and what they wanted—which is why I liked them so much. I was always offended that the women who worked as Bunnies were perceived as stupid, exploited women.

"Even today I feel protective about the Club. I saw a television film in which Tatum O'Neal played a Bunny. Her Bunny Dip was wrong. I went wild. I remember thinking, 'This is silly. Couldn't they do their homework?'

"We Bunnies felt special because many of us were chosen for individual qualities that did not necessarily include buxom or blond. Look at me—I'm a gangly 6'3" inches in high heels. My hair is still down to my waist, as it was when I worked as a Bunny. I wore no makeup. I was skinny and I certainly did not have what you would consider your classic, hourglass-shaped Bunny-type figure. Nor did I ever stuff my costume with plastic bags and Bunny tails. Everything I experienced at the Club contradicts this notion of the stereotypical Bunny.

"I bounced back and forth between the New York and Miami clubs until 1964, when I moved to Los Angeles. Through my friend Cher, I got a job as a production

In 1971, Farrah Fawcett appeared in her first Movie of the week, The Feminist and the Fuzz, portraying David Hartman's Playboy Bunny girlfriend. In the end, Farrah loses cop boyfriend Hartman to feminist Barbara Eden. Ironically, Tatum O'Neal, the daughter of Farrah's long-time companion Ryan O'Neal, later also played a Playboy Bunny, Canadian fugitive "Bambi" Bembenek, in the 1993 TV movie Woman On the Run: The Lawrencia Bembenek Story.

assistant on her television show. During the year I worked there, I met my future husband, Don Reo, who later went on to become one of the writer-producers of *M.A.S.H.* He encouraged me to start writing, and together we co-wrote an episode of *M.A.S.H.* One thing led to another and I sold a couple of pilots to NBC and CBS. After that, Don and I began to collaborate on a number of projects, including *Wizards and Warriors, Private Benjamin, Heartland, Blossom,* the *John Larroquette Show and Pearl.* Today I work with Don at Witt-Thomas Productions, writing and producing." ■

Jan Marlyn

I n 1961, when my mother and I visited my aunt in Miami, everyone was talking about the new Playboy Club that had opened on Biscayne Boulevard. I was a well-developed teenager with big breasts, and I had been in a few beauty pageants back home in New Jersey. My aunt told me I should get a job as a Bunny. I was only 17 years old, but I went for an audition and was hired. Nobody questioned my age or asked for a birth certificate.

"The first thing I noticed is that blacks weren't allowed in the Miami Club, either as customers or to work as Bunnies. Segregation was part of the landscape there in 1961, and Playboy had to conform. Nat King Cole was allowed to enter a club only because he was an entertainer. That law didn't sit well with Playboy because it sure wasn't their policy.

"I was fired almost immediately when they discovered I was underage. Afterward I worked as a 'Lambchop' at the Lamb's Club, a very elegant place patterned on Playboy.

We wore curly lamb's wool tails and little furry collars. But I was so devastated at losing my Bunny job that I decided to return to New Jersey. As soon as I heard that a New York Club was opening, I auditioned. By that time, I was 18 years old.

"As I walked out on the floor on the opening night in the New York

Jan in the Bunny Mother's office.

Jan and her husband, actor Robb Reesman, run The Kindness of Strangers Coffeehouse and the 50-seat Back Parlour Theatre in North Hollywood, a meeting place for writers' groups, where Jan has had several of her one-act plays staged.

Club, Keith Hefner saw me wearing a black costume with the skimpier 'Miami' cut that I had begged the seamstress to make especially for me. 'That costume is banned from this Club!' he said, and I had to go up to the dressing room and get refitted. It's funny now to think that the Bunny costume was then considered scandalous. It was far less revealing than what some people wear on the streets today. The way we wore the costume was strictly regulated, but the ears could take on real personality. The girls would bend and shape them to give more individuality, and we all wore masses of hair.

"For the first few weeks, my cheeks just ached from smiling. I loved being on my own, out in the world, and I was grinning all the time. My father, an Italian-American, brought friends to the Club; he was so proud of me.

"I was totally un-self-conscious. I cultivated that wide-eyed, bushy-tailed bimbette look and usually wore several pairs of eyelashes. When you're young, you love going to extremes and getting away with as much as you can. One night I was doing a High Carry with a tray full of Irish coffees and flaming mug drinks when a customer said, 'I'll give you a hundred bucks to drop that tray.' Without a second's hesitation I flipped my tray over. The busboys raced over to help clean it up and I tipped them out of the hundred dollars.

Ashtray with the Femlin motif designed by LeRoy Neiman.

"We'd all take little things home to furnish our apartments, like ashtrays and glasses decorated with the Femlin logo. Well, one girl had a complete set of flatware, dishes, tumblers, candles and ashtrays that she'd taken from the Club. One night she went out with one of the big shots and took him back to her place for the night. The next day, after sleeping with her, he had her fired for stealing all that stuff!

"I married and left Playboy in 1964 to have a baby. I returned to the Club when my son was 3 years old because I needed a good-paying job with flexible hours. Furthermore, the Playboy tuition program enabled me to enroll in a two-year liberal arts course

New Orleans

New Orleans

BUNNIES IN THE VIEUX CARRÉ

Joyce Nizzari opens the doors
to the New Orleans Club.

On October 13, 1961, a crew of Chicago Training Bunnies opened the brand-new, baroquely ornate Playboy Club at 727 Rue Iberville, just off Bourbon Street in the heart of New Orleans' Vieux Carré. Again, the usual contingent of Bunnies, Playmates, Playboy executives and members of the press flew in from Chicago and Miami for the festivities.

The Chicago Bunnies were the first to notice a problem: "When I worked at the opening in New Orleans, there weren't any black Bunnies," recalled Alice Nichols. "Blacks and whites weren't allowed to mix, and you were always made aware of that."

The franchise agreement forced Hefner to cede operational control of the clubs to the new owners. Unfortunately, the Playboy head did not take into account the social realities of the South in 1961, where racial discrimination was still a fact of life. Hefner learned that not only was the Club not hiring black Bunnies, it also was not accepting black membership. It was wholly antithetical not only to the sophisticated, liberal philosophy behind the Clubs but also to Hefner's personal and professional beliefs. Hefner tried to convince the franchise holders to operate within the framework of Playboy's policy, which was completely nonracial.

Linda Wickstrom, Joan Garber, Ellen Stratton, Carol Roski and Bonnie Jo Halpin.

"But we couldn't get to first base," Hefner recalled.

Joyce Nizzari and Nat King Cole.

The new franchise Clubs turned out to be public-relations disasters when the media charged that both Miami and New Orleans were racially biased, prompting comedian and Hefner friend Dick Gregory to quip that "Negroes with Playboy Club Keys found that the locks had been changed."

Hefner's solution to the impasse was a costly one. Ultimately, he bought back the franchise in Miami and operated the club himself. The transaction, completed in early 1962, put a whopping 150 percent profit on the original investment in the pockets of the franchise holders.

"A ridiculous move from the standpoint of good business?" Hefner said at the time. "Sure. But it was worth it. Now the Miami Club is open to every single one of our Keyholders, and I'm proud to say that we haven't had even a trace of a grumble from white members."

Still, the racial barrier remained in effect at the magnificent 18th-century Franco-Spanish New Orleans Playboy Club in the heart of the French Quarter. There, Hefner was up against a state law that forbade drinking, dancing or any kind of socializing between blacks and whites. "I know this is patently unconstitutional, but we have to have a liquor license to operate," Hefner explained. "We are doing everything we can to set the matter straight." In the meantime, Playboy arranged to buy back the New Orleans franchise, too. Once again, the price was steep: The franchise owners wanted a profit of $250,000 on an investment of $175,000. Hefner would not make the same mistake in New York.

The Playboy Club in the Vieux Carré.

CHINA LEE

S ophisticated. Tough. Straight, no-nonsense. Dangerous. That's how most former Bunnies remember China Lee, the only Bunny who always got to wear a black costume. She was known to the rest of us as a barracuda: Club slang for a Bunny you didn't want to cross.

The very self-possessed Chinese-American beauty, who already had posed as a *Playboy* centerfold by the time the New York Club opened, struck many of the other Bunnies as the ultimate insider. She arrived in New York as a Training Bunny from Chicago and was dating Matt Metzger, the general manager of the New York Club. She had also dated Victor Lownes III, Playboy's promotions director and a close friend of Hugh Hefner. China had been hired in New Orleans in 1960 when she was only 17 years old.

"When one of my brothers showed me the newspaper ad for Playboy Bunnies, I told

him maybe I should try for a job. He said they'd never hire me. I bet him they would. During my interview at Playboy I said, 'Tell me, do I have this job or not? Because I don't want to waste my time.' They hired me.

"I was brought up in an old-fashioned, strict Chinese tradition. It took strength to bump up against my parents. My father was prominent in real estate, politics and the restaurant business [New Orleans' House of Lee], and when I got the job at Playboy, he telephoned every influential person he knew because he didn't want me working there. The gossip in New Orleans was that, as far as my parents were concerned, I was lost to them when I became a Bunny and that they held a funeral for me—which was completely untrue.

"On opening night in New Orleans, I was a Door Bunny. The place was jammed, and during the evening a couple of the Bunnies working tables just fell out; they couldn't handle it. Matt Metzger pulled me off the door and told me I'd have to take over their stations in both

New Orleans Playboy Club, 1961.

the Playmate Bar and the Living Room. I agreed—and then discovered I would be serving 60-some customers by myself! I demanded my own busboy and went to work.

"People stared at me, so I must have been quite a sight. Oriental girls are usually small and fragile-looking, but I was buxom and strong. I came out of the service area carrying a big tray loaded with drinks and food over my head. The busboy followed in my wake with more trays. Matt said, 'I've never seen a Bunny work like you.' But with my family restaurant background, it was nothing new to me.

"At 19, I was one of Gloria Steinem's Training Bunnies at the New York Club. I didn't know she was working as a Bunny in order to write an article, but I knew something was up because she was well over the age limit and she didn't look like she belonged. She struck me as both aloof and insecure. I remember asking her how she got the job. 'Through a friend,' she told me.

"When Gloria's article came out, I was disgusted that she felt she had to put down the girls working at the Club. I think it was her insecurity coming out, her need to feel superior to us. Who knows what hang-ups made her strike out at us; victims often get even by victimizing others.

Today China, who is divorced a second time from political satirist Mort Sahl, owns racehorses. She works for Welink, Inc. in Los Angeles as a trader in foreign exchange, buying and selling currencies, and is also a distributor for "2001," a financial services program.

China Lee, star player in the Bunny softball league.

"During the seven years I worked for Playboy, I opened most of the Clubs: Atlanta, Baltimore, Cincinnati, Boston, New York, Detroit, Kansas City, Los Angeles, Phoenix, St. Louis, San Francisco, Denver, Great Gorge and Jamaica. In 1968, I was 25 years old and more than ready to leave. Smart Bunnies, the ones who didn't get hung up on false images of glamour and a superficial lifestyle, used the opportunity and went on to other things. We all fantasize, of course—I more or less run my fantasies in my head like a movie!—but you have to face real life.

"At first, it's fun to dress in the Bunny costume and see how people react. I felt like a thermometer taking everyone's temperature as I walked through the room. You soon start to realize how great the power of a woman's sexuality is—and how you're using it. Even as a teenager, I could tell so much about a man—if he's gay, straight, insecure, emotionally healthy, whatever—by how he reacted to me in that Playboy Club setting." ■

Bogus Bunnies

Above: Vietnam

A Bunny banner was hoisted above the "Saigon Playboy Club," a thatched roof American Service Club near the DMZ. The decor in the "Playmate Bar" was—what else?

Above: Yugoslavia

In 1963, *The Associated Press* reported a sighting of "Bogus Bunnies" in the state-run Putnik Nightclub in Novid Sad, Yugoslavia—business boomed.

Above: The Antarctic

The Navy canteen in Antarctica was said to have the coolest jazz—and Bunnies in long johns.

New York

STEP INTO THE SPOTLIGHT . . .
BE A PLAYBOY CLUB BUNNY . . .

An exciting new life awaits you if you're a pretty, young girl and you want to be a Bunny. You'll never be bored by routine. You'll earn far more than other girls. You'll have the opportunity to travel. You'll meet internationally famous people in show business, politics, industry and sports while you serve drinks, snap pictures or greet guests in the glamorous atmosphere of the luxurious Playboy Club soon to open in New York.

**BE
A
PLAYBOY
CLUB
BUNNY**

If you are pretty, between the ages of 18 and 23, married or single, and want a fun-filled, pleasant and always exciting job while you enjoy a new measure of financial independence, apply in person Wednesday through Saturday, between 2:00 P.M. and 7:00 P.M. at 25 West 56th Street, 6th Floor, New York City.

Please bring a swim suit or leotards.

At 2 o'clock on a windswept afternoon in mid-March, 1962, hundreds of young, attractive women who had seen the "Wanted" ad in the New York dailies jammed the sixth-floor Playboy offices at 25 W. 56th St., waiting to change into swimsuits or leotards and line up for the Polaroid pictures that would be stapled to their applications. Keith Hefner and Shelly Kasten, described by the *New York Post* as "well-dressed in the Playboy manner—slim-legged trousers, slanted pockets on the coat and narrow ties," sat at opposite ends of a long table. The women streamed past the table in a double line, one for Hefner and one for

Kasten, each applicant hitting a mark, posing for a Polaroid and answering a few brief questions from the two men. Appearances to the contrary, it was actually grueling work.

"We saw 1,100 women in five days," recalled Kasten, "but no more than 20 applicants were hired."

Among the hopefuls come to audition was Jan Marlyn, a "veteran." The brash and wily New Jersey-bred Italian-American had worked in the Miami Playboy Club while underage. Still a teenager, with luminous brown eyes and a big grin, Marlyn waited her turn wearing a fake rabbit fur coat and fishnet stockings, her favorite two-piece bathing suit tucked in a carry-all. Also in line was model and aspiring singer Marion Barker, a tall, elegant 24-year-old African-American who had already spent the morning on her rounds of the fashion houses looking for work as a showroom model.

Ling Quong, an exotic African-American Chinese woman known as "Mei Mei," showed up after a friend suggested to her that she audition.

"But when I mentioned it to my boyfriend, he said, 'Oh, no, they don't want girls like you—only tall, blond Midwestern types,'" recalled Quong, now Ling Maris, a Connecticut-based interior decorator and children's book author. "Well, I was intrigued. I thought even if they reject me I'll get

a chance to see what's going on. Keith Hefner and I hit it off very well, and I was called for a second interview. My boyfriend was shocked and told me I was just being set up for a big disappointment. He was on target; minorities didn't stand much of a chance back then. But Playboy liked the idea of having Bunnies with a wide range of ethnic backgrounds, and I was hired. At first there was some debate about putting me in the VIP Room as an 'International' Bunny, but I got hired to work all the rooms."

In fact, four black Bunnies were hired in those five days, including Barker,

Mei Mei Quong, 1963.

dubbed a "Bronze Bunny" in the caption that accompanied a news-wire photograph of her wearing a bikini during her interview at the Playboy offices. Barker was sent to work in Chicago until the New York Club opened.

"The building was just a shell under construction when Victor Lownes hired me to do PR," Barbara Harrison recalls. "And I remember that the press reacted with some surprise in the beginning when Playboy made a point of hiring black girls, and girls from various other racial groups, but that had been a long-standing policy of the organization."

By the time Harrison was hired, Lownes and Playboy had officially severed ties. Lownes remained as a consultant for the still unopened New York Club, but he had opened his own public-relations firm with offices on 53rd Street next to the Stork Club—with Playboy Enterprises as his first client. Harrison, an elegant, well-spoken, blonde New Yorker, had worked for Georg Jensen, the posh Fifth Avenue silver and crystal store, before joining Playboy. "They really wanted to create a certain image in New York," Barbara says, "and I think I was hired because

Cathy Young, Keith Hefner and Marion Barker.

I wasn't flashy-looking. New Yorkers are cynical and there is an alienation toward anything coming from the outside. Before the opening, there was an inclination among columnists to look down their noses and characterize Playboy as a kind of corny, hick operation. They called the guys from Chicago the 'brown-shoe crowd.' "

Despite the hard-boiled cynicism, it was obvious from the beginning the Club was going to be hot. By April 1962, the Club boasted 33,000 registered Keyholders in New York. But the opening of the $7 million, seven-story Playboy Club, at 5 E. 59th St., adjacent to the Sherry Netherland Hotel, proved a more torturous and time-delayed process than anticipated. There were the usual construction problems, compounded by hassles with the city and state's notorious bureaucracies. By spring, the official opening was postponed to September, then October.

Meanwhile, the Bunny hiring crept on at a snail's pace month after month. Newspaper articles, such as one claiming that out of some 3,000

Sandra Deetz

"Playboy was a steppingstone and I've never looked back," says Deetz, whose 15 minutes of Playboy fame was as the 20-year-old Bunny applicant featured in a *New York Mirror* article on the last wave of auditions a week before the club opened.

Sandra Deetz auditioning for a Bunny job, November 1962.

"I worked at the Playboy Club for three or four months to make enough money to take some classes at Hunter College. I didn't really have any goals back then, except not to go back to Ohio. I'm a natural people person, and I was just made for that kind of 'let's keep it lively, have a quick laugh, a drink, some fun, some food and move on.' I was good at it, but come on, it was a very undignified job. The big effort was all in putting your lipstick on.

"But I had a lot of fun there and met some great women who have been my friends for over 30 years. In 1976, I became a sports feature reporter for NBC, interviewing everybody from race-car driver Mario Andretti to Triple Crown Champion Seattle Slew. I'm Fate's godchild, and I've been very lucky to have done a lot of interesting things, like dancing in the Copa line, hosting a television talk show and doing a lot of traveling." ■

"would-be Bunnies," only 125 would be hired to work in the New York Club and make "lush earnings of $200 to $300 a week," enticed a steady stream of new applicants well into the fall. Seventeen Bunnies were hired in a four-day audition in late April. *New York Post* columnist Normand Poirier watched the girls "in an endless stream, flow past—dancers, models, actresses, 'hat chicks,' waitresses, students, nurses, salesgirls, stewardesses . . . 'Stand on your mark, please, pose for the Polaroid, click, thank you, dear, we'll call you if . . .'"

"Foggy"

Susan King, Martha Faberman, Deede Sterling
at the Playboy Offices, 25 W. 56th St.

A mong the first Bunnies hired in New York was Deede Sterling, now the owner of The Magpie's Nest, a quaint doll shop with ancient stone walls and rough hewn beams in the medieval cathedral town of Canterbury, England.

"I was quiet. Insecure. I was never your typical bubbly Bunny," recalled Deede. "Keith was always telling me to smile. Now *he* would have been the perfect Bunny. Always upbeat.

"I was so much in my own world that everyone called me Foggy, and that became my Bunny name. I was a million miles away, daydreaming. I could never quite remember which drinks went to which table. I did my job but in my own time. People eventually got their drinks, but I wasn't what you'd call a go-getter. I left Playboy in 1963 to work in the Bahamas, and that's where I met my husband, an Englishman. We married, had two children and, after moving to Canterbury, I opened my antique doll shop."

Deede was stunned to learn that the Clubs had been shuttered for more than a decade. "Really, fancy not knowing the Playboy Clubs had closed. No one mentioned it to me. I guess I really am still foggy." ∎

"I came from a small town in Pennsylvania," Sandy Kolosinsky Capasso recalls, "and it was a big deal to even think of auditioning to be a Bunny. In those days if a girl wore a short skirt, she was 'asking for it.' There was always that attitude. Women didn't wear bikinis to the beach; they wore two-piece bathing suits. Imagine what it was like writing home to your folks to tell them you'd gotten a job as a Bunny!"

In October the opening was postponed until Friday, November 23. The Club was nowhere near completion. Lee Hase, a tall, 20-year-old brunette, posed for a photographer, dressed in her satin Bunny costume and

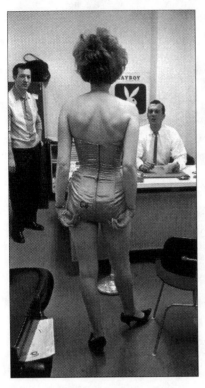

Shelly Kasten and Keith Hefner interview a
prospective Bunny, 1962.

ears and wielding a blowtorch at the construction site.

In early November, Hefner and Kasten still needed more Bunnies, and the auditions continued. The ads showing B.J. Halpin appeared again in the New York dailies:

Step into the spotlight . . . Be a Playboy Club Bunny. If you are pretty, between the ages of 18 and 23, married or single, and want a fun-filled, pleasant and always exciting job while you enjoy a new measure of financial independence, apply in person Wednesday through Saturday, between 2:00 p.m. and 7:00 p.m. . . . Please bring a swim suit or leotards.

Keith Hefner had pneumonia, so Shelly Kasten handled the remaining auditions on his own in a growing atmosphere of anticipation.

"Playboy coming to town was a big deal by then, and I had reporters and network TV crews all over the place while I was seeing girls," recalls Kasten. "I would go home hoarse from talking all day. Who would believe seeing hundreds of girls in bathing suits could be such hard work? I had one girl show up who must have weighed 300 pounds, stuffed into a bathing suit—and the cameras were on us, so I had to be really straight about it. 'Why do you want to be a Bunny?' I asked seriously. She couldn't even fit in the chair."

Finally, after six months of delays and rescheduling, the Playboy Club opened its doors at 5 E. 59th St. on Saturday, December 8, with a gala, black-tie benefit for the Parkinson's Disease Foundation. The entertainment, liquor and food for the event were donated by Playboy. But the Club's problems were far from over. At the last minute, both the liquor and cabaret licenses were pulled.

"The problem was that when Playboy came in to New York, they were told that certain people expected payoffs to make things happen," Barbara

New York Club opening, December 8, 1962.

Harrison explained. "Playboy tried to act in good faith—when in Rome do as the Romans do—but they acted on bad advice. They were eventually vindicated during the State Liquor Authority fraud trials the following year, but it was a bad way to open the Club. It didn't help that Victor was not particularly diplomatic, nor interested in what people thought of him. During a big press conference Playboy called to announce its difficulties in acquiring the cabaret license, we prayed Victor would simply read a statement and not make things any worse. Fortunately, he was on good behavior. Acquiring those permits was a tedious process that required some finesse. There were also several court appearances that involved Bunnies displaying the costume, which was specially altered for the occasion. Aside from problems with the liquor and cabaret licenses, there was also a newspaper strike that prevented any coverage at all. Everything seemed to go wrong."

But, seemingly, nothing could stop people from coming. The Keyholder applications swelled, and customers lined up outside the Playboy doors well into the night. And all proceeded under the capricious authority of Victor Lownes III, Hef's consigliere, confidant and alter ego.

"It was so different back then; men and women related differently," explained Harrison. "Victor Lownes was interested in any attractive woman who crossed his path, and women generally responded to him. He was funny, charming and attentive to the woman he was with—at least while he was with her. But his span of interest was very short. Lownes was the living image of the swinging bachelor playboy, the

Victor Lownes III reads a statement to the press concerning the procurement of a state liquor license.

embodiment of the magazine, and lived that lifestyle. Stylish. Urbane. Lots of women. Living well, with no particular regrets. And no long-range romantic plans."

After Playboy cleared out of the temporary space on 55th Street, Lownes opened offices on 53rd Street and later moved to quarters in the St. Moritz Hotel. There, he threw notorious parties, always packed with an eclectic mix of musicians, writers, artists, entertainers and, of course, lots of Bunnies. "I remember the manager of the St. Moritz calling Victor down to his office and telling him, 'We can't have this. You people have to leave. There's too much going on!' " recalled Harrison. "And I sat there trying to look demure, certainly not at all like a party animal, and promising the manager that there would be no more parties, no more noise, no more carrying on. And, of course, that wasn't the case. In the mornings when I came to work, I would find Polaroids of the previous night's activities displayed on the coffee table. The parties continued, and I found myself almost daily insisting to the manager that we would mend our ways and not cause any more trouble."

It was not all harmless fun. Some of the young girls who had come from less sophisticated backgrounds could not handle the pressure or the temptations of the new lifestyle. "Hefner didn't come into New York all that often, but when he did, there were rounds of parties," Harrison says. "I remember a party at his suite in the Waldorf Towers with the usual mix of celebrities, old friends and Bunnies. The following morning, long after Hefner and his friends had departed, I got calls from both the manager of the Club and the hotel manager that there were two Bunnies left over from the party the night before. I went to the hotel and found that one of the girls was hysterical. Words came tumbling out of her. She had come to New York with dreams of becoming an actress and thought being a Playboy Bunny was the launching pad. It was the old idea that someone—a producer, a celebrity—would walk into the Club or the party and see her and say, 'That face, I must have that face!' And she would be 'discovered.' It hadn't happened that way for this young woman.

"There were other girls who got themselves involved in romances with guys who were way over their heads. The most serious incident of that sort involved a Bunny who had become infatuated with one of the C-1 Keyholders and took LSD in his company. While under the influence of the drug she stood in front of a mirror and could not see her image reflected. She began to scream that she had lost her identity, that she was going to kill herself by jumping off the terrace.

"There were strict rules about Bunnies not dating the customers, and for the most part, that policy was enforced, but it was always difficult with celebrities. One young girl got involved with a well-known comedian who was often at the Club, and that relationship ended badly. The girl expected

Keyholders line up for the New York Club, January 1963.

more would come her way because she was a Playboy Bunny."

Gloria Steinem's article in May 1963 seemed to confirm the worst fears not only about Lownes but also about his friend Hefner's club. Ironically, it put Harrison in a very difficult situation, personally as well as professionally.

"I was then dating Paul Desmond, who played sax with the Dave Brubeck Quartet, and was a friend of Gloria's. He used to come to the Club sometimes in the evenings as I was about to leave and we'd have a drink together. I had been talking to him about writing a novel based on Playboy, which I ultimately did write some years later. But one night at the Club, a Bunny came up to our table and said, 'I'm your Bunny Marie, may I serve you?' When she left the table, Paul said to me, 'You know, if you want to write your book, you'd better do it in a hurry.' I didn't know what he was talking about until Gloria's article in *Show* appeared. Paul then admitted that Gloria had sworn her friends to secrecy and he didn't feel he could reveal to me what he knew.

"We were absolutely blindsided by that article. Gloria Steinem made a dramatic impact because of the way she looked and the manner in which she did the story. She was the first to focus on these issues of exploitation—and it was good that she did—but the article itself, I think, was unfair and demeaning to the women who worked at the Club. The great majority of the Bunnies were using the income they earned there to pay for schooling and prepare for a career. They had goals. I felt that her article ignored that aspect and was distorted and self-serving.

"At the time, I felt the best way to deal with the issue was to have various Bunnies do radio interviews and appear on television shows, such as David Susskind's *Open End*, to answer the comments inspired by her article.

"For a while, Gloria Steinem worked for Harvey Kurtzman, who created <u>Mad</u> magazine and did Little Annie Fanny for us. She was his 'Girl Friday.' Harvey got it into his head that Gloria and I were made for one another. He talked to me about her and told her about me—she had a reputation in those days for being pretty good at breaking hearts—with the result that in 1963, we came close to dating one another when I came to New York for one of the first State Liquor Authority meetings. I had an apartment in New York that was part of a photo studio, and we held a party there. Harvey invited Gloria. She was going to come, but then she didn't show up. She even wrote me a letter, which I still have, telling me she was sorry she missed me in New York and apologizing for not coming to the party. Harvey later called up to explain she didn't come to the party because she was already working undercover as a Bunny."

—Hugh Hefner

The Girl In the Brown Sweater

Bud Prager, a talent manager and music industry veteran, was a close friend of Victor Lownes in the early 1960s. The two men played backgammon together every night and shared a summer house on Fire Island. Prager remembers getting a call one day from Albert Grossman, "the manager of Janis Joplin, Bob Dylan, Peter Paul and Mary—the most important manager in the world at the time.

"He asked me if I would I see this young lady who wanted to be a Playboy Bunny. Albert knew I was friendly with Victor Lownes. I said sure. So, over comes this lovely young lady with brown hair and brown eyes wearing a brown sweater. She was really very 'homey' looking, the kind of girl that you want to marry. I said to her, 'you don't look like the Playboy Bunny type. You should do something else with your life.' She insisted she needed the job and said, 'please, if there's anything you can do . . .' So I said OK and spoke to Victor. This was the only time I ever asked him to 'do me a favor' about hiring somebody. 'Is she good-looking?' he asked. I said yes. 'Is she nice?' Yes, I told him, she'd be great. So Victor said he would take care of it and he did . . . she became a Playboy Bunny without going through the whole application procedure, without any complications, problems or anything else. It was done.

"Months later, there were these rumors about a 'Bunny exposé,' someone telling the inside story. Eventually, the article came out and I somehow knew right away that it was her. Gloria Steinem, the young lady in the brown sweater. The one person I happen to send over writes an exposé. The only thing I had to worry about then was Victor saying to me in one of his rants, 'You did this to us!' We were playing backgammon one night and he said, 'Didn't you have something to do with this girl who wrote this article?' I said no, never heard of her before. Thank God he had 20,000 things on his mind and he never pieced it together.

One Saturday many years later, I was on a bench in Flushing Airport on my way to the Hamptons and I saw a bag with the intitials 'G.S.' go by—and nice legs. I look up and there she is, after all these years. So I said to her, 'You used me.' That was the key expression all the feminists used in those days. She said 'How could I use you, I don't even know you?' I said, 'I'm the guy you came to see to get the job at Playboy.' She laughed and said 'You were the one?' She was just so charming. She was on her way to a fund-raiser in the Hamptons for Bella Abzug when she was running for office. I guess that was my contribution to Gloria Steinem's career—and Victor will now find out I was the guy who sent her over to Playboy." ∎

Her piece had raised questions in my mind, too. Bunnies were sex symbols. How did they personally feel about that? There were no ugly Bunnies. No fat Bunnies. Whatever shape each one had was rearranged to advantage by those costumes.

"Lownes took the article very badly. It didn't help when he surmised later that a friend of his may have helped Steinem land the job. If anything, the article led to more exploitation of the women in the press: There were some very disturbing calls from reporters wanting to talk to Bunnies as though these women were chained inside a brothel."

The article couldn't have come at a worse time for Playboy. In April 1963, five months after its opening, the New York Playboy Club, with an average of 2,700 customers a day, still did not have a cabaret license. This precluded the Club from presenting live entertainment, envisioned as its lifeblood, not only philosophically and aesthetically, but also financially. General manager Kurt Brods claimed to *The New York Times* that the city's refusal to grant the license was costing the club at least $90,000 a month. *Times* writer Thomas Buckley observed that, to some extent, the Playboy Club had itself to blame for the situation: "Its promotional literature emphasizes Bunnies, and the reader might be excused for inferring that considerable deviltry takes place on the thick broadloom amid the banquettes."

Open End's David Susskind with Bunnies Mei Mei Quong and Teddy Howard.

During the protracted legal battle to acquire the cabaret license, Playboy turned to Elaine Trebek Kares, then known as Teddy Howard, to counteract the image of the Bunny painted by Steinem and being propagated in the press. A quick-witted, engaging 19-year-old from Ohio, Howard was hired in December to help open the Club in Manhattan. The brown-eyed blonde, who bore a striking resemblance to '60s English fashion model Twiggy, was quickly recruited from the ranks as the perfect Bunny to model the Bunny costume—labeled "indecent" by the city—in court for a panel of jurists.

The legal controversy hinged on a regulation in the city's Administration Code stating that "female entertainers and female employees of a cabaret shall not be permitted to mingle with patrons or guests." The city contended that Bunnies were encouraged to mingle with the guests and push liquor sales, both of which are violations of the law.

"Playboy had spent $7 million renovating that seven-story building and opening the Club," Howard recalled. "Without a cabaret license, their showrooms were just dinner rooms, and it was very important to them to secure the license so they could present entertainment."

Appearing as "Exhibit A" at the hearing, Howard wore a specially designed emerald-green costume. "I always wore a lavender costume in the Club," Howard recalled, "but this one was cut a little higher on the bosom and a little lower on the hips. I never saw that costume again after the hearing."

Howard testified that every woman working as a Bunny had to sign a document that she would not date customers or divulge any personal information to a patron of the Club. Furthermore, she insisted, the Bunnies were not instructed to "push" drinks, and that there was a rigid code of behavior covering almost every aspect of their jobs, far more strict and comprehensive than any club or cabaret in the city at the time.

"I guess I charmed them and did a good job convincing the judge, because on my way out of the hearing room, Hef smiled and gave me a 'thumbs up,'" Howard recalled.

Finally, on April 19, 1963, Playboy was granted its cabaret license.

Ironically, Steinem's article had only added to the growing mystique around the Bunnies, and enticed even more young women to apply for the jobs. "The most amazing thing was the way people on the outside related to anything associated with Playboy," recalled Harrison. "I dated a fascinating physicist, but when we went to dinner parties, nobody cared in the *least* about what he did—everyone had to know about the Bunnies."

"No Gym Bloomers or Middy Blouses Required"

Representatives of Playboy, with a costumed Bunny as "Exhibit A," appeared before New York's Supreme Court December 22, 1962, to argue that the "scanty costumes" were not a valid reason for denial of a cabaret license. In denying the application December 18, City License Commissioner Bernard J. O'Connell had claimed, "It would appear to be quite clear that the applicant's main appeal to its customers is the lure of its scantily clad waitresses . . . the granting of a license would not be in the public interest."

Playboy contended that the costumes were "not as scanty as those of showgirls at the Copacabana or the Latin Quarter."

O'Connell's huffy reply: "The applicants widely advertised their intention to open a private club to be operated in the mood of the nation's most sophisticated magazine . . . a mere glance at the magazine in question [Playboy] would indicate that any approximation of its 'mood' would invite immediate police action." Application denied. The New York Playboy Club continued its court battle, meanwhile operating without entertainment in its showrooms.

On January 15, 1963, State Supreme Court Justice Arthur G. Klein famously overruled License Commissioner O'Connell, declaring, "To satisfy his personal moral code, it is not incumbent upon the petitioner to dress its female employees in middy blouses, gymnasium bloomers, turtleneck sweaters, fisherman's hip boots or ankle-length overcoats."

Bunnies Edie and Judy model the two versions of a Bunny costume.

Tony Roma, general manager of the New York Playboy Club, surrounded by Bunnies Erica, Jodi, Marta, Cathy and Marilyn at a press conference regarding the cabaret license, January 1963.

In describing the Bunny costume, Judge Klein stated, "Their work clothes, in addition to rabbit ears and a tail, consist of a short, tight-fitting costume, similar to that customarily worn by skaters and dancers. Sworn testimony indicates that this costume exposes no more of the upper female anatomy than is normally revealed by a bathing suit or a low-cut formal evening gown."

In a parting shot at Commissioner O'Connell, Judge Klein said, "He is neither a censor nor the official custodian of public morals, nor may he impose his own personal standards upon applicants. He is forthwith directed to issue a cabaret license to the petitioner."

Taking a cue from Judge Klein's colorful decision in favor of the Playboy Club and its Bunny costume, which stated that female employees need not be dressed in "middy blouses, gymnasium bloomers or fisherman's hip boots," Playboy produced a photograph showing what the Bunnies might have looked like if the court had ruled differently.

Banned in Boston

Members of the Massachusetts Alcoholic Beverage Commission took a look at a costumed Bunny and turned down the Boston Club's application. Geri Dougherty, 19, one of the original New York Club Bunnies, appeared before the Boston Licensing Board February 13, 1963, to demonstrate the type of costume that the "waitresses" would wear in the Boston Club. One commissioner didn't even dare look! Instead, he turned his chair around and stared at a wall during the presentation. But he voted against the Bunnies just the same. Another commissioner made the classic statement on *Playboy* Clubs: They are "definitely not a place to take children."

Above: A Bunny wearing a costume cut lower on the hip and specially designed for the Boston Club, dances in the Living Room to the music of jazz trombonist Kai Winding and the Russ Carlton Trio, Opening Night February 26, 1965.

Left: Bunny Geri appears before the Boston Licensing Board wearing a white Bunny-fur jacket over her costume.

Elaine "Teddy" Trebek Kares

A lice Nichols, the Bunny Mother, thought that I would be a good spokeswoman for Playboy, probably because I looked more like Twiggy than a voluptuous Bunny. So she sent me to see Hef, who asked me a lot of questions before deciding I was the image they wanted to present.

"When radio stations and newspapers wanted to interview Bunnies, the Club needed someone who wouldn't give them a surprise. I appeared on Johnny Carson's *The Tonight Show, What's My Line* and David Susskind's show *Open End*, among others. I was sent on a lot of promotions and made extra money from these personal appearances. I even went to Labrador with the U.S.O.

"I *was* a good spokeswoman for the Bunnies, and I gave answers that honestly reflected the women work-

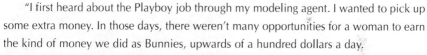

ing at the Club. For the most part, we were a fairly decent group of wholesome girls, and the few tough, hard-core types were weeded out pretty quickly.

"I first heard about the Playboy job through my modeling agent. I wanted to pick up some extra money. In those days, there weren't many opportunities for a woman to earn the kind of money we did as Bunnies, upwards of a hundred dollars a day.

"But it was hard work. The costumes were so tight that we would go behind the bar and use a fruit knife to cut threads in a side seam. The busboys then helped us pull out the stays; otherwise, those stays pressed against the hipbone in a way that cut off circulation. Your legs would start to go numb.

"On the whole, most of the younger Bunnies were just babes who didn't really know what was going on. We were agog at the older Bunnies working the night shift who tucked the costume up like a G-string in back. On moral grounds, I don't think that management cared if the girls went out with clients or not, but they certainly cared from a business point of view. They did not want to jeopardize their liquor and cabaret licenses. Any time there was a whisper about a Bunny dating a customer, the woman was fired immediately. And, of course, that policy worked to the Bunnies' benefit.

"We had special customers who came in every day, and we got to know them well. Emmanuel—we called him Ed—was a sports handicapper. Frank was a big-game hunter from Africa who used to send me souvenirs. And, of course, Giles Copeland, a widower who was in perpetual mourning for his wife, a former Billy Rose showgirl. He loved being around the tall, willowy Bunnies.

"For the most part, we didn't really notice men in any personal way, which surprises people. You would refer to a particular man at one of your tables by whatever he was drinking; the 'Chivas on the rocks' in the corner. I was nice to all my customers, despite the fact that we always said and heard the same things.

"We were major cock teasers, and that was our image as Playboy Bunnies. We never got too familiar, but we flirted. I remember that I once perched on a table—a major no-no in Bunny decorum—and Keith Hefner walked by. He was furious, and sent me upstairs to report to Alice Nichols that I'd been given a three-week suspension.

"You always heard the night-shift girls talk about the after-hours parties. Limos waited outside the Club after work to ferry certain Bunnies to Victor Lownes' penthouse in the St. Moritz Hotel. Finally, one night I went there. When I walked in, I saw group sex going on, an orgy. A Bunny I knew from the VIP Room called out, 'Hi, Teddy, come on in.' I couldn't help noticing there was a guy going down on her. I was shocked, but I still tried to appear sophisticated and ignore people all over the room in twos and threes, some heading off to bedrooms.

"Still feigning sophistication and not knowing how to leave gracefully, I walked to the bar and ordered a drink, striking up a conversation with a young guy who seemed to have chosen the bar for the same reasons I had. Neither of us wanted to be pegged as judgmental or moralistic, so we sat and pretended that these things were not happening all around us. It was like being in a Woody Allen movie. Today's young woman would probably say, 'I'm outta' here!' and leave, but I was intimidated and couldn't come up with a good exit line. My solution was to sit there and get smashed.

After leaving Playboy, Elaine Trebek Kares moved to Canada, where she became a talk-show hostess. Back in the U.S. she founded Adsert, a niche advertising firm, in 1985, and Scent Seal, a fragrance-sampling company, which she sold in 1995 to her largest competitor, Arcade. "I just can't seem to get away from Playboy. My Scent Seal offices in Manhattan were on the 24th floor of the same building that housed Playboy: I would look out my window every day and see their balcony below me." Elaine was married to game show host Alex Trebek for seven years, and is now married to film producer Peter Kares.

My bar pal eventually did find the proper exit line: 'I think I'd better get you out of here'—not surprisingly, since I'd just thrown up all over the wet bar. He found a cab, dropped me off at my apartment building and I never saw him again.

"Most of us were young and innocent, but in the club atmosphere, we savvied up pretty quickly. We knew how to draw the line on what to do and what not to do. There were only 125 of us, at most, working as Bunnies in the New York Club, and we were, at least in the early days of the Club, treated like celebrities all around Manhattan. For that brief time in our lives, we had a chance to savor the taste of being a 'star.' I was treated like a movie queen when I was on promotional assignments. Even though I would wear a white pleated skirt and black sweater with the Bunny logo on it rather than the satin Bunny costume, people would stop me and ask for an autograph. Inside the Club, we paraded like starlets in our showgirl costumes—we were the show.

"I worked there two years, and then left to get married. Years later, after I moved to California and had founded my own company, I was invited to the Playboy Mansion on a Sunday night to see a movie. I remember walking in the garden with Hef and Victor Lownes. I liked Hef and Victor; both of them were intelligent and charming. I thought of Victor as a kind of bright, charismatic villain.

"As we walked into the mansion aviary, I said, 'I don't belong here. It's 20 years later. You guys are still the same, the scene is still the same, and you're still with 23-year-old girls. When I was in my early 20s, you guys were in your 40s—and we had the best of you. Now you're in your 60s and the new girls are still in their 20s. I've outgrown this.'

"Victor stopped and looked at me. 'Teddy, you're no fun anymore,' he said." ∎

Sabrina Scharf Schiller

At the age of 15, I eloped with my high school algebra teacher, having decided that this was the man I would be happy with and that we could make a life together. But a significant factor was that I was pretty sure no one else would ever ask me so I'd better say yes! For three years I straddled two worlds—high school student and housewife—before the marriage was annulled in 1962. With a gasoline credit card in my pocket and my sewing machine packed in the trunk of my old De Soto, I traveled cross-country to New York.

"Shortly after I arrived in New York, I fell in with some people who were working at an off-Broadway theatre. I thought I was so lucky because I got a tiny role in a play. But during rehearsal, I experienced one of those grim moments, you know, when you see the director slide down in his seat. I knew then that I had to get acting training. I was told the Neighborhood Playhouse had the best acting program, but the school also had a strict rule that you had to attend as a full-time student.

"I had a job working for the developers of a game show based on Charades. A couple of girls who auditioned as contestants were talking about interviewing for jobs as Playboy Bunnies. As a lark, I went along with those girls to audition, realizing I could earn a whole lot more money there just working part-time."

Sabrina's diary: *Friday night. Nine p.m. November 30, 1962. Thoughts while on my way to apply to be a Bunny: These are the young years—may I spend them laughing.*

"As it turned out, I was hired and my companions were not. I can't explain it, except that I was straight off an Arizona ranch and had that wholesome look they seemed to like.

"The Club was jammed. The customers could get a drink anywhere in New York, but they would stand in long lines outside the club at 3 in the afternoon, determined to be served a drink by a Bunny. By the time these men got in the door and sat at a table, they were grateful just to be there. The atmosphere was charged, and there was a delicious kind of playfulness between the Bunnies and customers. We saw men at their most entertaining and

Bunnies Elka Hellman, Monica Schaller and Sabrina Scharf.

Monica Schaller Evans

"We all had our favorite customers. One of mine was Giles Copeland, a widower whose wife, known as Stuttering Sam, had been a tall, beautiful, dark-haired showgirl. Giles never got over her death. He'd come into the Club around 3 o'clock, during that lull before cocktail hour, and order champagne. He loved the lanky, statuesque brunettes who reminded him of Stuttering Sam. Even though I was petite, blond and bosomy, Sam's physical opposite, we got on well. He would give every Bunny on the floor a hundred-dollar tip.

"I also served Johnny Carson when he brought in a party for lunch and sat at a big circular table in the Living Room. He never played the VIP and appreciated the simple things that a cocktail waitress can do to make people feel comfortable. You'd have people eating out of your hand just by remembering their names and making them look good to their friends. In the days of the three- and four-martini lunch, a customer sometimes wanted a 'virgin' Mary but preferred that his friends thought he was drinking alcohol. If you said, 'Shall I bring your usual?' without making him specify a nonalcoholic drink, he would be so grateful.

"My one indelible memory of the year I worked as a Bunny was the day President Kennedy was assassinated. I was standing at the service bar in the Living Room when the bartender heard the news bulletin that the president had been shot. We were asked not to say anything to the customers until the report was confirmed. When the announcement came that the president was dead, we went to each of our customers and quietly told them what had happened. At first, no one could believe it. Imagine a Bunny coming up to your table and telling you the Club was closing because the president of the United States has been killed. Everyone was in shock and crying. After we closed, the girls sat together in the dressing room for a long time sobbing."

Today, Monica runs a California-based hair-products firm she founded with her late husband.

charming. I used to keep detailed lists of how much each of my customers tipped me. When they came back, I could address them by name, and they'd tip me more.

"When we walked onto the floor of the Club, we were on-stage. As a Bunny, you got a great sense of being in control, of having power. You could handle that tray, do your job. This was your space. You owned it. We learned to sit up straight, be aware that we were the center of attention. I learned about makeup and clothes. It gave me a bit of sophistication and some self-confidence. I felt pretty.

"When I took the job, I had promised myself I would work at the Club only one year. In December 1963, my year at Playboy was coming to an end and I was determined to keep my promise. One of the Bunnies was recruiting girls for the opening of a hotel on Grand Bahama Islands. A whole group of us from Playboy joined up. It was a beautiful resort, but there were no accommodations ready for the staff."

Sabrina's diary: *By December 27, we were here—Monica Schaller, Lauren Hutton, Johnnie Lynn, Sandy Deetz, Gloria Prince, Ginger Gibson, [many others] . . . and there was nothing here but us and the croupiers and a half-finished hotel.*

Sabrina Scharf Schiller, an attorney and environmental activist, at home in her garden.

"We were assigned spacious guest rooms in the hotel, but there were no linens. Lauren Hutton, who was in the room next to mine, pulled down the draperies to use as bedding. I was shocked, but by the second night, we were all doing it. Lauren was the only sensible one.

"Those were the days when you didn't really acknowledge your body and certain things just weren't talked about, but nothing was sacrosanct to Lauren—I couldn't even say the word *menstruation*, but she used to talk about her body—and every other taboo subject—while she was stuffing socks in her bosom.

"In September, I returned to New York to attend the Neighborhood Playhouse and signed with the William Morris Agency. The following summer, I went to California to meet the Hollywood agents. Within a couple of days, I had a contract with Columbia Studios and started working immediately. It happened so fast. I never went back for my second year at the Neighborhood Playhouse.

"One of my first films, *Easy Rider*, became an overnight classic. I did several more films, but I decided I really wanted to go to law school. In 1968 I married Bob Schiller, the sitcom writer [*I Love Lucy, Maude*], and we had two daughters. I passed the bar and immediately involved myself in environmental issues, particularly the Clean-Air Initiative. I ran for Congress in 1972. At the time, Bob and his partner, Bob Weiskopf, were writing *Maude* and drew on my real-life experiences when Maude ran for Congress.

"My daughters are now friends of the children of several women I knew as Bunnies. I saw Monica Schaller pushing a stroller on Beverly Drive and I recognized her immediately, although it had been years since I'd last seen her. Teddy Howard and her daughter lived with our family for a while when they first moved to California. All our kids know one another.

"There are friendships that happen in college, in war, in camp—a bonding process that takes place when you are part of a group sharing common experiences. Maybe Bunnies bonded because we were so identifiable—if you worked as a Bunny, you were always introduced as a Bunny. We were celebrities of a sort and everyone had strong feelings, one way or another, about Bunnies. It was like that from the beginning—and still is." ∎

Barbara Bosson

I arrived in New York at 18, almost the second I graduated from high school in St. Petersburg, Florida. I studied acting with Herbert Berghoff and Milton Katselas while working in a succession of bread-and-butter jobs to save enough money to attend the Carnegie Institute of Technology (now Carnegie-Mellon) School of Drama full-time.

"I was good at shorthand and typing, thanks to a high school class I took in order to earn money for college. I got a job as an executive secretary, which paid $75 a week. This job included, before any such practices were questioned, personal shopping for the boss, after-hours work, charming clients at lunch and whatever other chores needed to be done. I hated feeling like I was owned, so I started taking temporary office jobs.

"Then in 1962, one of my roommates was working as a secretary for a lawyer representing the Playboy corporation. She told me about the Bunny jobs. To me, that executive secretary job was far less honest than being a Bunny—and I earned a hell of a lot less money. I figured I had to wear high heels and look good as an executive secretary, so what was the difference? I went to one of the early huge cattle calls, although I had never thought of myself as glamorous or particularly pretty. I probably wouldn't have gotten the job if the lawyer hadn't put in a good word for me.

"At the time, my roommates and I were all poverty-stricken. At the end of the week, literally starving, we'd go out for dinner with guys we would never have dated if we weren't so hungry. When I began work at the Playboy Club, I wasn't used to the amount of money that we were making in tips—in cash. We were living in this crummy place on Sullivan Street in Greenwich Village and when I came home from work, I would throw the tip money into a dresser drawer in my room. One day, one of my roommates came in to borrow something. She opened my drawer and gasped, 'Oh, my God, where did this come from?' The drawer was full of cash, hundreds and hundreds of dollars.

"The whole time I worked at the Playboy Club, I felt like a fish out of water. There was a track for those girls who you knew were going to be asked to pose for the centerfold, and then there were the shleppers like me—you know, just hop into the Bunny suit and go wait on tables. I was a 32D, so I was well enough endowed without padding. But a lot of girls weren't so they would stuff plastic cleaning bags into their costumes and then wonder, after a busy night running around waiting on tables, what had happened to their breasts. One girl said to me, 'What's with this? My breasts are getting even smaller!'

"I never went to the parties or dated customers. But a couple of girls I worked with intimated there was more going on than I knew about. Early one morning, we were all called in for a Bunny meeting in the Penthouse. The Bunny Mother got up on stage and, in very dramatic tones, said, 'Somebody—we won't name names—was caught last night soliciting.' Three-quarters of the Bunnies there didn't even know what the word meant. While girls all over the room were murmuring, 'What's she talking about?' one of the tougher, older Bunnies bellowed, 'Hooking!'

"A musician I was dating at the time kept saying, 'Oh, I'd really like to see you in your Bunny outfit.' I was glad he wasn't a Keyholder, because I didn't particularly want him to see me in my costume. But one night he managed to get into the Club and surprised me as I was walking down the stairs from the Penthouse. He looked at me in my orange satin outfit with the ears and said, 'You look awful.' I started to cry. When I told that story, everybody's reaction was, 'How cruel of him.' But at the time, I understood how he felt and shared his assessment. I could never enjoy being a Bunny, and had a hard time smiling when men said things like 'Hey, can I touch your tail?'

"However, I never apologized for working as a Bunny, either. For me, it was completely pragmatic, a means to an end. There were girls there, of course, who wanted nothing more than to marry someone rich, wear diamond rings and live a glamorous life, which is what they thought Playboy was all about. That was fine. That was what they wanted. As in every job I've ever had in my life, you are thrown together with people completely different from yourself, people you wouldn't think in a million years you'd have anything in common with, but you find you do and you like them.

"At first glance, you would think Tony, a room director who was the sweetest guy in the world, was a gangster. He would often drive me home, and he never, ever came on to me. He'd tell me, 'Barbara, listen, you gotta be careful where you live. Dere's a lot of drugs down dere.' Then he'd make sure I got home safely.

"Finally, in 1964, when I'd earned enough money, I auditioned for the acting program at Carnegie Tech. By the time I enrolled, I was a 26-year-old freshman. After my junior year, I decided to transfer to the San Francisco Playboy Club to earn the money for my senior year at Carnegie. On my way to the Club, I happened to pass the theatre where The Committee, an improvisation company that did political satire, performed. There was a casting session going on. I walked in as the director was saying, 'Have I seen everybody?' I said, 'No.' I went up onstage, auditioned and got the job.

"The Committee was very prestigious and a difficult company to join. The *San Francisco Chronicle* asked for an interview, during which I mentioned that I had come to San Francisco intending to work at the Playboy Club. The next day's article was all about [how] the new Committee member is a Bunny! In the entire piece, there was nothing about college or being an actress, just my job as a Bunny. As a result, of course, everyone in the company tormented me about it for a long time. But the Committee marked the beginning of my professional acting career and the end of my days both at Playboy and Carnegie Tech.

Barbara Bosson on the set of *Scattering Dad*, a television film she wrote and produced (CBS, 1998).

I stayed with the company for three years, eventually moving with the show to the Tiffany Theatre in Los Angeles. Stephen Bochco, whom I'd known as a classmate at Carnegie, came to see the show and we started dating.

"Stephen and I married, raised a son and daughter, and worked together [*Hill Street Blues, Cop Rock, Murder One*]. Three or so years ago, I stopped being really fulfilled by acting and started to write. I wanted to create and deliver a whole piece of work, to participate in every aspect of production, rather than just wait to be hired as an actress. *Scattering Dad*, a CBS telefilm, which I wrote and produced in 1997 and which aired in 1998, was one of the most incredibly fulfilling experiences of my life—a lot like having my children.

"Looking back, maybe I don't credit Playboy enough. Being a Bunny got me where I needed to go to have a life that I have really loved. I didn't have a lot of options when I started out. Nobody did. But all the rules that applied in those days don't apply now.

"When the New York Playboy Club closed in 1985, CBS *Morning News* asked me to be a guest on the show with Gloria Steinem. Gloria's point of view was that this bastion of male chauvinism was closing and that it was indicative of the times—how much better things were for women now and all of that. I had about one-and-a-half minutes to speak, and I didn't want to say to her, 'You're wrong,' but I wanted to make my point that the rewards were worth it. Working at the Club gave me the opportunity to do something I had always dreamed of doing, which would probably not have happened otherwise. Everybody has to make their own deal in life. Working as a Bunny enabled me to go to drama school and have the career I wanted so much." ∎

LinÅa "Jill" DurhÂm

From my first day as a Bunny, I thought someone had made a mistake hiring me. I never felt in the least attractive enough. My recurring fear was that Hugh Hefner would one day appear in the Club, see me across a crowded room and point a finger saying, 'What is *she* doing in a Bunny suit?' Then he would tear my ears off and send me home.

"Eventually, I was chosen Bunny of the Week many times. I still felt insecure. No one ever said, 'She's too ugly to be a Bunny,' but I could never shake the notion that I wasn't pretty enough to have been chosen in the first place.

"I was one of the original New York Bunnies. I was 19 years old and a theatre major at Ithaca College when I decided to get married and move to New York City with my husband. I had been a professional actress from the time I was 13 and had started working in musical theatre, but I couldn't hold out for an acting job. I needed to work. An employment agency found me a job dressing up in a pussycat suit and handing out flyers in front of Macy's department store. Someone stopped me on the street and asked if I'd like to be a Bunny. At first I thought it was a joke.

"But I was hired in November and began training almost immediately for the Club's opening. Playboy brought Kelly Collins from the Chicago Club to train us, and, boy, did we have a lot to learn. When Ed Sullivan ordered a Scotch and soda from me in the Penthouse on opening night, I served him tonic water instead of club soda. I didn't mistake the bottles. I just didn't know the difference. He was furious.

"I was relegated to the lunch shift, anyway, because I was too young to work nights. Among my

Training Bunny Marion Barker
demonstrates the Bunny Dip
to Bunny Jill prior to the New York
Club's opening in 1962.

Bunny Mother Joan Howard teaches novice Bunny stylized service.

regular customers in the Living Room was a businessman who would brief me in advance about the clients he would be bringing in. As a prank, he'd have me pretend I recognized one of them as an old acquaintance.

"There were a lot of misconceptions about Bunnies—one being the assumption that we all lived together in one big dorm on the top floor of each Club. Another that persists to this day is equating Bunnies with Playmates. I take great pains to explain that I wasn't a centerfold. My son remembers that when he was a toddler, he heard someone mention that I was a Bunny, and his image was that his mother actually turned into a little furry animal.

"But some of the wild stories were true. A good friend, a German Bunny who worked in the VIP Room, once called me at home to ask if my husband and I would like to come to a party that Victor Lownes was throwing in his hotel suite. She said that there would be some other nice couples there and that Victor would send his car for us. Well, we accepted, thinking it would be great to go to a swanky party hosted by one of the Playboy executives. We got all dressed up. My husband put on a suit and I wore a cocktail dress with a mink stole, and soon a limo arrived to take us to the hotel. We knocked on the door of the suite and waited a long time for anyone to answer. Finally Victor, looking very disheveled, opened the door and said, 'Have a seat here and we'll be right with you.' It was obvious what was going on. We could hear people in the various bedrooms, and there was a stack of Polaroids on the coffee table, pictures of Bunnies I knew, without their clothes on. It was clear that we were expected to join in and switch partners. That kind of party life was always available if that's what you wanted. We didn't and we left.

"Like a lot of Bunnies, I was making more money at age 20 than my father made when he was raising a family. I had fun, and I learned a lot of valuable lessons as well. Years later when I moved to Santa Fe, New Mexico, I realized that the city had only a souvenir art market. I had lived in Greenwich Village during my years as a Bunny and made friends with the art crowd. So I decided to open the Durham Gallery to show the works of fine, contemporary artists.

"I also created a workshop called Creative Business and the Artist to give artists a better sense of how to operate in the crazy contemporary art world. Oddly enough, schools of business and management—not art departments—recruit me for lectures in which I point to my Playboy Club days as my own personal business school. So much depends upon having a strong sense of yourself and confidence in your ability to accomplish something. When I was setting up my own business, it helped to keep in mind the relationships I had with some

Linda Durham at her Contemporary Art Gallery in Galisteo, New Mexico.

of my customers who were executives of big corporations. I talked to them as equals, and they treated me with respect. If you feel intimidated, it will communicate itself; that in itself is an important lesson.

"On my last day as a Bunny, I went into the wardrobe room to say good-bye to Betty, the seamstress, and told her I couldn't bear to turn in my costume. I managed to keep the whole outfit, including the ears, collar, cuffs, cuff links and bow tie. Around the time I

turned 40 and was feeling lonely, I came across my old Bunny costume in a trunk where it had been for years. I thought, 'I'm going to try it on, and if it doesn't fit I'm going to be really depressed.' But it did fit.

"I wouldn't want too many people to see me in it, but I'd like everyone to know that I can still get into it." ∎

HeleN HiTe

Novice to Bunny? People who hear that I went from life in a convent to being a Bunny in the Playboy Club ask me how I could have managed such a transition. Actually, it wasn't as traumatic as it sounds. In terms of discipline, the Bunny Mother functioned much like a Mother Superior.

"As a teenager in South Carolina, I had won eight beauty pageants in a row. But when my mother died, I became very involved in the church. After seeing the movie, *The Nun's Story*, I decided I should give up everything and devote myself to God. I lived in a convent for a year before realizing it was not the life for me. I was pretty much on my own by then because my father had also died. "When I saw the ad: 'Girls! Be a Bunny!' I sent a letter with a few beauty-pageant photographs to Playboy. I got a letter back telling me I was hired, and in March 1964 I started at the New York Club.

"I remember sitting in front of the makeup mirror in the Bunny dressing room, carefully gluing on three pairs of false eyelashes, and laughing so much. Everything about being a Bunny was a hoot! Madeleine Tarr and I were invited to be mascots for the Philadelphia 76ers. Wearing our Playboy promotions outfit (white skirts, black sweaters and black satin ears), we sat on the bench with the players at every game throughout that basketball season.

"Madeleine and I were saving our money for a trip to Europe, but friends suggested we should become stewardesses and travel free."

After two years as a Bunny, Helen quit Playboy to become a Pan Am flight attendant. "One difference from the Club was that in the sky I didn't have a room director I could go to and say, 'Table 32—out!' At 35,000 feet, you can't do that to the obnoxious passenger in seat 32."

During the three years she flew for Pan Am, Helen married and had her first baby. "I was then fired because, at the time, airline regulations wouldn't permit a woman to work as a flight attendant if she had children. By that time, I had become interested in natural childbirth and trained to be a midwife. I've now delivered more than 500 babies."

Helen Hite at home in her kitchen sewing the hats she's designed for Denver Broncos fans.

"In 1974, I received a letter informing me that I had been wrongfully fired and was offered the opportunity to return to work as a flight attendant. My daughter Nimi was then a year old. I've now been flying with the airlines for more 30 years, first with Pan Am and now with United.

"I've been married and divorced twice and I have three children, my youngest daughter born when I was 40. I'm single again and haven't had a date in five years. I think I've gone back to being a nun!" ∎

LAUREN HUTTON

The girls who became Bunnies in the early '60s were pioneers. We were pre-feminist, pre-hippy era explorers and extraordinarily brave for the time. I don't think any of us at 18 or 19 felt we needed permission to do anything, yet we had grown up in an age when girls absolutely had to have permission for everything. Before there was any press attention given to the idea of a woman owning her own sexuality, we had already started figuring out for ourselves what real sexual freedom was about. Entering a milieu that was then misconstrued to be in the 'B-Girl hooker' category—fearlessly—we were basically all learning together what was good and bad.

"We came from every sort of background. My own was very chaotic. I never knew my father, Laurence Hutton, who abandoned my mother before I was born. I grew up with a stepfather and took his surname, Hall, although I was never legally adopted. My mother, who was well-born and came from a privileged background, had three more daughters. We had little money. There were problems with alcohol. My mother, who was afraid of everything, couldn't protect herself or us, which is why it was basically left to me to raise my younger sisters. I just couldn't be afraid because it became my job to protect my sisters and take care of the household. And I couldn't wait to get out.

"Back then, everything was a giant adventure. After a year at the University of South Florida, I headed for New York. I saw the ad for Bunny jobs in *The New York Times* and was hired in 1963, not long after the Club opened. There were three other Bunnies with my given name, Mary, so I opted for Lauren, after my father, Laurence. I was hired as a Lunch Bunny, because I was too young to work at night. Lunch Bunnies were there to be looked at—to smile, chat and, incidentally, to serve drinks.

"We all had our little opening routines. When customers heard my name, they would ask if I was named for Bacall, and I'd say, 'No, for D.H. or T.E. Lawrence.' It was sassy and a hint that I was literate. You never wanted to get too personal, but at the same time, letting them know you had some education was a way of protecting yourself, code for 'I'm not a hooker.' You were saying, 'Don't look at me *that way.*'

"I quickly became the Demerit Bunny. My ears were crooked, my tail not on straight, whatever. Every time I had 97–98 demerits and almost got fired, I'd somehow win the bartenders' Bunny of the Week contest. That would give me enough good points to lower the demerits and I wouldn't be fired.

"One of my favorite customers was a white Russian prince, who was head of some company and really fancied me. I liked him because he had the manners of the great old gents I knew as a little kid growing up down South. He was old and sad and full of stories. I became very attached to him, but I never saw him outside the Club. Mysteriously, I started receiving in the mail million-dollar insurance policies, with me named as the beneficiary. Those were the days when airports had machines that sold air-travel insurance. I discovered that before every business trip, he would take out a policy and send it to me.

"The Night Bunnies, the big, bad girls who came in to work as the Lunch Bunnies were leaving, were a tense group. They'd just bump us out of their way. It was all very exciting, kind of dangerous. They were the ones who went to the parties and met all the big shots. Toward the end of the time I worked at the Club, someone in the hierarchy got an eye for me. I started getting invitations to Playboy parties. It frightened me. The hits started coming too hot and heavy. I think I might even then have been worrying about my own attraction to that life if I stayed in it too long. I still think what *if* I'd slept with one of those very rich, powerful guys? Would I have ended up getting married or being kept? I didn't want to get pulled into that world, and I knew it could happen.

"After about a year, I wanted to move on. I was working in a dark club while the sun was shining outside. It was depressing. Also, I was in my very first relationship, a bad one, with a disc jockey I'd fallen in love with in Florida. He was an older guy, and he had a lot of control over me. One reason I never went to parties or saw the other girls outside the Club is that he wouldn't let me out of his sight. So I finally left Playboy in January 1964, and I went to the Bahamas to work in a resort casino with a lot of other former Bunnies. The Italian croupiers used to make pasta for us and they'd sling the spaghetti against the wall to see if it was *al dente*—if it stuck, it was cooked enough. I thought it was the most European thing I'd ever seen. And an English croupier who had records by some group called the Beatles told us, 'They're bigger than Elvis, they're going to take over the world!' Then I was fired shortly before the resort's big grand opening because I wouldn't sleep with one of the guys who owned the place. It was a Saturday night and all the cruise ships were coming in, but the other girls went out on strike in support of me. Everybody quit *en masse*.

"I eventually wound up back in Manhattan and found myself standing with two suitcases in front of Tiffany's on a Sunday morning, not knowing what to do. Then I remembered a Bunny I'd worked with, and called her. She and her boyfriend, Arnie, a great born-in-Brooklyn kind of guy, let me sleep on the couch until I could figure out what to do. I needed a job, but I just couldn't be a cocktail waitress again. Arnie looked in *The New York Times* ads and said, 'Here. You can be a house model for Christian Dior.' You had to be 5'8" and I was 5'6 1/2", so I went in wearing very high heels and got the job.

Lauren Hutton, the supermodel, actress and talk-show hostess; above, wreck-diving in Pearl Harbor.

"Later, when I was modeling for *Vogue* in the 1970s, I was asked to be one of the speakers at a feminist rally held in front of the New York Public Library. Gloria Steinem and Betty Friedan were there, and I was very proud to be asked. I stood in the crowd listening to the angry words, and it struck me that I was hearing nothing but a tirade blaming men for everything. I couldn't relate to all that hostility. I turned around and left. My idea of being a feminist was making your own way in the world, being responsible for your own decisions and taking care of yourself, not looking to a man to take care of you.

"When we became Playboy Bunnies, the '60s hadn't yet really started. I think we were probably the last ones to come out of an era when women had to make a clear choice between being either smart or sexy—one couldn't have both brains and beauty. As a little girl, this all came home to me with Marilyn Monroe, who was soft, warm, the essence of femininity—but people laughed at her. She had to be a joke because she was sexy. There was also great hostility toward Bunnies. But, of course, a Bunny was sexy, so she, too, had to be dumb and a joke. No choice there. I wondered even as a kid why a real woman couldn't be both smart and pretty.

"But Playboy protected us. In the early 1970s when I was a *Vogue* model and had just signed a contract with Revlon, Hugh Hefner got in touch and said, 'We've got nude pictures of you. Do you want us to run them?' I said, 'Huh—what nudes?' He sent me copies and then I remembered what had happened. Ten years earlier, shortly before I started working as a Bunny, a photographer paid me $15 an hour to do a local newspaper ad for plastic garbage cans. After we finished the ad, he told me he wanted to test a 'nude modeling light.' I had no idea there was no such thing. I was leery about it, but he assured me that since I was under 21, he would never be able to publish the photographs anyway. Could I help him out? I signed the release as Mary Hall, my name then. The photographer's wife made me up and there I was posing in cloth drapings for these pathetic '40s-style art pictures.

"When I saw the photographs, I told Hefner, 'No, please don't publish them.' And he didn't.

"We were young women on the move, out there pushing a new frontier. We were like sisters learning together how to take charge of our own lives. We protected each other. We were a rare bouquet." ∎

Susan Sullivan

I t was summertime, and I was working in Manhattan as a showroom model for a month or so to earn money for my junior year at Hofstra University. The fashion houses always took on extra girls to show the new fall lines, but I needed a part-time job when I went back to school, too. It was then that I saw a huge, full-page ad in *The New York Times* announcing jobs as Bunnies in the Playboy Club. The Playboy Club to me was about *Playboy* magazine, which represented something illicit and erotic. I didn't read it, but I found it sexy to look at when I would see it in some guy's apartment. I suppose it comes from an Irish Catholic background, but the taboo aspect of sex was very erotic to me. The idea of working at Playboy as a Bunny titillated all of the voyeuristic aspects of my nature.

"I never seriously thought I would be hired, but I decided I would at least go and apply for the job. I wanted to see the club, and I figured this would be the only way I ever would.

"It was *really* an adventure. I went on my lunch hour. I borrowed a dress from the line, a very clingy, simple crepe sheath dress. And I wore all of this padding because, to me, the image of Playboy Bunnies was bosoms. So I went in there with my large padded breasts for an interview with some man who was in charge. But then he told me he was going to send me down to see the Bunny Mother.

" 'You know, I'm going to be quite honest with you,' I said. 'I don't think this is going to work out because actually I'm going back to school in September.'

" 'Oh, that's fine,' he said. 'You can work on the weekends.'

"And I said, 'Well, I have a scholarship I have to honor. On the weekends, if I'm in a play, I'll have to be in the play.'

"But he said, 'That's not a problem. We're very flexible, very accommodating.'

"There was another reason I knew it was never going to work, but I certainly didn't want to say to him, 'Look, I have no bosom!'

"He said, 'Just go down to the Bunny mother and try on a costume.'

"I said, 'OK.' I went to the Bunny Mother and told her, 'Listen, there's not much point in my doing this because actually I have no bosom.'

"She said, 'We pad everybody. Nobody has much of a bosom. It's no big deal.'

"So I thought, 'Well, wait until she sees me.'

"I put on this costume and, sure enough, I learned about Bunny padding. You know, they carry on about this new Wonderbra. Please! They have nothing on what those costumes did. In my case, the costume pushed me up from my thighs and pushed me in from . . . well, everywhere. And by the time I was through, I ended up with bosoms.

"But everything's relative, I guess. Once, there were these two guys sitting at my station, and one of them had just come out of a seminary maybe a few months short of becoming a priest. He very shyly said to me, 'You know, Bunny Sue, I really admire you because all these girls are walking around here showing everything they've got and you, —Well, Bunny Sue, you are subtle.'

"I just said, 'Thank you.'

"My phobia about not being busty probably had to do with growing up in the '50s, when the ideal figure was a bosomy gal. So while I always felt deficient in that area and very aware of not being busty enough for the costume, I did think that my legs sort of compensated. I liked that long, leggy look. In fact, I never thought that the Bunny costume was such a terribly bizarre outfit. I'm an actress and I liked the idea of being in a costume and not being myself. I even altered my name—I became Bunny Suzanne.

"Apparently, I did feel a little uncomfortable about the whole idea behind being a Bunny, though. It would manifest itself in that I would always try to tell people that I was in college. If I could slip it in, I would. I would go up to table and say things like, 'Forthwith, my Lord, here is your gin and tonic. I'm working on a Shakespearean play in

Susan Sullivan, the two-time Emmy nominee has starred in numerous series, including *Falcon Crest* and *Rich Man. Poor Man*, and most recently ABC's *Dharma and Greg*. She co-starred as the mother of the bride in *My Best Friend's Wedding* with Julia Roberts.

school and I'm just practicing.' I felt the need to let them know that I was a college student and this was not my life. So a part of me clearly felt uncomfortable about being thought of as somebody who would be doing this work as a profession.

"The fact that I was a Bunny was soon known on campus, and that became a big thing. I was already well-established at Hofstra as an actress because I was in all of the plays. Then a big picture of me in my Bunny outfit appeared in the school newspaper. I had been dating a very popular guy and we had broken up. But I remember him seeing the picture of me as a Bunny and saying, 'Oh, my God, what's going on here?'

"And that pleased me. I was in school, doing something of significance, yet I was also capable of doing this other thing on the side. I was 'pretty enough' to do it. It added a bit of an edge. I never thought of myself as being terribly pretty, so getting hired to be a Bunny served as confirmation that I was a 'sexy' female.

"During Bunny training, Keith Hefner kept emphasizing that we couldn't date customers or meet a man anywhere near the Club. Well, a man sat down at my station, a Texan, and I did what I always did: 'Hello, I'm Bunny Sue and I'm applying for a Fulbright. What would you like to drink?' Well, this man became fascinated with me and wanted to help me get the Fulbright. He was very intent on meeting outside the Club and, of course, I told him that wasn't possible. I do not know how he did this, but he followed me on the train to Long Island, and when I got off at my stop, there he was. And all he wanted to do was to give me this set of books, Best American Plays, which I still have. He also showed up on the campus at Hofstra a number of times.

"In 1964, the Beatles came to New York and stopped in at the Playboy Club. I don't know how I got to be their Bunny, but I found myself serving Scotch and Coke to the Beatles. It was a table of 12 people, and there was a disc jockey in their party. They were charming and very funny. Of course, I knew their songs and knew all about them, but what made it really nice is that, for them, I was somebody special.

"Many of the gals working at the Club were not necessarily beautiful. They were not the prettiest and didn't have the best bodies, but they were bright. That quality seemed to be of greater importance to the Club when they hired Bunnies. Initially, a lot of the women they selected were college students. I remember meeting a lot of European girls there, and a good many very highly motivated women.

"When the Women's Movement came around and one thought about these things, I had to admit that I personally had never felt subjugated as a woman. It wasn't in the nature of the work I did as an actress. It's a profession where they need women. I was sort of surprised when all that consciousness raising started to happen some years later, and then I began to question that I had once walked around in that really provocative outfit as a lure to bring men into the Club. 'Was I being used and abused and tattooed on the *Camino Real?*' Hmmmm. Then I thought, 'Gosh, no, that wasn't really the way it was.'

"No one working for the Club ever made a pass at me that I recall. I always imagined that the top guys had a bevy of gals that met somewhere to party or something, but that I just wasn't in the loop. I had no desire to be there—and I'm sure I thought I wasn't sexy or pretty enough to be asked. But, you know, you always tend to wonder why you haven't been invited to a party even when you really don't want to go to it anyway.

"I never felt ashamed of being a Bunny. I thought, I'm articulate, intelligent, a professional actress—here's something counter to my normal image, and it's amusing. The experience of working as a Playboy Bunny provided good material later when I was a guest on Johnny Carson's *Tonight Show*.

"I worked at the Club a little less than a year. Then I graduated from Hofstra University in 1964 and went to the Cleveland Playhouse.

"At the time I worked at the Club, being a Bunny was not the main thrust of what was going on in my life. But now, when I look back at it, I'm glad I had the experience, because it was just that—an experience. A little round section of time. So much of your life goes by with a sameness, but the experience of being a Bunny has a sharp, electric blue kind of color.

"The same color as my costume." ∎

Francesca Emerson

I was a single mother with two kids and practically living on welfare in Brooklyn before I became a Bunny in 1963. The following year, I made so much money that I was audited.

"When I first started at Playboy I couldn't hold a tray—my arm was too weak. So I was put in the gift shop, where you earned a fixed salary. China Lee came to my rescue and told Keith Hefner, 'I'll train her. She can do it.' It was do or die for me, and I managed to make the grade.

"In that time of Sexual Revolution in the '60s, we were independent women, supporting ourselves and sometimes children, husbands and boyfriends, and trying to make something of our lives. That's nothing to be ashamed of. Free love, sex and drugs—everything was going on at the time. But I never saw drug or alcohol abuse among Bunnies who were my friends. I was 26 years old and living in Los Angeles before I ever had a drink. I didn't smoke.

"Bunnies were part of that era, but we were way ahead. Even today, when people hear, 'You know, Fran used to be a Bunny,' they're interested. Their eyes get wide and they want to know all about it. Why? I guess because they remember it now as part of the Sexual Revolution.

"A week or two after I started working, a customer who was with BBD&O advertising agency asked me if I was interested in modeling. I said I hadn't ever thought about it. He gave me a card, and several of the girls told me I should check it out. I did, and one of the first black modeling agencies signed me. They changed my name from Francine Barker to just 'Francesca.' At a time when blacks were just beginning to appear in advertising, I ended up doing a couple of television commercials, including a national spot for Dial soap.

"So much happened for me during that first year when I worked as a Bunny. I went from doing print modeling to television commercials, and Playboy was the catalyst. If I hadn't become a Bunny, I might still be living in Brooklyn, getting along on welfare. The Club experience put me in the mainstream, meeting people I would otherwise never have known.

"In late 1964, I moved to Los Angeles. I was getting a divorce. I called China Lee, who was training Bunnies for the opening of the Playboy Club on Sunset Boulevard. She put in a word for me with Keith Hefner and got me a job as a Training Bunny.

"I took leave as a Bunny after I remarried and got pregnant with my son. I came back to work while I was still nursing, but I'd gained a lot of weight. I just couldn't get trim enough to continue working as a Bunny, and eventually I was fired. I knew I must get training to do something else. I was still fragile; my second marriage was ending, and I had kids to support. My high school diploma wasn't enough.

"I was always interested in cameras and photography, and I'd been taking some film courses at UCLA. One of my friends, who had earned her M.A., considered herself an intellectual and was into the Black Panther Movement. She was working for a film producer. I asked her for advice about becoming a film editor.

" 'Oh, I didn't know Playboy Bunnies were interested in such things,' she said, and then directed me to a film editing program. Thirty years later, we still laugh about how she put me down for having been a Bunny.

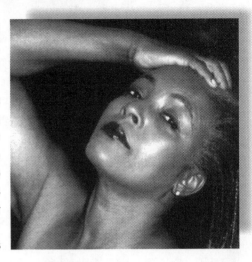

Filmmaker Francesca Emerson.

"During my training, I worked at MGM, Fox and Universal Studios, gaining experience in all facets of film editing. When I completed the course, I was hired by Universal. I've worked in film editing ever since. Beverly Sawyer, a screenwriter and my former apprentice in film editing, is working with me on a documentary about female friendship, focusing on five women who met as Playboy Bunnies 30 years ago." ■

B.J. Ward

After graduating from high school in Wilmington, Delaware, I headed straight to New York to launch an acting career. I needed a bread-and-butter job, so I auditioned for the Playboy Club—twice. I thought Bunnies were supposed to look sophisticated, so I pulled my hair back and wore a lot of makeup. They turned me down. Then I went back with the fresh-scrubbed, all-American-girl look and they hired me. I wrote to my parents about the job; they didn't consider it good news. My father sent me one of the two letters I ever got from him. The first was a wonderful letter when I was born and he was serving in the military overseas. The second broke my heart because he equated being a Bunny with prostitution. I had felt so good about getting a job in such a glamorous place. If you were an actress, like me, waiting for your big break, it was certainly better than working in some dark, crummy bar.

"I found the Bunny Training amusing. Just the idea of calling someone Bunny Mother—like Reverend Mother!—was strange stuff. I remember laughing so much toward the end of

B.J. Ward, the current voice of Betty Rubble on *The Flintstones*, combines comedy with opera in her acclaimed one-woman show *Stand Up Opera*, which she's performed throughout the country, in such venues as Washington's Kennedy Center and New York's Carnegie Hall.

the training film when they showed a sequence about projecting the Bunny Attitude. 'When you walk to work, don't look down . . .' and in the film you saw piles of crap in a gutter. Then you heard this bouncy music and the camera panned to the sky. 'Look up! You're a Bunny!'

"I relished playing the role of 'good girl' wearing a provocative costume: 'Come hither, but don't touch.' But as my acting career started taking off, I lost interest. In April 1963, I married Jeremy Steig, a flautist who played with Bill Evans, and we lived in Greenwich Village. I was studying acting with Sandy Meisner and Phillip Burton. I was taking voice classes. My life revolved around rehearsals, auditions, music and friends in the Village. But every day, I would head uptown to 59th Street to work as a Bunny. It seemed surreal. I took a leave of absence to do summer stock in Cooperstown, New York, and when I returned to New York that autumn, I could no longer cut it as a Bunny.

"I was fired. It happened the day I was working in the Piano Bar of the Living Room and the 'Tallest Man in the World' walked in. He had hands like shovels. Of course, all the shortest Bunnies were rounded up to be photographed with this giant. I'm 5'3" tall, so I qualified. There were the usual corny remarks: 'Any more in the hutch like you?' and 'I could use ears like that on my television set.' It finally got to me. I'd had it. I tipped a drink on a guy. I said, 'Oops!' but that was it.

"Not long after I left Playboy, I was hired to play The Girl in *The Fantasticks*. I was invited to do a segment of ABC *Nightlife* March 10, 1965, with Shelley Berman as the guest host. When I mentioned I'd been a Playboy Bunny, the audience howled with laughter because I didn't look at all glamorous in my kneesocks and a bulky sweater. People love to cling to stereotypes." ∎

Honey "Brigitte" Lieberman

Remember 'A little dab'll do ya?' I was the girl who came out of the tube in the Brylcreem TV commercials. I had come to New York from Austria to be a model, and my father, who was a police chief in Vienna, flew over to visit me. I told him I needed to earn extra money to live on and was working as a Playboy Bunny. I thought my father might chop my head off when he saw me in the costume, but he liked it. He spoke only a little English, but all the girls came over to his table and made such a fuss over him. My father was proud of me and still talks about that visit.

"America was and, even now, is very Puritanical. I think Playboy eased people into a more normal, relaxed attitude toward sexual things. Europeans don't cover up all the time. Nudity isn't embarrassing to us and we don't have some of the sexual hang-ups that come with covering up. But what was most troubling to many was that Playboy combined the wholesome, girl-next-door image with sexuality. A Bunny was the girl you shouldn't take home to mother—but could."

Today, Honey, the mother of four children, lives on a Long Island horse farm. ∎

Chialing "Jolly" Young

I was an army brat, born in Chunking, China, where my parents, both Chinese-Americans, were stationed. My father, a famed mountaineer, was a major general in Chiang Kai-shek's Chinese Nationalist Army prior to Pearl Harbor, and later a Brigadier general in the American Army. Living a peripatetic childhood in various army bases all over the world, I learned to adjust quickly to anything that came my way. However, when I enrolled at Hunter College in New York City at age 16, immediately after graduating from high school, I just took on too much. After a year slogging through a heavy course load as a math major, I needed a break. I decided to take a job and reduce my class schedule.

"I saw the ad for Bunny jobs in the summer of 1962 and thought, 'This is it. Perfect.' I was hired and then waited six months for the Club to actually open. It was great to see those ads in *The New York Times*: *An exciting life awaits you if you're young and pretty* . . . and know you already had the job. During Bunny training, Alice Nichols asked me if I'd had dance training. I proudly said 'Yes.' She said, 'I thought so. You're doing a plié, which is the last thing you want to do when Bunny Dipping!' At first I wore very little makeup, but before long, like everyone else in the dressing room, I was gluing on multiple pairs of eyelashes and piling on more hairpieces. The glamour was fun.

"I began working as an assistant Bunny Mother soon after the Club opened, helping out with office work. Management was convinced Playboy was being targeted by people who wanted to close the Club down, and I'm not sure there wasn't a conspiracy of sorts. During one hectic week in the spring of 1963, both the police and the FBI interviewed me, throwing out questions about drugs, prostitution, wild parties, Mafia ties and a bizarre tale about the psychiatric unit of a particular hospital claiming to have a so-called special 'Bunny Suicide Watch' ward. The bottom line was that Playboy couldn't afford trouble and took pains to run a straight operation. One way to shut our doors was to prove that Bunnies were fraternizing with the customers, in violation of the licensing

Wally Elmark, Lauren Hutton and Jolly Young, 1963.

laws. Playboy hired Wilmark agents to pose as Keyholders to ferret out the Bunnies who would accept dates. For the most part, the Wilmark reports were quite dull: 'Bunny X did not smile and didn't use her flashlight to check the member's key.' But their undercover operations were quite inventive. One agent left theatre tickets at the Club, and the girls who showed up to claim those seats were fired.

Chialing "Jolly" Young.

"But that office job also set me on my career course. At the same time I was in charge of Bunny scheduling, a tedious, time-consuming task using pencils, erasers and a messy mimeograph machine, I was taking one of the early courses in computer programming at Hunter. So many factors came into play with scheduling: school and child-care commitments, age (only women over 21 could work the night shift), ability (only top girls could handle the Showrooms), costume color co-ordination (we couldn't have only girls in blue costumes working) and myriad individual Bunny requests and preferences. One day, when a hand-written master list disappeared, we were lost. I had to start from scratch. There had to be an easier way: the Bunny schedule became my class project and first computer-programming challenge. Unfortunately, the program I developed was useless because few companies (including Playboy) had computers. Yet, as a Bunny calling in drink orders, checking a Keyholder's credit and totaling bar checks, I could see all the uses for a computer.

"The Playboy job was seductive and lucrative, but after almost three years working as a Bunny, it was time to think about a career. I credit my mother for stepping in and saying, 'What are you going to do with your life? You need a challenge.' But there wasn't a math field, including teaching, that appealed to me. When I discovered computers, I was so excited about this new technology that I left Playboy in 1966 in search of a job where I could develop these skills. Blue Cross hired me on the basis of an aptitude test.

"I've worked with many companies in my 30-year data-processing career. I would describe my work today as 'troubleshooting:' an outsider with a fresh viewpoint and no political ties who can take over large, high-visibility 'bet-your-business/reputation' projects that are generally behind schedule, over budget and with a high probability for legal action. I generally have about two weeks to assess, renegotiate, restaff, repair, revitalize or shut down.

THE BUNNY BITES THE BIG APPLE

"I learned negotiating skills as one of the small group of Bunnies fighting to stave off management's efforts to bring in a 'sweetheart' union. Workers are often only too happy to comply with unionization without examining the actual benefits. The experience was an important lesson for me in the delicate process of neutralizing emotional responses to rumors and intimidation. The time I spent as an assistant Bunny Mother and working with the Bunny softball team gave me my first taste of scheduling resources and team building—putting together groups that play to everyone's strengths. I also learned that you have to have more going for you than a pretty face—in that rarefied working place, I was surrounded by pretty faces!

"What Playboy did *not* prepare me for, however, was being a pioneer in a male-dominated work environment. I had come from a workplace where a teenage, female workforce held power and earned more than their immediate male superiors, the room directors. For many years, I was the youngest participant and the only female in management meetings and advisory councils. At Playboy, ethnic diversity was prized: I was unprepared for being looked upon in a corporate environment as a 'token,' filling minority quotas. In the corporate world, good looks worked against you. For years, I did not answer the phones if I worked late with male colleagues so I wouldn't cause suspicion among wives and girlfriends. It was often a surprise to wives attending company functions to discover that I was a) nonclerical b) management c) single or d) their spouse's boss.

"In the three years that I worked at the Club, I was never in a position where I had to fight off advances: Clearly defined rules and penalties eliminated a lot of unsavory situations. Since leaving Playboy, one of the most difficult experiences of my working life was to recognize my inability to resolve a sexual-harassment situation without having to resort to legal action. After two years, and considerable strain on my marriage, I recently accepted an out-of-court settlement. The man I filed the complaint against was promoted.

"I live in Texas, but I'm usually on the road. I love my work. The challenge of problem-solving is very gratifying to me. I still keep in touch with several of the women I worked with at Playboy 30 years ago.

"Was it the most exciting, glamorous time of my life? You bet. I met the Beatles at the Club, appeared as a guest on several TV talk shows, played a role in the movie *How to Murder Your Wife*, dined with Steve McQueen, gave interviews for magazine and newspaper articles—and was 'the Chinese Bunny' who stuffed her costume with gym socks, according to Gloria Steinem in her irritating piece in *Show* magazine. I received fan mail, had my own male 'groupies,' made more money than I ever dreamed of and had more close girlfriends among the Bunnies than I had in high school. I felt like a star. And my stint at the Club led me to an exciting, challenging career." ∎

A Club of Their Own

y 1963, it was clear that Hugh Hefner had plugged into something deeper in the American psyche than just the need for an exotic private club. While the one truly "guy thing" about the Playboy Clubs in the early years was that women could not become Keyholders—a regulation that was eventually abolished in 1967—the long-held policy of excluding women from membership had the effect of eliminating the Clubs as venues for picking up girls. At swinging private disco clubs, just coming into their own in the early '60s, attractive unescorted young women were readily ushered past the velvet ropes. At the Playboy Clubs, women—girlfriends, wives, mothers, sisters, daughters—were welcome guests as long as they

Equal Rights!

In 1967 the Playboy Club welcomed women members. Qualified female applicants could own a key and were entitled to all rights and privileges, including those of entrance sans escort to any Playboy Club.

Ava Faulkner dancing on the piano in the Living Room of the New York Club, 1970.

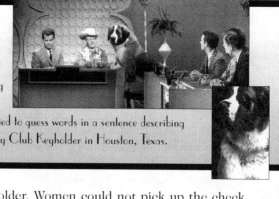

were accompanied by a Keyholder. Women could not pick up the check. They could visit the Gift Shop, where any number of items were specifically designed for "her." And, of course, one of the most publicized features about the Clubs was that members COULD NOT TOUCH THE BUNNIES! much less date them. Despite the brouhaha in the courts regarding the scanty costume and fears that Bunnies would "mingle with the customers," the Playboy Clubs were, curiously, one of the least sexually threatening destinations available.

The American geisha, wearing Bunny ears and a cottontail, smiled, served drinks and cast her winsome presence over every sort of occasion from business lunches to first dates and anniversaries. But more than a metaphor, a Bunny was the flesh-and-blood embodiment of a male fantasy fulfilled. Frequently, the Keyholder who brought his business associates to the Club for weekday lunches returned with his wife in the evening so she could meet "his Bunny." A Bunny, with no last name or address, served as an amiable stand-in for any number of roles: a disarming young woman who listened, remembered you, reminded you of your college sweetheart, made you feel young again—or grown up—and made you want to come back another day in the hope that maybe, just maybe, she, in turn, secretly harbored lustful feelings for you. Yet Bunnies were skilled in putting wives, girlfriends and other women accompanying the Keyholder at ease. They quickly established a sympathetic, nonthreatening air of collusion with women guests, a kind of unspoken acknowledgment that they were co-conspirators in satisfying male fantasy needs.

But less obviously, Bunnies also embodied the fantasies of other young women—here was a fun job with good pay that required minimal training, but no career commitment. As with airline stewardesses of their day, the job was also perceived as having the caché of glamour and sex appeal. It was cool to be a Bunny. Women visiting the Club and coming upon a Bunny invariably asked privately, "So, c'mon, what's it really like?" And, in some cases, "Do you think they'd hire me? How do I get a Bunny job?"

The Playboy Bunny as glorified waitress and unattainable, nonthreatening sex object had entered the pop lexicon. Bunnies were popping up everywhere, as familiar an icon as the Hula Hoop and the Corvette Stingray, and serving as almost accidental poster girl for the blastoff into the '60s Sexual Revolution. The Bunny-as-Girl-Next-Door made her way into the newspapers and onto local television programs, as Bunnies appeared at community, charity and sporting events. There was the Bunny softball team, which had started as a charity event against the local Chicago Jaycees to raise money for a handicapped high school youth. In Bunny Baseball, an antic version of the sport that would have confounded Abner Doubleday, the game's originator, "stealing a base" meant actually stealing a base—but always for a charitable cause.

China Lee and Teddy Howard play the WNEW Good Guys, 1963.

The idea spread throughout all the Clubs and though the point was fun and philanthropy, the girls showed a competitive edge sharp enough to get the New York Club Bunnies into the prestigious Broadway Show League in Manhattan, which played every Thursday at noon in Central Park. In 1963, the New York Club's Dream Team, sporting black tights and orange sweatshirts with the Bunny logo, vaulted to supertar status in a showdown against the WNEW Good Guys that drew a crowd of 5,000 spectators. The Bunny 9, boasting a 9-0 record behind the pitching of China Lee, won the League Championship with a 7-6 victory. "We were very strong from carrying the heavy trays," China recalls, "and everyone loved watching the Bunnies play ball."

"The game had to be stopped in the third inning because the crowds were so enormous," recalled Teddy Howard, who played second base. "The mounted police tried to control the crowd, but they were afraid we were going to get hurt in the crush. In order to get us out of there, the cops lifted each one of us onto the back of a horse and rode us out of the park. We were literally saved by the cavalry."

By 1965, Bunnies and various Bunny teams were regular fixtures in charity events around the country. Bunny basketball originated with a team of Chicago Bunnies playing a team of high school coaches from Gary, Indiana, to help pay the hospital and educational expenses of a young boy who had been shot while trying to prevent an armed robbery. There were Bunny touch football and broom-ball hockey teams, scooter races, snow-ball fights, horseshoe matches, bicycle relays and bowling competitions that raised money for, among others, the March of Dimes, Muscular Dys-trophy Association and American Cancer Society. Bunnies volunteered at local hospitals and community events while wearing white skirts and black sweaters with the Playboy logo.

A chorus of Bunnies danced at the Carnegie Hall Celebrity Tribute to Sammy Davis Jr. for the Leukemia Foundation. "I'd taken dance classes, but I certainly wasn't a professional dancer—none of us was," recalled Marcia Donen Roma, the Bunny who eventually married the New York Club's manager, Tony Roma. "The Bunnies just volunteered and then rehearsed like crazy." Eva Nichols, a former teenage Freedom Fighter and refugee from the 1956 Hungarian uprising, remembers, "We opened the show with a song and dance number from *Hello, Dolly!* and everything went perfectly. The applause was thunderous!"

The charity events, aided by the show-business patina of the Clubs, dramatically elevated the image of the Playboy Bunnies; it also had the effect of forging strong bonds among the women themselves, who began to feel more protective of their role in the Clubs—and of their own welfare.

At the top of that list of concerns was the increasingly unacceptable "Saturday Night" massacres in which Bunnies would show up to work only to find that they had been fired without warning or redress.

Elaine Freeman

I was 20 when I graduated from college. That made me only a few years older than the students I would be teaching at New York City's Junior High School 71. Although I had always been a good student myself, I was totally awful at teaching and entirely too young for the responsibilities. I had to find another line of work. In the teacher's cafeteria one day,

161

Bunny Ball Games

China Lee.

Above: Los Angeles, 1965. Bunny Alice Nichols makes a basket.

Left: Bunnies Bobbi Goodley, Teddy Howard and Emma Patterson on the Bronx ski run.

Below: Always Stand in Against the Curves. The '63 Bunny Dream Team: Jonnie, Ginger, China, Teddy, Nan, Charlotte, Carol and Lisa.

...and Benefits

Touch football in Central Park, 1963: Bunny Ginger Gibson scored all three touchdowns against the Rinky Dinks, a group of television and advertising execs . . .

. . . when Bunny tackle Francesca Emerson lost her false eyelashes during a scrimmage, a penalty was lodged against a Rinky Dink lineman.

"Don't touch my tail!" Angel player Jim Purcell and Alice Nichols.

Right: St. Louis Bunnies
Sandy, Margie and Bunny
Mother Dorothy deliver
clothing for
St. Francis Girls Home.

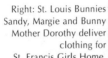

Left: Bunny Stacy serves a gourmet meal to a Victory
Memorial Hospital patient in Waukegan, Illinois.

Below: Bunny chorus line at Carnegie Hall, 1964.

I was discussing the job market with several friends when one of them said, 'Well, you can always be a Playboy Bunny.'

"I couldn't type. I didn't know steno. So I stuffed my bra with tissue paper, and I walked into the Playboy Club cold off the street one day in March 1964 and said, 'I'd like to be a Bunny.'

"Being hired threw me into a state of shock. I had always been academic. My mother, who was a liberated woman, stressed that I should make it on my brains. Now I'd taken a job where I would be making money off my looks. It was quite alien to me. I was shy about my body and had to get used to the idea of standing half-naked while changing clothes in the Bunny dressing room. I remember picking up my costume one day and seeing a notice from the Bunny Mother on the bulletin board: 'Girls, please remember to douche. You are at crotch level with the customer.' It was a new world.

"In a way, it was like coming into the theatre every night and becoming this creature in a play. Women of every background and description were thrown together in the intimate, intense atmosphere of the dressing room. Dozens of Bunnies with rollers in their hair sat half-nude, wearing black panty hose while putting on their makeup. You'd start out with this bare, pedestrian face—at least mine was—and try to make something of it, sharing your makeup and advice about hairstyles and false eyelashes with everyone else around you. We were always fussing with one another and sharing our innermost secrets.

"Ironically, being a Bunny got me interested in being a therapist: Your regular customers would come back time and again to unburden themselves. I'm a born *yenta*. I was always

Elaine Freeman in her office at
Yorkville Dialysis Center.

really interested in people's stories and
in helping them solve their problems.
And I finally said to myself, People are
giving me a few bucks in tips and
blowing smoke in my face when I
could be sitting in an office dispensing
advice properly. I returned to school
for an advanced degree in social work.

"I worked six years at the St. Luke's/
Roosevelt Hospital Rape Intervention
and Crime Victims Program to aid victim's of sexual assault, domestic vio-

In what would become known as the Valentine's Day
Purge, on Valentine's Day 1966, two-year veteran
Bunny Elaine Freeman, a doctoral candidate in English
Literature at NYU, and described in the New York
Journal-American as "only 24 and on the slim side,"
was fired by Bunny Mother Lynn Smith along with
15 other Bunnies at the behest of general manager
Tony Roma, who claimed the women no longer
projected the "Bunny Image." Among them was Kelly
O'Brien, a 115-pound, 5'3" 25-year-old, who was
told she was overweight and too old. "I just can't understand why they did this to us—suddenly, cruelly and
without reason," the blonde mother of two told the press.
"Maybe it's because
I wouldn't join the
company union they
tried—unsuccessfully—
to foist on us last year."

lence and crime. We provided individual and group therapy for rape survivors, trained rape crisis volunteers,
testified in court cases and ran work-
shops in schools for students, teachers
and counselors. I spent several years
in outpatient mental health and now I
work with hemodialysis patients.

"But every once in a while, something comes back to me from my
Bunny days that involves my work as
a therapist. I remember a tall, beautiful, very glamorous Bunny who told
us that she could eat anything and
not gain weight because she always
threw up after eating. At the time I
thought, 'Isn't that clever? She can
eat a big steak dinner and just up-
chuck all those calories.' I'd never
heard of bulimia back then." ■

The Bunnies Strike

A master pact covering all Club employees had been signed between Playboy and the Hotel and Restaurant Employees & Bartenders International Union, but the New York Bunnies soon deemed the Dining Room Employees Local 1 a "sweetheart union" and demanded the right to join a union of their choice. Marcia Donen and Nancy Phillips represented the Bunnies in union contract negotiations and, when talks broke down, the women staged a walkout on Saturday, February 4, 1967. *New York Post* columnist Earl Wilson quoted one Bunny as saying, "I'd rather be a Teamster."

On Sunday, February 5, the 42 striking Bunnies received a Western Union telegram stating: *Your failure to work as scheduled or notified was in violation of the collective bargaining agreement and gross violation of your obligation to your employer. You are therefore discharged effective immediately.* [signed] *Alan Spiers, General Manager, New York Playboy Club.*

Striking New York Bunnies.

The walkout on that busy Saturday night did not go unnoticed. On the following Monday, Earl Wilson visited the Bunnies on the picket line and noted, "It was by far the prettiest picket line in New York history, and caused many men to take a new interest in labor relations."

He also reported management's admission that at a salary of $1.45 an hour, a Bunny's basic pay for a 40-hour week was $68, not counting tips. At issue was the fact that on the previous Wednesday, the Club had eliminated signed tipping and substituted a 15 percent service charge. In return, Bunnies would no longer have to pay $10 a night in bar fees to be shared by untipped colleagues such as service bartenders and busboys; that would subsequently be a percentage of the service charge. The economic reality was immediately apparent to every Bunny; the cash tip would soon be history.

One important benefit of the walkout was that Bunnies were able to reveal, through the press, the effect of the Club's new tipping policy on their incomes. Bunnies would not be getting any of the 15 percent service charge on the first $70 worth of drinks they served and only a portion of the service charge thereafter. And, after all, tips were the reason everyone donned the tail and ears.

In response, Playboy management flew in 30 reserve Bunnies from Clubs in Boston, Baltimore and Atlanta who raced to get fingerprinted for their Cabaret licenses so they could cross the picket line. Tony Bennett, singing at the Copacabana around the corner, telephoned his regrets that he would not be visiting the Playboy Club; he refused to cross the picket line.

Richard Leahy reported in the *New York World Journal Tribune* on Wednesday, February 8, that "those 42 poor Playboy Club Bunnies who got kicked out of their hutch for picketing are due back today in their little rabbit costumes." An arctic blizzard had shut down New York City, including the Playboy Club, the night before, but the striking Bunnies had nevertheless met at the Waldorf-Astoria to discuss a truce with management while the National Labor Relations Board studied the situation.

That same Wednesday, "Shop Steward" Marcia Donen received another telegram from Western Union: *Several girls have contacted the New York Playboy Club with the hope of being rehired as Bunnies. In order to be fair to all of those involved in the current difficulty, a meeting will be held with top Playboy Club executive Arnold Morton at the Club on Thursday afternoon February 9 at 3 p.m. All those interested should attend.* [signed] *Hugh M. Hefner, President, Playboy Clubs International.*

Marcia Donen Roma

I became involved in labor relations when I got tired of seeing girls learn they'd been fired by not finding their names on the weekly schedule that was posted every Saturday night in the Bunny dressing room. The girls would cry their eyes out. Individually, they didn't have the means to fight for their jobs, and yet nobody was joining together to do anything about it. It was a matter of principle with me, and I felt that we ought to be represented by a union that would protect us.

"Management had brought in Local 1 of the AFL-CIO, but girls were still being left off the schedule for not having the so-called 'Bunny Image.' Another Bunny, Nancy Phillips, and I started talking about how we could change things, and soon the other girls elected us to represent them. We took our existing contract to the National Labor Relations Board and discovered that, up to a certain date, we had the option of bringing in another local. We went to the Teamsters. When Playboy balked, the Bunnies decided to go out on strike, and the Teamsters helped us organize the walkout.

"We set the strike for a Saturday night because we knew that would really hurt business. A lot of the customers supported us and didn't cross the picket lines. It was bitterly cold. L'Etoile, the restaurant next door, gave us hot onion soup. Bunnies were brought in from other Clubs, although none of the New York Bunnies really let us down. For a couple of the girls, the job was their life and they didn't go out on strike because they were afraid of retaliation. That was sad. Otherwise, the girls were all fabulously supportive.

"After the strike was settled, the other Bunnies gave Nancy and me engraved peace-sign pendants and cards with all their signatures. In fact, we went on to help negotiate the union contracts for the entire Playboy chain. I continued to work as a Bunny for 10 years. Finally, the New York Club closed for renovations in 1974, and everyone was laid off. But at least I didn't find out about it by seeing my name missing from a work schedule tacked to the wall!"

Ironically, Donen ended up on management's side. Several years after she left the New York Club, mutual friends reintroduced the former Bunny to her former boss,

New York real-estate agent Marcia Donen Roma near her Upper East Side office at Fox Residential.

restaurateur Tony Roma, who had managed the New York Club for a while before establishing his chain of rib restaurants. Years earlier, Roma had spotted Marcia as a teenager eating ice cream at the Flick Ice Cream Parlor with a friend. He had handed them both business cards, telling them that they should audition for Bunny jobs. Donen ultimately took his advice. After becoming reacquainted in the late 1970s, Donen and Roma married. Now divorced, Marcia is raising their daughter Sarina and working as a Manhattan real-estate agent. ∎

Lisa Aromi

A lot of the Bunnies had been talking about going on strike, but I didn't know they had actually decided to do it. I hadn't been working for a few days, and when my cab pulled up at the corner that Saturday, I saw the picket line. Some of the girls didn't think that I would join the strike because it could jeopardize my livelihood, and I had a child to support. I said, of course I would join, that this work stoppage was for the benefit of all of us—for women in general and even my daughter's future. After all, it was because of my daughter that I took the job in the first place.

"If I were to meet Gloria Steinem, I would say, 'Thank you very much.' My marriage was over and I was a young single mother living in Brooklyn in the late summer of 1963 when my mother showed me Steinem's article in *Show* magazine. After reading the piece, I realized the Bunny job would be perfect for me because I could work at night and stay home with my daughter during the day. I put on a sheath dress and, because I had done some modeling before I got married, I brought along my portfolio for the interview. While I sat in the Bunny dressing room waiting to be interviewed, I watched the girls come in off the floor and listened to their banter and complaints. I was mesmerized.

"I failed the written test. I had no idea what a *Cuba Libré* was and I didn't know the names of any liqueurs. The only cocktail I'd ever had at that point was a brandy Alexander—and I wasn't even sure what was in that. Keith Hefner called me into his office and said, 'We really want you to work for us and we're going to go over this Bunny Manual together.' He was very patient. He could see that I really needed the job and that I was very insecure.

"The rules for Bunnies were strictly enforced. Without any prior warning, women were let go when management determined they had lost the Bunny Image. The weekly schedule was posted in the dressing room on Saturday night, and if your name wasn't on the list, you were out of a job. We considered it a cruel and unfair labor practice that was stressful for everyone, but especially for the Bunnies who were students or single mothers, like me. When the Bunnies decided to strike, I chose to walk the picket line instead of going in to work.

"Customers were lined up around the block—it amazed me that they stood calmly watching us marching in the freezing cold, carrying our picket signs. If we had been truck drivers or postmen, would they cross that picket line? Many people waved at us and called out, 'Good luck, girls!' as they went into the Club. My mother thought I was crazy, but during the day I brought my daughter along, because I wanted to show her what we were fighting for. She sat at the top of the steps at the door of the Playboy Club wearing her little muff and hat.

"My mother was with me when the telegram arrived telling me that I was fired because we had gone out on strike. She said, 'Oh, you foolish girl, now look what you've done! How are you going to support yourself?' I told her, 'You don't understand. We have to stick together and not accept a union chosen by management. We need a union that will support our grievances over pay and working conditions.' With all the publicity we attracted, I wonder that Gloria Steinem didn't volunteer to join our picket line, too. Changes needed to be made, and that's what we had set about doing.

"After the strike, we all got our jobs back. But when the Club closed September 1, 1974, for renovation (and did not reopen until February 29, 1976), we knew that many of us would not get our jobs back. It was in the Club's best interests to reorganize the operation and replace as many people as possible. They could hire a completely new staff of fresh faces and keep a few senior Bunnies to train new girls. That, of course, is what happened.

"Any woman who had worked at the Club for 10 years was presented with a watch. Unfortunately, I got the watch and a letter from Hugh Hefner congratulating me on my job performance at about the same time I was fired. The tribute was decidedly bittersweet. I thought, 'Well, I'm being patted on the back and shoved out the door at the same time.'

"However, I had worked as a Bunny for 10 years, and the experience changed my life for the better. The job enabled me to live independently and care for my daughter. Today, my best friends are women I met working at the Playboy Club. Recently, when Al, my longtime companion, passed away unexpectedly, they were the friends who saw me through that terrible time." ∎

Lisa Aromi, a collector of vintage movie wardrobe and memorabilia, is a consultant for Kirn McGuire, LLC, a Manhattan antique shop.

A Bunny Mother's Tale

"In 1964, I was selected New York City's Bunny of the Year, and six of us were given a grand tour of Paris and London as a prize," says Liz Yee. "Four years later, I was told I no longer fit the Bunny Image, but I was offered a job as a Bunny Mother."

*T*hose were tumultuous times to be the Bunny Mother. Morale was low. The turnover rate in staff throughout the Club was outrageously high. Thirteen Bunny Mothers had preceded me, and during my six years in the job, I worked with several different general managers. While attending a Bunny Mothers' training conference in Chicago, I was called out of a meeting and told to have my suitcase packed, my airline ticket in hand because the Bunnies were on the verge of a strike at the New York Club.

Elizabeth "Jadee" Yee.

"That particular strike was averted, but the problems remained. I had to work in the Club from opening through closing hours seven days a week in an effort to restore good relations between management and the Bunnies. For one thing, there was friction between the Bunnies and room directors, who were in charge of assigning stations and seating customers but never made as much money as the girls. Meanwhile, the senior Bunnies had turned into barracudas protecting their territory; they were deeply resented by the new girls. It was survival of the fittest. But the bottom line was that these women were the sole reason any of the Playboy Clubs made money. People came to see Bunnies, not to drink or dine or see a show. When you realized that it was the girls who made the money for the Club, you realized how essential it was that they were protected."

KELIA WAGNER

The stylized service was a performance, choreographed with precision. We were taught how to introduce ourselves ['Good evening, I'm your Bunny . . .'] and it set the tone. You could size up your audience by their reaction as you approached the table, and we all developed our own individual 'shtick' to entertain the customers.

"The training was hard and incredibly thorough. We had to carry the ounce-and-a-half shot glasses, with separate water or soda backs, and actually pour the drinks at the table—using a backhanded pour while doing the Bunny Dip. You learned never to 'claw' a glass by picking it up from the top so your fingers touched the rim. You always used a napkin and handled the glass in the middle. You never jammed a glass into the ice machine; you always used a scoop. You always 'capped' an ashtray with another ashtray before you removed it from the table—and you never dumped ashes in a dinner plate!

"The Showrooms were so crowded, you had to be able to do the High Carry for safety's sake. We had strict rules about handling and serving food. Even if you had to quickly deliver eight dinners to a table before show time, each plate balanced on your tray had to be completely separated; 'No Food Touching Food' was the rule. When you set down each plate, the meat had to be positioned directly in front of the diner.

"Today, I run a Manhattan advertising agency with my husband, but I still find time to work two nights a week as a cocktail hostess—only now I wear a black designer dress to serve drinks. Part of what I loved about working at the Club was moving to music. The place where I work now, a quiet, elegant cocktail lounge, has a pianist. I love to talk with customers. People come and go—maybe you'll see them again, maybe you won't. It's relaxing, and a good balance to my daytime career. I really think it keeps me young and alive." ∎

"But the major problem was job security in a job where there was very little security. Nobody wanted to be terminated, but nobody could be a Bunny for 50 years, either. Management was simply not geared to dealing with an aging workforce of Bunnies. In 1968, there were a good number of women still working as Bunnies who had been hired when the Club first opened. Most still looked slim and youthful, even, in some cases, after several pregnancies. But they watched their friends fired for no longer having the Bunny Image.

"Those terminations were a double-edged sword for all the Bunnies. Even as a Bunny comforted a friend who had been fired and was thinking, 'That could be me,' she realized a very high standard had to be maintained.

"The Bunny costume, for example, looked simply ridiculous on a mature woman no matter how youthful or fit she appeared. Most of the girls were very clear about that and accepted it. It was painful but unavoidable. The aging problem was the same for professional models, ice skaters, ballerinas or tennis players. You have your day—and you must prepare for the end of the ride while you are still going top speed."

EMMA PATTERSON

In September 1967, when I was 21, I married a musician and transferred from the Chicago Club, where I'd worked for two years, to the New York Club. I was still a Bunny when I was 33, even though 30 was considered the cutoff age. The Bunny Mother was in charge of checking Bunny Image. If a girl had crinkly skin, a crepey neck, circles under the eyes, laugh lines or crow's feet, she no longer had Bunny Image. I thought the policy was unfair because a lot of the women aged very well, but when I became a Bunny Mother in 1980, I could see the situation from management's side. A lot of Bunnies still looked good, but they had just been in the job too long and didn't have that youthful attitude and sparkle. I don't want to see a grandmother working in a Bunny-type job, but I have very mixed feelings about the age and image issues. I really do.

"Playboy tried to smooth the transition to other jobs and opportunities by picking up tuition fees for Bunnies. I took journalism courses at Hunter College because I wanted to be a food critic. I've always been interested in food and got into the catering profession through Playboy.

"I also took advantage of the opportunity to travel. The London Playboy Club was my base while I traveled through Italy, Spain and France. I stayed with Playboy until the New York Club closed for renovation in 1974. When the Club reopened, I went to the 're-evaluation,' bringing a bathing suit, as requested. They chose five or six veteran Bunnies out of the hundred or so who applied. I wasn't one of those chosen, and I didn't care. By that time I was an assistant restaurant manager at the Statler Hotel, but by showing up I did get my severance pay from Playboy.

"I've managed restaurants in San Francisco, London and New York, and I'm now the catering director for an off-site firm in Manhattan.

"To this day I can't figure out why I stayed so long in the job, but it was a very comfortable way of living and working. The Bunnies in New York stuck together and socialized, and some of them have remained friends for 25 to 30 years. We joke about becoming senior citizens and moving into one big nursing home together." ∎

> ## The Bunny Manual-Tuition Aid
> Playboy provides a continuing program of training for all employees and maintains a climate in which personal development is encouraged and rewarded. The company will consider tuition aid for permanent, full-time and part-time (20 hours per week or more) employees.

Left: Breakfast Bunny Emma, 1965.

Above: Emma Patterson today in the kitchens of
Neuman & Bogdonoff, a Manhattan off-site catering firm.

"The pressure on these young women was terrific," says Liz Yee. "From the girl's point of view, she was thrown into a situation where the job required that she wear something very revealing, wobble around on 4-inch heels while carrying a heavy tray with drinks and appear very beautiful. She was soon drawn into the competitiveness of the job: making the most money, staying beautiful, being the best. You had to be quick, bright and strong to keep up. Of course, even among sophisticated and beautiful young women, there were those who couldn't handle being a Bunny, and it was apparent almost immediately."

Jodie Brockway

I thought I was sophisticated, that I could handle anything. I graduated from Boston University in 1965 and got a job in New York earning $90 a week as a trainee for the Metropolitan Life Insurance company. I was 22 years old. In those days, you went to college to party, find a husband and get married. I didn't really have my eye on a career. I figured I would probably work for two years, settle down and have kids. What I really wanted to do was go to Europe, and I needed money.

"Somehow I heard about the Bunny jobs and the great money the girls earned. I went in for an interview wearing office clothes, a knee-length brown jersey dress with a turtleneck and leather belt—and I'm sure I wore a girdle. In those days, we thought it was really tacky to walk around without a girdle. I thought I looked really sophisticated.

"The woman who interviewed me was cold and professional, not at all what I expected. 'Fill out this form, we'll call you in a few days.' But my biggest shock came a few weeks later when the Bunny Mother called me in for a costume fitting.

"The minute I walked into the Bunny dressing room and saw the other girls, I got my first inkling that I was in another league entirely. These women—most of them dancers, models and actresses—walked around half-naked, not at all self-consciously, putting on their makeup and costumes. I was out of my element. I was terrified. Having always been so confident of myself physically, I was shaken at the thought of having to expose my body like that.

"I didn't last three weeks. Getting picked was the best part of the job. I took Bunny training and worked about nine evenings serving cocktails.

"I had thought I was so hip. From the time I was 12 I had a good body—and I never had a problem getting a date. I was not at all shy or backward, so it bowled me over that I could not handle being a Bunny. While I was in college, I had worked as a waitress during the summer months, but this was different. I can't claim that it was because I was a feminist, either. Whose consciousness was raised at that time?

"Getting by on your looks is a double-edged sword. I knew I could get what I wanted with my body, but I never respected that and I didn't feel good about it. Working as a Bunny did awaken something in me in that it was the first time I came up against something I couldn't even pretend to handle. It stopped me cold. Five years after I had worked at Playboy, I spent a summer on Fire Island writing a novel, *I'm Your Rabbit, Rhonda.* It was my take on Hugh Hefner and Bunnies. Forty publishers turned it down. It was pretty dreadful, but then it was one of my first writing efforts.

"At 30, I turned a corner. I married, had children and started thinking in career terms when I became an editor at *Harper's Bazaar.* When my son was about 4, I got into television development, first with Dick Clark Productions, then with Lorimar. I was at Hearst Entertainment for seven years. I joined NBC in 1993, and I'm now head of long-form drama and miniseries." ■

"Drinking or drug use came easily to some girls, especially those who had problems before working at the Club. A nightclub atmosphere presented quite a feeding ground for the sharks who prey on young, unsophisticated women. Needless to say, a few girls succumbed to the pressures.

"When I hired the girls, I told them they were going to make a lot of money, but that they had to prepare for they day they moved on. To get them in the habit of saving money, I arranged for a clerk from a nearby bank to set up a table in the corridor outside my office on payday and accept savings account deposits from the Bunnies. The clerk was ecstatic; he used to win prizes at his bank for opening the most new savings accounts.

"I always worked around a Bunny's class schedule and gave her extra time off around exams. Education was very important to me, and I did whatever I could to help these women prepare for another career."

LindA KisH

I n art school, I met a college guy who got drafted. President Kennedy had made married men exempt so my friend asked me to marry him to keep him out of Vietnam. I did it to help him out. I think we were together for about a year before we split up. I knew I was at a crossroads.

"In 1963, I moved to New York and got a job as a stewardess with TWA. I was living with five other girls in an apartment, all of us broke. The pay was low, but out of our earnings we had to buy our own uniforms—$400 for the winter coat and suit, and $25 for the shoes. The regulations were also getting under my skin: Hair couldn't touch our collars, and we were supposed to wear girdles. There were stipulations about being married, and we had to sign a document stating that at age 30 we would retire. When I was on standby, I would often get a call in the middle of the night for a 6 a.m. flight. I was unhappy enough in the job, but when four stewardesses I had trained with and two pilots I'd worked with were all killed in a plane crash, I started thinking about other job options. Shortly after I had an emergency on one of my own flights, I quit.

"In 1966, I applied at Playboy, a dream job and a definite improvement over the airlines. I could make a hundred dollars a night in cash. I did not have to pay for my Bunny uniform, only for the dry cleaning. In an airplane, if a passenger got unruly, you were stuck with him for the rest of the flight, but if a Keyholder got out of line, you just called a room director to bail you out. Really, I never understood why people thought *Bunnies* were exploited.

"But, of course, Bunnies were supposed to 'retire' gracefully, too. A good many of us were on the verge of turning 30 at the time of the strike. I wasn't at all interested in union matters, but I thought since I was on the cusp of 30, I'd better get on the picket line. Besides, I was truly angered by the age cutoff; I was starting to look my best at age 30.

"Although we managed to change the policy so that Bunny Image wasn't based on age alone, I really couldn't fault the airlines or the Playboy Club at the time for wanting to fire women who gained weight or had a sloppy appearance. Part of the job description was 'looking good.' I once had an accident that left a small gash on my lip and I was afraid I would be suspended, but Jadee, bless her, said, 'I don't see a thing; go out on the floor.'

"If I had any regrets about my seven years as a Bunny, it would be that I didn't take advantage of Playboy's tuition program or invest my money. Other Bunnies were going to school, setting up businesses or launching careers. But I never looked ahead. I'm a let's-see-what-happens sort of person, one of the flaky ones.

Linda is a portrait artist and lives in a California beach house with her husband.

"I left in 1973, when my husband and I moved to Marblehead, Massachusetts. I set up a studio and began to paint, doing portraits on commission." ■

Carol "Pixie" Wilbourn

I was in two totally different worlds: a per diem substitute teacher by day and a Bunny at night. It was hard enough, but because I was short, had long hair down to my thighs and wore no makeup, the Playboy Club got calls and letters complaining that I was underage. In fact, I was 25 years old, and a graduate of NYU. Jadee, the Bunny Mother, finally had to ask me to give her a copy of my birth certificate to keep on file.

"In the autumn of 1965, I gave notice to Playboy so I could begin teaching full-time. Jadee asked, 'Why not stay on and work weekends?' I've always loved animals, and my avocation at the time was finding homes for cats. I had discovered that

Carol Wilbourne, with "Jack," is a consultant for the New York Humane Society, author of *The Inner Cat, Cat Talk: What Your Cat Is Trying to Tell You* and columnist ("Cats on the Couch") for *Cat Fancy* magazine.

the Playboy Club was a great source for placing cats with customers. Besides, I liked working weekends and making extra money.

"I stayed more than seven years, through marriage, divorce, remarriage and a bicoastal Malibu/Manhattan lifestyle. Every time I left New York, Jadee would say, 'We don't care how long you're away as long as you come back to us.' In 1973, my second husband, a veterinarian, and I decided to open New York's first cat hospital in Greenwich Village. It was an unusual clinic that provided feline psychological treatment as well as physical care." ■

"The problems inside the Club only reflected what was happening outside. The times were changing radically in the early '70s. We were a favorite target and constantly in the news. A reporter for an upstate New York radio station wanted to interview the Bunnies. I could see that his attitude was distinctly negative, that he was there to poke fun at the 'dumb Bunnies.' I asked him to tell me the sorts of questions he intended to ask, and he very smugly showed me his list. It comprised the usual round of fatuous pseudo-intellectual questions, dripping with sexual innuendo and designed to make the girls sound foolish no matter how they answered.

"To his surprise, I told him that I approved the questions and insisted

What Dumb Bunnies?

Mensa, the international organization for people whose intelligence places them in the top 2 percent of the world's population, held regular Tuesday lunch meetings at the New York Playboy Club, beginning in 1964.

179

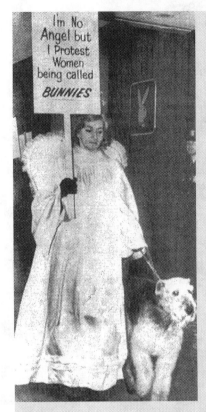

A protester pickets the Detroit Club.

he interview each Bunny as she arrived for work. He stared at me and waited for the other shoe to drop. I smiled and said, 'That's it. None of the girls will have any advance warning. Go ahead. Ask your questions.' He stood in the hallway outside the dressing room and asked his questions. Every Bunny had a sharp answer, an interesting opinion that reflected some thought, a little wit and some humor—after all, these were women who were used to talking to strangers trying to put them on. He came into my office a while later and said, 'I owe you an apology.' I told him, 'No, you owe the girls an apology. These are women who talk to 90 people a night and then go to college or pursue other careers during the day. Do you think we store them in a closet and bring them out at night to show their boobs?'

"The Women's Libbers, as they were called, also started to picket the Club around this time. These were very tough-looking women who would picket every day and scream at the Bunnies arriving for work: 'What's wrong with you? You're being used!' The Bunnies would try to brush them off with, 'I'm here by choice. What's wrong with that?' Sometimes, when I arrived for work in the morning and they were shouting at me, I'd try to talk with them. I'd point out that the Bunnies weren't dragged into the Club in chains. We didn't lock them in. 'They are earning a living, so leave them alone.' The libbers were outraged that I, a woman, would attempt to justify working at Playboy to another female.

"The general manager, Mario Staub, called me into his office one morning to tell me that the libbers had climbed up on the roof the night before and thrown a banner over the side of the Club.

" 'How did this happen? How did they get up on the roof?' he asked.

" 'How would I know?' I replied. 'Do you think I stay here all night?'

"He put me in charge of finding out and told me he didn't want it happening again. I had no idea then or later how they did it. Maybe it was an 'inside job.' Because of the type of women picketing the Club and their militant stand, you had to keep a sense of humor. Yet, there were many things that warranted change and, of course, one could argue the issues of sexual exploitation.

"The gender discrimination issues at that time also prompted several guys to come in for Bunny interviews. Some of them were transvestites, others just men pushing the parameters of hiring guidelines. A man I later discovered was a reporter came in and asked if I would give him a Bunny application. I said of course and set up an interview. I told him I would have to see him in the full costume and high heels before I could determine if he had the Bunny Image. He balked.

"Playboy had an incredibly long run. But, in the course of time, styles changed in food, entertainment, décor—and the whole idea of a pretty girl wearing ears, a tail and high heels while serving you dinner became passé. I worked at the New York Playboy Club from its opening in 1962 until the Club closed for renovation in 1974; six years as a Bunny and six years as a Bunny Mother. It was time to move on. So many things in our society were changing."

—Jadee Yee, 1997

Just Call Him Bunny Frank

On September 1, 1970, reporter Frank Swertlow, "a men's libber who had tried to invade the world of women as a Playboy Bunny," appeared as a guest on To Tell the Truth, hosted by Garry Moore, to stump panelists Bill Cullen, Peggy Cass, Kitty Carlisle and Gene Rayburn.

Elizabeth Yee, managing director of *VEA New York*, a quarterly Spanish language magazine.

By 1967, the Vietnam "incursion" had become a War, gradually expanding into Laos and Cambodia and swamping Lyndon Baines Johnson's Great Society. Love-ins and anti-war protests took the place of football rallies on college campuses across the United States. Hippies battled hard hats. Women burned their bras. And, inside the Playboy Clubs, the dimly-lighted fantasy world of sex and the good life found that it, too, could no longer keep out the gray light of a harsher, "real" world. Anna Lederer and Ava Faulkner both recall the day when two soldiers arrived at the Club to inform one of the Bunnies that her husband had been killed in Vietnam. Bunny Mother Jadee was summoned to break the sad news.

Sakina Mohammed

During the Vietam War, the Club sponsored special evenings in the Penthouse for disabled soldiers. It was heartbreaking to see the horrifying injuries these young men had suffered. At first, I didn't know what to say to them. One young man smiled shyly at me when I brought food and drink to his table—and I then realized he was paralyzed. As I fed him and held his drink so he could sip it through a straw, we began talking, both of us enjoying the conversation and feeling at ease. That experience, and many other encounters like it, taught me so much about dealing with people.

"Playboy really was the best of times for me. I was 19, married and already had a 2-year-old child when Bunny Mother Lynn Smith hired me in 1966. I grew up in Queens, in an extended, loving family. I'm American born, but my parents and grandparents had come from Calcutta and West Bengal, India. When I told them I would be working at Playboy they were absolutely shocked. They tried to persuade me to find another job, but I loved being a Bunny. For the first time I had some sense of independence.

"I went to school throughout my eight years working at Playboy, earning an associate degree in early childhood education and a four-year degree in humanities. After I left in 1974, I taught inner-city children in pre-kindergarten classes. Many didn't have the stable home life that I grew up with and had provided for my own children. Some of these kids didn't even know how to eat with a spoon or fork. It was incredible to me that I had to teach basic skills that most kids learn in a family environment.

"I now have a master's degree in elementary education, and I'm working toward a master's in school psychology while teaching fifth-graders. Teaching children is my vocation in life; listening to them, giving a hug and letting them know somebody cares are the most important lessons I've learned." ■

Deborah Harry

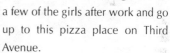

I came from the sticks and wasn't at all sophisticated. I was born in Florida, but grew up in New Jersey. The Bunny job had an aura of glamour. I thought I'd give it a try, figuring that it might be interesting and fun, certainly lucrative.

"Before Playboy, I'd worked as a waitress at Max's Kansas City, a major '60s hangout. The backroom became famous as the hangout for Andy Warhol's crowd. After Max's, I joined a band for about a year and a half and recorded an album. After a second album we recorded didn't go anywhere, the band broke up.

"I sampled a lot of things trying to find out what to do next. Becoming a Bunny in 1968 was part of that period. I was quiet. I did my job and I kept my eyes wide open to everything. Bunny training was more complicated than I expected. I wondered how I'd remember everything and if I could carry all that stuff on a tray without spilling anything. The usual doubts. Then, once I got going, it all became routine. I was very much in my own little world during that time, and I wasn't very sociable. But sometimes I'd hang out with

a few of the girls after work and go up to this pizza place on Third Avenue.

"Playboy was smart in constructing its operation. There were strict codes of behavior for both employees and customers. Bunnies had to maintain a certain decorum in relating to customers; if you overstepped the parameters, you were out of the game. The rules worked both ways. If a customer got out of line, he lost his Club membership. You knew that management backed you up and that

Hatcheck Bunny Deborah Harry.

you were protected. As someone who had worked as a waitress before, that was a shocking revelation!

"The Club was popular and especially busy on weekends. The girls who had worked there for a while had the prime spots, the Showrooms, where the money was really good.

The lead singer/songwriter for the band Blondie has been touring for the past three years with the Jazz Passengers, and pursuing her acting career. She starred with Liv Tyler in *Heavy*, a film written and directed by James Mangold, in 1995, and *Six Ways to Sunday* in 1997.

Initially, I worked downstairs in the Playmate Bar. I also worked in the Hatcheck and as a Door Bunny. By the time I'd been at the Club long enough to be scheduled in the Showrooms on the weekends and make the big money, I was ready to move on. The experience had been worthwhile. But the time demands were excessive for a job that wasn't leading anywhere. Besides, I broke up with a boyfriend and decided to leave New York. I tended to move in radical leaps at that time. I quit, packed up and left for California. It wasn't a decision I spent time considering, but I remember that period of my life as fun and intriguing.

"There's no one now that I really stay in touch with among the Bunnies. I know Lauren Hutton from just being on the scene in New York. When I was a guest on her television show *Lauren Hutton and . . .*, we talked briefly about both being Bunnies. But I told her my wildest experience was a pre-Bunny one at Max's when I had sex in the phone booth with rocker Eric Erickson while I was supposed to be waiting tables.

"Being a Bunny involved a rare combination for a woman in the workplace. It was an unusual perception of women that they could be beautiful, feminine and very sexy, and at the same time ambitious and intelligent. At Playboy those women had a place where they could use those attributes to make money—and also be really valued as employees. Bunnies *were* the Playboy Club." ∎

Anna Adamira Lederer

I left Trinidad in 1967 to study in Paris, but after a few days in New York, I decided to stay. When a friend suggested I go to Playboy for an interview to be a Bunny, I felt very rebellious even considering such a thing, but it was all very glamorous to me. I'm Indian, Chinese and Spanish, and I thought they would only want tall blondes, but even though I was small and dark, I was hired immediately.

"On my first day in the gift shop, I hid behind a pillar until I was given the little fur jacket that Door Bunnies wore to cover myself because I felt so naked. But then one of the customers stopped to chat and I saw that he was talking to me, not staring at my breasts. I stopped being self-conscious, and realized that people were not looking at me as a sex object, but as a person.

"I'm a chatterbox, and customers loved my British accent, so I enjoyed being a Door Bunny and greeting everyone who came to the Club. I had long chats with James Baldwin, Woody Allen (who was introduced to me as an 'up-and-coming comedian') and the Thai Ambassador, a delightful and fascinating man.

"I married an attorney during the three years I worked at the Club, and moved with him to Geneva, Switzerland, when I was 21 years old. I have always been interested in politics, so I went back to school and studied International Relations at the University of Geneva. While living in Europe, I got letters from my friends telling me that feminists had begun picketing outside the New York Club, claiming that Bunnies were being exploited as sex objects. Social changes were altering people's perception of Playboy, but I couldn't help but think that one had to experience the job to have a true perspective." ∎

Anna Lederer now lives in Washington D.C., and works as a political fund-raiser. She is also writing a book about Trinidad.

Dr. Elizabeth "Dana" Clark

O n the night of the famous New York City blackout, November 5, 1965, I was working hatcheck in a restaurant near Central Park. Sometime around midnight, a group of people came in, and you couldn't miss the fact that there were about 12 beautiful women with two or three men.

"One of the men came up to me and said, 'Hi, honey, how long you been working in this joint?' I'd been there about two or three months. 'How much you make here, sweetheart: $20, $30?' I was embarrassed, but I told him, 'Yeah, something like that.'

"Well, how would you like to make a hundred dollars a night?' Then he gave me his card and introduced himself as Joe Palazzo, Party Room director at the Playboy Club. 'Call up Lynn Smith, the Bunny Mother, and tell her I told you to call.'

"I was kind of horrified and realized all these girls who came in with him were Bunnies. I'd never been to the Playboy Club and at the time equated Bunnies with hookers. But Joe introduced me to a couple of the girls in his party, and they seemed like nice human beings, not at all like my Southern small-town notion of a hooker. I went for an interview at the Playboy Club and was hired.

"I had grown up with five sisters in a sheltered, rural environment in Mississippi. I had been shy and not terribly popular in school. One of the greatest influences on my life was an elderly maiden aunt who took me under her wing and taught me the gracious old-world manners of a genteel Southern lady. I went to France during my junior year at college and loved it, but nothing could compare to the wide range of people and experience I later encountered while working at Playboy. In part, I think, that's what spurred my interest in studying psychology.

"I wonder if Playboy management had any idea how well they designed the competitive aspects of being a Bunny. I'd competed with sisters, so I had some preparation for the jockeying. The Bunny of the Week contest was based on drink averages. The Big Guns who had the highest drink averages got the best schedules. We were always striving to keep up in order to stay in the Showrooms where you earned the most in tips. I can still remember my great sense of triumph when I walked in on Monday to find out that I was Bunny of the Week.

"The entire time I worked as a Bunny, I continued to take various courses at Hunter College. In 1972, I met a professor who encouraged me to return to college for an advanced degree in psychology. In the summer of 1974, I took a leave of absence from

Today, Elizabeth is raising her son and working as a psychotherapist at the Women's Foundation, while also teaching at UCLA.

Playboy to do observational research in a primate lab in Georgia. Shortly after I returned from studying the monkeys, the New York Playboy Club closed its doors for remodeling. I collected unemployment and continued with my studies. The whole time the Club was closed, I collected unemployment, which meant I could continue in graduate school. When Playboy didn't rehire me (I was no longer 'Bunny Image'), I didn't fight it. I was thrilled because I then got severance pay. It was a very generous amount because I had been a Bunny for eight years. The money enabled me to sail through several years of graduate work, virtually subsidized by Playboy." ∎

Karen Barnes Bartolotto

I think I've based my whole outlook on life on a comment I first heard in Bunny Training: You can look at the world two ways—up at the blue sky or down in the gutter. Attitude guides your behavior.

"I had been working in the garment center as a model, a terrible job. In March 1965, three days before my 19th birthday, my boyfriend saw an ad in *The New York Times* for Playboy Bunnies. He dared me to go for an interview.

"I still remember standing in front of the mirror looking at myself in the Bunny costume and thinking, that's me? I was shocked I looked as good as I did. Tall and skinny—but with a shape! But when I was told I was hired, I turned the job down. I was still living at home with my German immigrant parents, farm people who went to bed at 9 o'clock. I knew they wouldn't go for it. The Bunny Mother and the general manager persuaded me to bring my parents in for a free lunch and a VIP tour. I went home and begged, pleaded and promised. Over lunch in the VIP Room the following day, every Club rule and policy was explained to my parents. Before we left, I had a job as a Bunny and my father had bought a Playboy Key.

"Two years later, I celebrated my 21st birthday by working in the Penthouse, finally old enough to work nights in the Showrooms. Nancy Phillips, Judy Bruno and Marcia Donen gave me the Royal Test. They did everything to reduce me to tears: dropping one of my glasses in the ice so that the entire bin had to be changed, pushing me to the end of the line because I didn't call my order in correctly or fast enough. In the end, I came through with flying colors and the girls invited me to Tobo's after work to celebrate. You always had to be invited to Tobo's. I tripped and fell as I walked in, and got a standing ovation.

"You weren't allowed to 'hustle' at the Club, but somehow you were expected to sell a three-drink average. The competition among the Showrooms every Friday and Saturday night was really fun. The room directors posted the drink averages on the following Monday and there was always this terrific rivalry between the Playroom and the Penthouse. The amazing thing about Playboy is that with all those beautiful, ambitious girls competing, I don't recall a fight. We had such camaraderie.

"I remember the night Pat Collins, the Hip Hypnotist, was doing a show in the Playroom and hypnotized Bunny Joi Kissling—who stayed under. We thought she was clowning as she kind of floated around. Toward the end of the night, we realized Joi hadn't

collected any of her checks. They were all still open and nobody had paid. By that time, Pat Collins was back at the Plaza Hotel. She had to return to the Club, her hair in rollers, to snap Joi out of it.

"On the night of the blackout, New York City's major power failure, November 5, 1965, Tony Roma, the general manager, had scheduled a Bunny meeting in the Penthouse. Tony was angry because of a rash of walkouts: girls not showing up for work and quitting without notice. The meeting was over and everyone was slipping out,

Karen Barnes in the Piano Bar
in the Living Room of the
New York Club.

heading for the elevators. Tony's last words had been, 'There'll be no more walkouts or else!' Moments later, the whole city shut down. A complete blackout. I was stuck in an elevator packed with Bunnies and a gay busboy, who kept saying, 'Why me? Oh, God, every other man's dream and it has to be me!'

"During my five years at Playboy, I had done the Jerry Lewis Muscular Dystrophy telethon and appeared on both *What's My Line* and *I've Got a Secret*. My God, I've never felt more like a celebrity in my life. Bunnies were a novelty: All over town, doors were open to us. It never failed that when a group of us went to a discotheque after work, we were ushered past a long line of people waiting to get in. It was a fantasy.

"We weren't allowed to date Keyholders. But let's face it, the rule that we all broke was not to fraternize with other employees. Well, who the hell among your friends are you going to hang out with around 4 a.m. when you get off work? The people you work with. In June 1969, when I was 23 years old, I left the Club to marry Joe Bartolotto, one of the room directors. Together, we opened a restaurant." ■

Gloria Hendry

Working at night almost ruined me. I would get off work at 3 or 4 o'clock in the morning and go out to eat. You're tired and your feet are killing you, but you don't want to go to sleep. You're so high with energy that it's like your day is really just beginning. You sit in a club drinking whatever you drink. At the time, wine was not the 'in' thing. I drank Chivas Regal. On the rocks. Or a mixed drink like a grasshopper or a brandy Alexander. Oh, the headaches!

"When people phoned me at 11 a.m.—or later—I'd still be in bed. I'd get up at 2 or 3 o'clock in the afternoon, with just enough time to do some errands and run back to work. You're around alcohol and food all night and, after a while, you find yourself joining the party. You start eating french fries. You find yourself mixing an extra drink on that tray of yours just for yourself. That was a merry-go-round I had to get off!

"In high school I studied to be a secretary. I wanted to become an attorney, but my counselor told me to 'be realistic, be a secretary.' I went to work for the NAACP in New York, then became an executive assistant in an advertising firm. One day, my boss took me to lunch at the Playboy Club just around the corner. The moment I walked in, I was in awe of the place. I was raised in a run-down area of Newark, New Jersey, and the New

Gloria Hendry in a Los Angeles production of *Lady Day at Emerson's Bar & Grill*, a one-woman musical drama about the life and times of Billie Holiday. Gloria and her husband, jazz pianist Phil Wright, are also collaborating on a number of musical projects.

York Playboy Club really did represent glamour to me. That's what I wanted in my life: beauty, glamour and neon lights. I didn't want to deal with the real world.

"After the boss turned down my request for a raise, I told him, 'You know, I'm going to be a Bunny.' He laughed at me. He thought it was funny. But I did it.

"I was breaking out in cold sweats on my way to the interview at Playboy. I was sent in to see Betty, the wardrobe woman, who told me to take off my clothes and try on a costume. I come from a conservative, religious background and I had never undressed in front of anyone. Betty just pushed one of my breasts aside and said, 'This is how you stuff your costume—take these old stockings and . . . believe me, after you work here a while, honey, you'll rock and roll with everyone else standing around the dressing room getting ready.'

"The Club was hot and the music was jazz. Live musicians—not piped-in stuff—played jazz on all five floors. Hefner loves jazz, bless him. The place was so alive! Those shoes we wore as Bunnies were cruel, but even today I will only wear high heels when I go out. My feet may look like hell, but I love those shoes.

"As a legal secretary at the NAACP, I had dealt with the reality of prejudice and racial slurs every day. It was such a different experience working at the Club as far as color was concerned. My skin color was glorified, and I felt good about myself. When Easter came around and I was called a chocolate Bunny, I thought of it as positive and fun. I experienced prejudice at the Club on only one memorable occasion. Unfortunately, it had to happen when my father came to celebrate his birthday one Labor Day weekend. My father was sitting at one of my tables in the Penthouse and, just before the show started, a man was seated at a table next to his. As I began to say 'Good evening, I'm your Bunny Gloria,' the man interrupted. 'I don't want you waiting on me.' My father knew instantly that the man was objecting to my color and I was mortified. I had been telling my family that things like that didn't happen at the Club. I went straight

Gloria, a dedicated bodybuilder, has co-starred in 14 motion pictures, appearing
opposite Roger Moore in the 1973 James Bond film *Live and Let Die.*

over to the room director and reported the incident. The man was asked to leave and his
member's key was confiscated. The Club really stood behind all of us, but I was so sorry
my father had to witness that one sorry episode.

"I left when the realization finally hit me that I couldn't be a Bunny for the rest of
my life. I wasn't going to be young forever, and I couldn't waste time. I began studying
acting in earnest in the late '60s. Before long, I was doing
print work and filming television commercials." ■

DeeDee Bradley

People forget that young women working in trendy
New York restaurants and cocktail lounges in the
mid-'60s usually wore some funny, skimpy outfit with
high-heeled shoes. My first job was at the Flick Ice
Cream Parlor, where I had to wear a silly shorts outfit. At
the Rolling Stone I wore a leotard and black tights. At
the Gaslight Clubs, the girls were wearing Gay '90s-style
satin corsets.

"I left Baltimore at 18 to study acting in New York, but once I got there, I was so intimidated I just couldn't handle it. I studied with Bill Hickey at the Herbert Berghoff School for a while, but I remember becoming terrified my first day in class hearing everybody talk about auditions. I didn't even have an agent. It wasn't until several years later, after I had moved to Los Angeles, that I really pursued an acting career.

"In New York, becoming an actress took a back burner; the social life at Playboy soon took precedence over any ambition I had. I went out every single night, and that became my life. I would get off work at 2 or 2:30 in the morning, stay out until maybe 7 or 8, then sleep until about 3 and go back to work in the late afternoon. I had a great time, lots of friends, pretty clothes and plenty of places to go.

"There were a lot of women working at the Club who were going to school. Playboy liked the idea that women who worked as Bunnies were interested in pursuing other careers. Girls were always given flexible schedules and time off to pursue careers; that policy enabled the Club to hire more interesting, intelligent women. It was fascinating to see schoolgirls come into the dressing room, just as plain as could be—no makeup, straight hair—and turn themselves into Bunnies.

"I worked at the Club nearly four years, and I think I saw the last of the best of it. By the time I left in 1970, there was no longer a crush at the door. The psychedelic phenomenon was sweeping the country by then; there were discos and topless bars. Bunnies were no longer special.

Hollywood casting director Deedee Bradley
in her Warner Bros. office.

"The Playboy Club was not for everybody, and it was clear that some people just didn't approve of it. I think the point of view expressed by the women's movement is healthy and necessary—and so is Playboy's—in our society. Eventually a middle ground is found. I think you can be a feminist, and also be sensual, sexy and your own woman. We need both Gloria Steinem and Hugh Hefner in our lives.

"I left Playboy to get married and move to Florida. I applied for a receptionist's job with a Miami pediatrician and gave the Playboy Club, my last employer, as a reference. The doctor looked over my application and started laughing. 'I've got to hire you!' she said. The following year, she delivered my son." ■

Denise Schweighardt McAdams

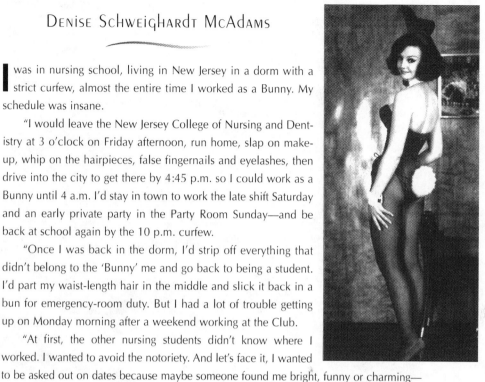

I was in nursing school, living in New Jersey in a dorm with a strict curfew, almost the entire time I worked as a Bunny. My schedule was insane.

"I would leave the New Jersey College of Nursing and Dentistry at 3 o'clock on Friday afternoon, run home, slap on make-up, whip on the hairpieces, false fingernails and eyelashes, then drive into the city to get there by 4:45 p.m. so I could work as a Bunny until 4 a.m. I'd stay in town to work the late shift Saturday and an early private party in the Party Room Sunday—and be back at school again by the 10 p.m. curfew.

"Once I was back in the dorm, I'd strip off everything that didn't belong to the 'Bunny' me and go back to being a student. I'd part my waist-length hair in the middle and slick it back in a bun for emergency-room duty. But I had a lot of trouble getting up on Monday morning after a weekend working at the Club.

"At first, the other nursing students didn't know where I worked. I wanted to avoid the notoriety. And let's face it, I wanted to be asked out on dates because maybe someone found me bright, funny or charming—

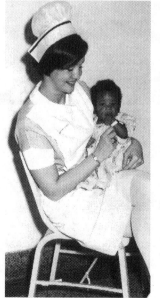

not because I was a status symbol, a Playboy Bunny. But one Sunday night, the Big Sister assigned to me at school called my parents to find out where I was. My father accidentally let it slip that I was a Bunny. The news spread like wildfire. One instructor gave me a hard time, but my grades were excellent. My mother even wrote a letter to the school to back me up.

"I completed the three year program and became an R.N. in 1969. Then, while continuing to work as a Bunny, I went for the two-year baccalaureate degree through a private program at Farleigh Dickinson University. Later, I got my master's degree in psychiatric nursing.

"I was caught in an incredible period of change during the eight years I worked as a Bunny. The antiwar, flower child/hippie movement was followed by the femi-

Student nurse Denise Schweighardt.

nist movement. It was a time of activists working to stop the war, while others wanted to just drop acid and drop out. Drugs and dropping out didn't appeal to me because I had gotten a taste of what money and independence could do for me. The Bunny job was the best thing that could have happened to me at the time. I could make my own decisions because I was earning enough to pay for everything. Even those girls working the Playmate Bar and Living Room, not the Showrooms, were making a hundred to a hundred-and-fifty dollars in cash a night. It was an awful lot of money in those days. I knew that as a woman, I could never make that kind of money any other place. In a nutshell, that was the lure of being a Bunny. Where else could I make that much money an hour—unless I was a psychiatrist?

"I didn't buy into the feminist thing, either. Women are women. Throughout the centuries they've put themselves into bustles and hoops, wound bands around their breasts and worn peculiar shoes—whatever the fashion of the moment decreed. Compared to all that, the Bunny costume was an artistic mas-

A Letter From Home . . .

. . . I would certainly appreciate your kind consideration in permitting my daughter, Denise, to have knowledge of her school schedule two weeks in advance so that she could continue and fit in other duties she is engaged in.

It is my impression that you have been misinformed about her type of outside work in typing her as a "go-go girl." This could not be further from the truth and I would like to clarify this appellation here and now; she is not a "go-go girl." As her mother, who has reared her in respectability, thank God, I would be the first to disapprove of such an avocation.

Denise happens to be working as a waitress at the Playboy Club in New York City, and this is certainly nothing to be ashamed of. Girls who are employed there are thoroughly screened by the management and must be the zenith of respectability; their work is by no means a sinecure, as any dedicated girl so involved will vouch . . .

Sincerely yours,
Julia B. Schweighardt

terpiece. But Bunnies made a good target for women who wanted to picket for equal rights and equal pay. They were angry, rightly enough, but we were the wrong target. They decided we were being exploited without taking into consideration that we were exercising choice.

"Besides, it was a great adventure—and very glamorous. I remember waiting on Judy Garland and one of Bing Crosby's sons.

"A friend once introduced me to his mother who had been a Ziegfeld Girl, a lovely, animated woman who was full of stories about the bootleg days. When we met I was in my early 20s and she was in her 60s, but we talked together like contemporaries, discussing the mystique of glamour and the quality of making everything look effortless.

"There is no question some women stayed on past their prime as Bunnies. Some of us began to think of ourselves as celebrities rather than cocktail waitresses, and didn't want to give up that status. Once Playboy became more than a short-term means to another career goal, being a Bunny was a pretty dismal prospect. I experienced that emotional pitfall. Once I'd completed my education, I put it off looking for work in my field because I was hooked on the excitement, money, connections, glamour and everything else about the lifestyle I'd come to know as a Bunny. Some of us just had to be booted off the merry-go-round.

"When the Club closed for renovation in September 1974, our union negotiated severance pay for those not rehired for the reopening. I was asked to return but decided to take the severance pay instead and finish grad school. It was time to do something useful for society—and me. I was motivated to get my master's degree in psychiatric nursing as much to help myself as anyone else. Jadee Yee, the Bunny Mother, stood up for us—and gave us a wake-up call when we needed it. I owe her a debt of gratitude for rocking me out of my complacency.

"Now that the youngest of my three sons is in elementary school, I'm going back to my nursing career." ∎

Patti Colombo

I felt like a starlet. Only the *crème de la crème* were hired to be Bunnies, and it made me feel very special. I worked as a Bunny from 1963 to 1974, and it took me another 10 years to get over not being at Playboy.

"Before becoming a Bunny, I had been modeling junior boutique clothes on Seventh Avenue. My fiancé took me on a date to the Playboy Club, which had just opened a few weeks earlier, and said, 'Why don't you get a job here?' I was married most of the time I worked at Playboy. My life changed so little in those years; instead of modeling clothes, I put on a Bunny costume and served drinks. But the money was better; men who were supporting families did not earn the kind of money 19-year-old Bunnies made at Playboy.

"I loved going to work every day and being among the other girls. I felt good about myself.

"We had to weigh in every day; if you gained weight, you were suspended until you dropped the pounds. It was the price of being a starlet. I remember going in for costume fittings and begging Betty, the seamstress, to 'make it tighter, as tight and skimpy as possible!' Everyone wanted the smallest waist in town. You had your costume made so tight that your legs would fall asleep. And you would stuff, stuff, stuff your bosom.

"I was nervous, absolutely terrified all the time, that I'd come to work on a Saturday night and find myself off the schedule. I'm not sure it's a bad thing to be kept on your toes. I liked having to abide by the rules because it meant everyone else had to do the same. It kept the standards up.

"We knew management was dying to get rid of the senior girls. One day Jadee, the Bunny Mother, told me that I'd probably be one of the Bunnies let go soon. Each day I'd go to work feeling terrible, afraid the end was near, but happy for whatever time I had left. Week after week, I'd find my name still on the schedule. Months later, when I was finally told I was working my last day as a Bunny, I was devastated.

Patti Colombo, president of Patco Software Supplies, in her Manhattan office.

"That day, Ricky Waller, my best friend, and I stuffed my costumes in a bag and walked out. Ricky and I went to one of the nearby restaurants to have a drink and agonize over the fact that I wasn't going to work at the Club anymore. I cried. I was hysterical. I hadn't looked for another job. As the weeks wore on, I had deluded myself that I could prolong the end forever.

"I understood room had to be made for the new girls. Those of us who had racked up seniority made more money because we were able to choose our own schedules. Seniority, in fact, was one of the issues we had won through our union, but I was one of the women who didn't walk the picket line because I was afraid it might jeopardize my job. After I was terminated (and that was the word management used), it was incredible to me that I was no longer a Playboy Bunny. I was 32 years old.

"I've stayed close to the other Bunnies; it was a sisterhood. At first I worked at the English Pub on Seventh Avenue with a lot of the other ex-Bunnies and room directors, and also modeled shoes. I then turned my life around completely by entering the burgeoning computer business. A few years ago, I started my own company, Patco Software Supplies. Although I'm proud of my success in this field, I'm still amazed I didn't go into some aspect of the beauty industry. Glamour has always been my thing. When *Dynasty* was on the air, I loved being stopped in the street by people mistaking me for Joan Collins. I still wore false eyelashes until 1995, when I finally gave them up. But everything is deglamorized now—even I wear jeans and T-shirts.

"Recently my mother threw away one of my costumes—and this was a woman who saved everything, so I thought they would be safe with her. When I discovered the loss, I cried and screamed like a lunatic. I never have cross words with my mother, but I said to her, 'You just threw away part of my life! How could you have done such a thing to me?' Fortunately, I have one costume left, and a set of cuff links, collar and cuffs. As recently as two years ago, I could still fit into it." ∎

JACKLYN ZEMAN

In 1967, at the age of 15, I graduated from high school and entered New York University on a dance scholarship. I switched to a premed course at NYU and worked part-time as a cocktail hostess at a bar in the General Motors building across the street from the Playboy Club. One day Oliver, the bartender, told me I ought to be a Bunny because I'd make a lot more money. Well, as a teenager in suburban New Jersey, I was fascinated by the image of glamorous, beautiful Bunnies in the pages of *Playboy*. I used to watch *Playboy After Dark* while baby-sitting. The women wearing slinky dresses and sitting around playing backgammon on the show represented a whole sophisticated, grownup world to me. I wanted to be a part of all that. Oliver got me an appointment with Jadee, the Bunny Mother, and I was hired.

"The only problem was I had to wait nearly a month until my 18th birthday before I could start work as a Bunny.

Jacklyn Zeman of *General Hospital*.

"The Bunny thing was so easy. You showed up, did it, left. A no-brainer work-wise, and a perfect job if you were going to school. And it was a lot of fun. It was all the rage to wear lots of make-up and tons of hair, which we'd slap on very quickly. Even though I had naturally long hair, I'd slick it back and then attach a long fall upside down so layers of hair would cascade even fuller over my shoulders. We really 'glammed' out.

"Most of us were just kids going to school, having a good time together. Some had boyfriends, a few were married. We picked up extra money modeling, doing trade shows, filming television commercials, whatever came along. If a girl was offered a job she didn't have time to do, she'd pass it on to someone else in the dressing room. We were family. I never felt bad vibes or competitiveness among the girls. We'd all come in early, taking turns bringing in doughnuts, and spend time together talking until the Club opened. It was exciting to live in New York then, and it was a surprisingly innocent time.

"I think a lot of people mixed up Bunnies and Playmates. My father, who subscribed to *Playboy*, was fine about my working as a Bunny, but he was concerned that I might pose for the centerfold. 'Promise me you won't do that,' he said, 'because you are so young and it could have ramifications on the rest of your life.' I told him OK, 'I can make

Bunny Baseball Team: Johnnie Gordon, Mary Chipman, Libby Wickes, Leigh Jefferson, Marcia Donen,
Tia Mazza, Lynn Passenger, Judy Bruno, Jackie Zeman, Geri Haywood and unidentified Bunny.

that promise.' But years later, after I became a soap opera actress, Mario Casilli photographed me for *Playboy* in a lime green scarf I wrapped around myself. To this day, men
mail me copies of that picture to autograph.

"During those years I worked as a Bunny, I wasn't sure what direction my life would
take. I was single and free. I could go anywhere, do anything. At one point, I considered
transferring to the London Club to train as a blackjack dealer. But I decided against going
after I met Murray Kaufman, the disc jockey who was known as the 'fifth Beatle.' I was
still working as a Bunny when I was hired to be one of the "K-Girl" dancers in his nightclub revue. We hit it off and eventually married.

"I played third base on the Bunny softball team, and we made about $2,000 a game
for various charities. Jadee, the Bunny Mother, also gave me an opportunity to do various Playboy promotions, for which I was paid a day rate. We wore white pleated
miniskirts, high heels and a black sweater with the Rabbit logo on those occasions instead of the Bunny costume. I began to enjoy doing the talk shows and personal appearances more than working at the Club.

"One of the most glamorous events I attended was a celebrity-packed, black-tie opening of the Playboy movie theatre in New York. Hugh Hefner was dating Barbi Benton at the time, but he arrived in a limo escorting a gorgeous Playmate. Most of the women were dressed in skintight, low-cut dresses, but I was wearing the miniskirt-and-sweater outfit. It was all very exciting, with cameras flashing everywhere. I was selected to pose next to Hefner, offering him a bag of popcorn. Seconds after his arrival, another limo pulled up and Barbi appeared. Hefner, the perfect gentleman, raced over to help her out of the car. Flashbulbs popped. The centerfold and I regrouped. Hefner smiled at me and I took that as a cue to thrust the bag at him and say, 'You want the popcorn?'

"I watched *A Bunny's Tale* on television and saw it strictly as one person's point of view. It certainly wasn't mine. I really enjoyed working at the Club. The philosophy behind the Playboy Club, on a human level, was about making people feel welcome and giving them a good time. The customers felt important because they were members of an elegant, sophisticated Club, and the Bunnies felt good about themselves because management was protective and kept up standards. I can't think of anything comparable to it today. People weren't doing drugs, getting drunk, tearing the place apart. The Bunnies were all so close that if someone was taking drugs, drinking, going out with customers—we knew.

"I took a lot of pride in being able to support myself. I came from a comfortable, middle-class background, so accumulating 'stuff' wasn't as important to me as the fact that I earned the means to live the way I wanted to. I was independent. The money was so good that it really was hard to leave Playboy, but eventually it was time to move on.

"After two years at NYU, I dropped out of premed. I wasn't dedicated enough to become a doctor. I remember sitting with Murray in a Bagel Nosh in New York wondering what I should do next and saying, 'You know what? I love soap operas and I want to be on one.' From the time I was a little girl when I'd come home from school for lunch, my mother and I would eat sandwiches off trays and watch soaps together.

"I auditioned for one soap and was just devastated when I didn't get the job. Then I auditioned for a role on *One Life to Live* and was hired in 1975. In 1977, Murray was a consultant on the Broadway show *Beatlemania,* which was going to open in Los Angeles. At about the same time Murray left for California, I got a call from Fred Silverman and Jackie Smith at ABC offering me a role on *General Hospital.* 'You don't have to test,' they told me. 'If you want the role, it's yours.' I flew out the next day to get fitted for wardrobe and start shooting. In January 1997, I celebrated 20 years on *General Hospital.*

"I've been married to my second husband, a businessman, for 10 years. I'm at a point in my life now when being a good mom is the most important thing to me. Everyone tells me what's coming—'Mommmm, are you really going to wear *that*!'—but right now, at 5 and 7 years old, my daughters want me around to hold their hands and take them places. There are some long days when I can't be home for dinner (we shoot 90—100 pages a day, and we don't go home until the show is finished), but then I have days off when I can spend lots of time with them.

"But 25 years after I left Playboy, two of my closest friends, Cheryl Glickman and Lynn Passenger, are women I met as Bunnies. Now we compare notes as moms." ■

MARY CHIPMAN

My experience at Playboy forced me to examine personal issues in a way that a normal job never would have. My generation was right on the cusp of the changing world: raised with traditional '50s values, but first on the scene for the so-called 'Sexual Revolution.' I was swept along by the tides.

"I was a rebellious teenager. At 17, I was already discouraged with my career as a ballet dancer and felt like a total failure. I took up with a much older man and lived with him in Beverly Hills for two years. He was one of those Hollywood 'hangers-on' who liked the lifestyle of the rich hippies, and we hung out at the Candy Store disco every night. Then Jay Sebring, the famous hairdresser who was part of our circle, was killed with Sharon Tate by the Manson gang. After the murders, the nights were full of shadows for me, and I wanted desperately to get out of Los Angeles.

"A friend wrote a show that was opening on Broadway, and I leapt at the chance to dance in it. The show closed after one night, and that's how I ended up in New York in 1971 with $6 to my name. I had no clear idea of what I wanted to do with my life, and I was woefully unprepared to go out and get a job. But, if you had looks and charm and could fit into that absurd outfit, you could get a job as a Playboy Bunny.

"The Bunny dressing room was the most interesting place in the Club and, of course, where all the great dramas were played out, from insufficient weight-loss confrontations with the wardrobe ladies to screeching hysterics over boyfriends. I saw girls fight so hard to hold on to their Bunny jobs, and I could never understand it. I thought, 'Get a grip and move on.' There was terrific stratification among the Bunnies, with the younger girls despising the older girls with seniority who got to work the Showrooms, where you could make the best money. I was one of the jealous junior girls, eyeing all the prime Saturday night spots that the older Bunnies were hogging. The Bunny dressing room was also the place where you had to get yourself psyched up to go out on the floor, always a trauma for me.

"Working as a Bunny radicalized me; I quickly became a card-carrying feminist. When you get dressed up in an outfit like that, it makes you question what the role is that you're really playing. You see that you get treated in a certain way by men and you stop taking those things for granted. Heaven forbid anyone whistled at me when I walked down the street on my way to work; I'd rip their eyes out!

"I think the girls who did well and had fun at the Club already had a strong sense of themselves, and could take it all with a sense of humor. Those of us who were on shakier ground with our egos ran into various troubles. I'm surprised I lived through it, quite frankly. I had been experimenting with drugs for a long time before working at Playboy, street drugs and chemical props to evade reality. I was a shy person. I drank to lower my inhibitions—not just at the Club, but at other waitressing jobs I'd had, too—just so I could go up to a table and talk to customers.

"Eventually the drugs were no longer recreational, but a necessity. The names of doctors who would prescribe drugs were freely circulated in the dressing room. The booze became necessary because, once you got to work, you needed a drink to relax and take the edge off the diet pills. You had to take sleeping pills when you came home at 4 a.m. because you were still buzzing from the diet pills and booze. I almost died from all that, but fortunately Jadee, the Bunny Mother, and Mario Staub, the Club's general manager, stuck by me and helped me clean up my act.

"I went into Jadee's office one day moaning about my life. I made up an elaborate metaphor about bobbing on the sea of life, drifting aimlessly. She interrupted me and said, 'Well, at least you're not sinking—yet.' It stopped me cold. Jadee, with more common sense than any five people I know, sent me to a doctor for treatment. I went into therapy, too, and eventually chose life over dying in stages by smoking, drinking and using drugs.

"When the Club closed for renovations, I worked at the Gaslight Club, then transferred to the London Playboy Club to be a croupier for six months. Afterward, I worked in a variety of typing and bookkeeping jobs. An interest in the mechanics of word processing led to an interest in programming, and I got a certificate in microcomputer technology through Columbia University's

Mary Chipman, a senior consultant with MCW Technologies, is co-author of the *Microsoft Access and SQL Server Developer's Handbook* (Sybex, 1996) and the new version of *SQL Server* (Sybex, 1998).

Continuing Education program. During a seven-year stint at Morgan Stanley, I further developed my skills working on exciting projects in New York, Tokyo and Hong Kong.

"Today I'm a senior consultant at MCW Technologies, a company I co-founded that specializes in creating software using the latest Microsoft database and programming tools. The dawn of the computer age gave many women like me an opportunity to find really exciting, rewarding careers. I'm a Microsoft-certified developer and train-er, and frequently speak at conferences. I'm also a contributing editor for the *Access-Office-VB Advisor* magazine.

"But even now, I can't walk past the Hong Kong Bank that occupies the old Playboy Club building in New York without a shudder, recalling the personal crisis I went through. Working as a Bunny exacerbated all my feelings of inadequacy and lack of identity; however, that experience also propelled me into a voyage of inner exploration that is ongoing and very rewarding. I'll always be grateful to Mario and Jadee, who tossed me a rope when I was drowning." ∎

Cheryl McArthur

For me, coming from a working-class background, the Playboy Club was magical. When I arrived in Chicago in 1969, I felt I had been emancipated. I could make my own decisions, have fun and spend my money on the things I had wanted for a very long time.

"Moving into the Playboy Mansion was thrilling. There were about 25 Bunnies living in the dorm, women from all over the world, who were bright, pretty and a lot of fun. Everything was new and exciting. I'd never seen a private indoor swimming pool before. Or tanning beds. There was a 24-hour kitchen serving anything you wanted. We had maid and butler service. On Sundays, we watched first-run movie screenings in the Ballroom. Rent was only $50 a month.

"Hefner was brilliant, but I found him intimidating. I loved to listen to him when a group of us sat together talking in front of the fireplace. I was awed by his ability to discuss a wide range of topics and ideas. I didn't get to know him well because I never felt I had the background, education or the confidence in myself to really engage him in conversation.

"There were always celebrities arriving at the Mansion: the Rolling Stones, Bill Cosby, Paul Newman and Warren Beatty. I worked long hours and didn't really go to any parties. Besides, I was young and in love, and so wrapped up with my high school sweetheart back in Toledo that I didn't date anyone else.

"I have three sisters, two of whom worked with me as Bunnies. Mary Jo worked nights, while Joyce and I worked during the day. Joyce worked at the Club only a year. I remember when I drove her to Chicago; she cried the whole way. She was young and just wasn't prepared emotionally to work at the Club. She cried a *lot*. Customers upset her. But then a talent scout for the Wilhelmina Model Agency came into the Club for lunch one day and discovered Joyce. She signed with the agency and moved to New York to work as an international model for eight years. For the past 12 years, she's had her own very successful women's apparel firm in New York, designing and manufacturing shirts.

"You had to be strong, physically and emotionally, to work at the Club. What got you through was a sense of humor and an upbeat attitude. I learned how to handle people,

Cheryl McArthur with her sisters Joyce and Mary Jo, Chicago Club, 1973.

Cheryl McArthur, co-founder and former CEO of McArthur/Glen, the leading developer of designer outlet malls in the United States.

not only because I really did want them to have a good time but also because it helped me get a good tip.

"After my husband finished dental school, he worked for a year in Chicago before we decided, in 1975, that we wanted to get away from the cold winters and start a new life together. We moved to Phoenix.

"My big opportunity for success came from the convergence of three areas of business I'd worked in. I had gained some experience in consumer marketing working in a Chicago advertising firm. In Phoenix, I worked in real estate, first selling new homes and later developing neighborhood strip malls.

"Seven years later, after my divorce, I moved to New York, and I set up a business importing knitwear, thereby gaining knowledge of the fashion industry. I later moved to Washington D.C., and in 1986 established McArthur/Glen with real-estate investor Allen Glen. When a leading apparel manufacturer came to me to discuss developing outlet centers, I knew I had found my niche. As a world-class shopper myself, I knew what women wanted: bargain prices for top-notch designer goods sold in beautiful stores with lovely landscaping in a secure, safe environment. The outlet malls we developed also had flattering lighting, piped-in music and baby-changing stations in the ladies' rooms.

"McArthur/Glen became the leading developer of designer outlet malls in the United States, building 21 centers in 19 states over a nine-year period. On October 14, 1993, we went public, and I became one of the few female CEOs to head a New York Stock Exchange company. At the ripe old age of 45, I retired. I had been working seven days a week, and I wanted a personal life. I remarried and now devote myself to oil painting and working with a number of organizations I've joined." ∎

The World's Most Beautiful Walkout

In stark contrast to the bitter 1965 union strike waged on Manhattan's frigid Fifth Avenue by Bunnies wearing fur coats and snow boots, the 1975 walkout by Chicago Bunnies was a frolic on Playboy's Michigan Avenue doorstep. Television crews and press reporters were invited to what was billed by Playboy as the "World's Most Beautiful Walkout"—a sunny afternoon display of costumed Bunnies marching along a sidewalk, laughing and wielding "Bunny Lib!" placards. The staged walkout was all for a good cause, heralding policy changes supported by Bunnies and Playboy management alike.

"The things we wanted," said Chicago's 1975 Bunny of the Year, Laura Lyons, at the time, "were pretty basic. Freedom to date Keyholders if we want to, freedom to use our real names if we choose and freedom to patronize the Club as Keyholders whenever we wish."

An open letter spelling out these desired policy changes was sent by the Chicago Bunnies to Hugh Hefner, President of Playboy Enterprises:

We love being Playboy Bunnies, and most of the time we love you, but there are times when we think you are a Male Chauvinist Rabbit. Those are the times when, because of the archaic rules you have decreed for Bunny behavior, we are made to feel like strange objects out of step with our times.

While you are, admittedly, the leader of sexual liberation, you have set the cause of Bunny Lib back 10 years. Our private lives should be our own. For example, we're not allowed to date Keyholders. We are human beings with human feelings and passions. Yet, you have decreed that Keyholders can "look but don't touch." In short, you have created a caste system through which we Bunnies have become America's "Untouchables."

We can't use our real names and even when asked we can't give out our last names. This, Hef, is medieval. You have prohibited us from enjoying the pleasures of the very place we work. We are not allowed to come into the Playboy Club as private citizens. This is anti-Bunny discrimination. We should be honorary VIP Keyholders, in fact. Also, we ask you to reconsider your outdated mandates. We believe you to be a kind, considerate and progressive-thinking person. We expect to hear from you in a positive way. Until we do, we intend to let the outside world know that we are unhappy. We have nothing to lose but our tails and ears.

The Chicago Bunnies

Hugh Hefner responded:

I have received your letter dealing with Bunny Lib, and I have to admit that I am both distressed and pleased. I am distressed because many of the ideas you propose are ideas that have discussed and then allowed to be tabled for some future consideration, and nothing has been done about them. But I am pleased that these ideas can surface in the Club. And I am reassured that the company is one where employees feel they can express themselves without any fear of reprisal.

For a long time, I have been thinking that some of the rules and regulations instituted in the early '60s make little or no sense in 1975. Some of these rules came about because of specific legal restrictions in certain areas, and these, of course, we must still impose. Other rules were considered sound public relations where and when the public thought there was something suspect about the Bunny concept. But I agree that you have proved to the world that Bunnies are mature, responsible young ladies fully capable of leading their own private lives without bringing any discredit to themselves or to the company. And I agree that is exactly the way you should be treated.

I agree and am enthusiastic about your suggestions for the Chicago Club and any other Clubs where there are no legal problems. Therefore, as of today:

1. *All Bunnies are honorary members of the Playboy Club and are entitled to use all its facilities.*
2. *Bunnies are free to date whomever they choose.*
3. *Bunnies may use their real names, and full names if they choose, in the Club.*

In short, we are making Bunny Lib a reality rather than just a slogan, and I will welcome any additional suggestions you may have.

Hugh M. Hefner

P.S. Really, Bunnies, I'm not a male chauvinist rabbit and I love and respect all of you. Maybe I've been just a wee bit overprotective.

Liz Doyle

Playboy paid my college tuition; I studied banking, credit and finance at a community college in New Jersey. I was married during the four years I worked as a Bunny. My husband, who is a musician, put together a musical act for us. I began working part-time so I could continue taking classes and also travel with my husband performing. I was a Training Bunny, working in the VIP Room on weekends, and also found time to do promotional work for Playboy.

"After I graduated, I felt I had gone as far as I could at Playboy. It was time to turn the page and start a new chapter in my life. I wanted to have a family life and start a business with my husband. I turned in my costume and we left for a three-week vacation in Europe.

"Many years later, when I was running my own special-events company, one of my clients found out that I had been a Bunny and blurted it out

Liz Doyle is executive vice president of Corporate Styles, a multimillion-dollar New Jersey-based company specializing in planning, designing and managing corporate events.

during a dinner meeting. I thought, 'Oh boy, here goes.' I stepped up to the microphone and said, 'I want you to imagine me doing this 15 years ago when I was 15 pounds lighter.' I put water glasses on a tray, went over to the president of the company and demonstrated the Bunny Dip. No problem. I had done that Dip so many times it was a piece of cake. Everyone just roared. They loved it. I never took being a Bunny seriously. I always looked at it from the lighter side.

"Even the way I got the job in the first place was a lark. One night in 1970, I went to the New York Playboy Club with some friends. We were standing in the lobby checking our coats when the Door Bunny came up to me and said, 'We're interviewing girls right now—how'd you like to be a Bunny?' Well, this became the topic of conversation for the rest of the evening. My friends were saying, 'Oh, this is so funny, you could never get a job here,' and 'I dare you to try out!'

"At the time, I was 19 years old and working at CBS in executive personnel, a strait-laced corporate job. I went for the interview with the Bunny Mother on my lunch hour. I could always go back to CBS, but I'd never get another chance to be a Bunny. I was young and spirited enough to give it a shot just to see where this adventure would lead. I was hired.

"My father is English and a ship's captain. He was so concerned when he heard I was working as a Bunny that he went over to the Club to check it out. He took a look around and said, 'All right, go ahead. It's no big deal.'

"The more I got into the training program and saw how protective all the rules and regulations were for the girls, the more I liked the idea. I realized I could easily fall into the mold. And that's what I did—until one day when I was approached about doing the centerfold for the magazine. At the time *Playboy* was paying $5,000, but it was just not worth it to me to pose nude.

"I never lived in a college dorm but, in a way, being a Bunny made me feel like I was in a sorority. A few years ago, I was on a business trip to Florida to do site inspections for some resort properties and had a meeting with a woman who was in charge of the catering department. In her office, there was a picture of her in a Bunny costume. When I asked her about it, she said, 'Oh, that was me a long, long time ago in Chicago.' Telling her that I had worked as a Bunny in New York only a few years later really opened the door for me. After that, it was a whole new ball game, sort of an 'old girls' network.'" ■

Dr. Polly Matzinger

I t was a great job," professor Polly Matzinger recalls about her days as a Bunny in the Denver Playboy Club in 1969. Today, she is the head of the T-cell Tolerance and Memory section of the National Institutes of Health's Laboratory of Cellular and Molecular Immunology, and the scientist who came up with the groundbreaking theory she calls the Danger Model.

The daughter of a French mother, who is an ex-nun, and a Dutch father, who is a painter and former KLM steward, Polly immigrated to the U.S. at the age of 9. The family's first home was a rented bungalow in the heart of Hollywood. Before her senior year in high-school, the family moved to Laguna Hills, where Polly's classmates voted her Most Likely Not to Succeed. "I didn't fit in very well," Polly says, "and quit going to classes. But then, my parents believed that in America if you want something and you're willing to work for it, you can have it—and my career is kind of an example of that." Polly, who left school at 16 without a high school diploma, enrolled in a local junior college to study music and become a composer. She found work as a carpenter and a bass player with a jazz group, and she considered becoming a veterinarian.

In 1969, when she moved to Boulder, Colorado, with a boyfriend who was in graduate school, she looked first for a waitress job. "The problem was that all the good restaurants only hired men as waiters, so I went to Denver—and there was the Playboy Club." The Club, on the 14th floor of the Hyatt House, had opened in December 1967 and featured a rooftop pool.

"I was struck by one of the questions on the Bunny job application: 'What do you feel yourself to be an expert in?' Playboy used that information to select the most suitable Bunnies to do various promotions. I had never been asked that before, and it made me think what I would be most qualified to talk about. My answer was Dogs. Yes, I felt I was an expert on dogs. Many of the women were students going to school, an amazing group. Bunnies weren't just pieces of flesh, but interesting women, able to talk to people.

"We also participated in athletic charity events. On one occasion, the Denver Playboy Bunnies played the United Airlines Clipped Wings, a group of retired stewardesses, in a game of broom hockey. Like most of the Bunnies on our team, I couldn't ice skate, but was willing to give it a try. The Clipped Wings had been practicing for months. During the game, there were Bunnies scattered everywhere falling on the ice. We were at such a disadvantage, even given a handicap of two goalies, that we lost 6—0.

"I made the most money playing billiards as a Pool Bunny, earning 40 cents an hour salary and a dollar a game, with the first $17 going to the Club. If you play a hundred games a night at the same table night after night, you get pretty hard to beat. Then you make some crazy triple bank shot and everyone wants to play you because they think you couldn't possibly do it again. I was able to save a fair amount of money."

Curiously, it was Polly's waitressing work that led her, at the age of 26, into a career in science. "I got to listen to a lot of great conversations. Two professors would come in and talk science. One day they were talking about animal mimicry—how one butterfly will mimic another butterfly and how a

Polly as one of the "Easter Bunnies" delivering baskets to Vietnam veterans at Fitzsimmons Hospital.

good-tasting butterfly will mimic a bad-tasting butterfly to avoid being eaten by birds." Polly, who had studied biology, asked them a question she'd wondered about for years. "Why has no animal ever mimicked a skunk? A raccoon with a stripe down its back would have a selective advantage. Their mouths fell open—a cocktail waitress asking this sort of question? They didn't know how to answer it.

"One of the scientists launched a personal campaign to persuade me to go to university and take up science. This man convinced me that science was actually something I could do. Otherwise, I could have worked as a cocktail waitress forever because it was a job that never got boring." After 11 years spent earning a college degree, Polly enrolled at the University of California at San Diego and got a government fellowship for graduate

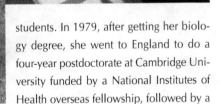

Polly's day begins at 5 a.m. at her Maryland farmland home near the National Institutes of Health. She also volunteers many hours at local hospitals with her Border collie Annie, an officially licensed "therapy dog." Weekends are often spent at sheepdog trials.

students. In 1979, after getting her biology degree, she went to England to do a four-year postdoctorate at Cambridge University funded by a National Institutes of Health overseas fellowship, followed by a six-year fellowship at Hoffman-LaRoche in Basle, Switzerland. By 1989, she was ready to take up residence at NIH.

There, with a colleague, she began to develop her theory, ultimately called "The Danger Model," described by the *London Telegraph* as "potentially the most far-reaching development in immunology this century." She and her colleagues had become convinced that a really effective immune system would only attack things it perceived to be dangerous. But they didn't know how the system figured out what was dangerous.

Months later, "I was in the bath and . . . all of a sudden—there it was! I jumped out of the bath totally naked, dripping water all over the house, unable to sit still." Her breakthrough realization? "The way the immune system could discriminate between things that are dangerous and things that aren't is that things that are dangerous do damage. It sounds so simple and it had taken so long."

If proved correct, her theories, grossly oversimplified here, have important implications for the treatment of cancers and transplants. Even now, several scientists and doctors are putting her findings into practice with promising results.

"One of the things I didn't know when I went into research is that you have to be willing to live a life that's 90 percent depression and 10 percent elation because 90 percent of what you do fails. Part of the reason for that is that we're working on the edge. We fail again and again, but every so often, one of those failures gives us a glimmer of how to try something a different way. That bit of elation keeps you going.

"If I'm right, we'll have a new treatment for cancer. I hope I am right, because after all the billions of dollars spent on cancer research, we still treat cancer the same way we did 20 years ago—radiation, chemotherapy and surgery."

Still, the remarkable Bunny-turned-breakthrough-scientist has her critics, partially as a result of her readiness to talk to the press. "People are afraid of what they don't know. As a scientist, I feel we're shooting ourselves in the foot if we don't go out and talk about these things." However, when the BBC was preparing a documentary on her, she almost backed out upon finding they were so interested in her Bunny past.

"I don't mind that—it's part of my life and I'm completely open. I was worried at first because it wasn't clear whether they were going to use the oddities of my personality to illustrate science, or use the science as an excuse to talk about this odd person. At 50 I'm still seen as the young ex-Bunny. How old do I have to get?"

A last bit of confirmation for the former Bunny and high school dropout voted Least Likely to Succeed: a British journal recently got in touch with her for an article on "The Most Influential Women in the World." ∎

Celebrity Bunnies

Hugh Hefner, a *Saturday Night Live* host in 1977, with
"Bunnies" Gilda Radner, Jane Curtin and Laraine Newman.

*A*mong the many actors and celebrities who have dressed up
as Playboy Bunnies over the years: Steve Allen, Kirstie
Alley, Chastity Bono, Johnny Carson, Carol Channing,
Cher, Jane Curtin, Bill Dana, Phyllis Diller, Farrah Fawcett, Sally
Field, Carrie Fisher, Bob Hope, Penny Marshall, Tatum O'Neal,
Laraine Newman, Dolly Parton, Gilda Radner, the Smothers
Brothers, Nancy Walker and Flip Wilson. In 1963, Barbara Walters
donned the Bunny costume and worked in the New York Playboy
Club to report on her experiences. Appearing in Bunny ears on the
Today show, she commented to Hugh Downs, "secretly I was kind
of pleased."

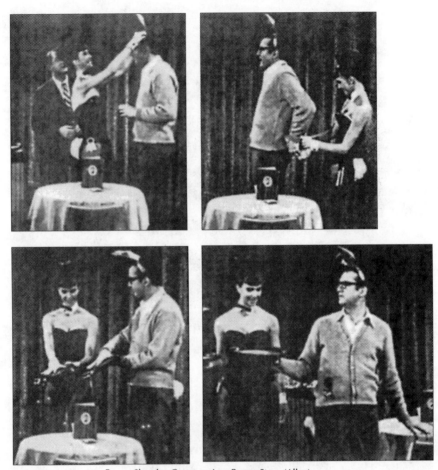

Bunny Sheralee Conners gives Bunny Steve (Allen)
instructions in the Bunny Dip, 1961.

Below: "Bunny" Nancy Walker with Durward Kirby and Garry Moore on the *Garry Moore Show*, 1963.

Above: Bing Crosby and "Bunny Geraldine" (Flip Wilson).

"Bunny" Johnny (Carson) celebrating his first anniversary as host of the *Tonight Show*, 1963.

217

Right: Sonny and Cher and their daughter Chastity Bono, 1965.

Left: Kirstie Alley as "Bunny Marie" (Gloria Steinem) in *A Bunny's Tale* (ABC-TV, 1984).

Barbara Walters and Hugh Downs on the *Today* show, 1963.

Above: Hugh Hefner with Betty White and "Bunnies" Carrie Fisher and Penny Marshall on *Laverne & Shirley*, 1982.

Right: Academy Award-winning actress Sally Field posed in the Bunny costume for the March 1986 cover of *Playboy*, which celebrated the 25th anniversary of the Playboy Bunny.

Los Angeles

Los Angeles

BUNNIES ON THE SUNSET STRIP

Joyce Nizzari conducting Bunny auditions for the
Los Angeles Club, November 1964.

he Los Angeles Playboy Club—the 11th in the nationwide chain that claimed more than 300,000 Keyholders—opened New Year's Eve 1964, in the heart of the Sunset Strip. At the celebrity-packed, black-tie charity benefit, guests Tony Bennett and Count Basie joined the bandstand in the Penthouse just for fun, while Jack Jones and Sammy Cahn were introduced to the audience in the Playroom. Just before midnight, as party favors were handed out to the guests, the Bunnies were asked to leave the floor as a safety precaution—and returned to work moments after the boisterous revelry that brought in the New Year. Within a month, more than 40,000 Keyholders and their guests visited the new Club.

Patti Murphy

O ver a thousand women applied for Bunny jobs at the new Los Angeles Club in November 1964. The newspaper ad had said auditions would be held in the evenings from 6 to 8, but the interviews went on until 2 a.m. I had left my children with a baby-sitter, and when I saw the mob of applicants standing in line, I knew I was in trouble. I called the baby-sitter and she said, 'Oh, don't worry, your daughters can spend the night with me.'

"I was working in a savings and loan as a secretary and when I heard about the Playboy Club opening in Los Angeles, I thought, What do I have to lose? I was separated from my husband and living in California with my two little girls, working hard to make ends meet.

"Keith Hefner and three Bunnies from other Clubs were handling the interviews. I filled out a long application, had a Polaroid picture taken and was given a number. While I stood in the hallway waiting, a man came up to me asked what number I had. I said, '139.' He said, 'Fine. You've got time to have dinner with me.' It was getting late and I was starving, so I went with him to a coffee shop across the street for a sandwich. After a while, he made phone call and said, 'Well, your number is coming up, so I'd better get you back.' He was tall, dressed in black, and I never saw him again. By the time my number was called, it was 11 p.m.

"The interview was like a scene from *A Chorus Line*. I stood against the wall in a group of 10 girls, all of us dressed in street clothes. Three of us in my group were sent to a dressing room to put on our leotards or bathing suits, and the rest were sent home. After we changed, we paraded through the room, and a few of us were discreetly asked to stay behind for an interview with Keith. Within two weeks, I was training to be a Bunny.

"Shortly before the Club opened on Sunset Boulevard, my husband arrived from Chicago hoping to mend the problems in our marriage. I decided to move back with him and asked for a transfer to the Chicago Club. Of course, I told nobody that I was married with children. The Bunny image of a beautiful, desirable, 'available' young woman didn't fit with the idea of a housewife raising two kids. I lived in two different worlds, coming home from this glamorous job in a nightclub to face the dishes in the sink at home. My marriage lasted another 15 years, but it was always difficult.

"After I had worked at Playboy about six months, I was caught in one of their 'house-cleanings' and fired along with a quite a number of other women. We were told we no longer projected the Bunny Image. I was 21 years old. At the time, I was devastated that they let me go. I was earning such good money. The job didn't interfere with my home life, and it was exciting, glamorous and fulfilling. I went through a very bad time after-ward. Normal, everyday life without that job was a miserable existence. I loved being a Bunny. It had been an escape, a release, for me.

"It took me a while to get my life back together. I became a model for three years, some-times working as a spokesperson at trade shows. That was just as tough to do while raising children. If I had to leave early for a location or fly off to New York for a job, I always seemed to be cooking at night and leaving instructions about food in the freezer. After a time, I came to realize how much strength and initiative being a Playboy Bunny had given me. Nothing is forever, and there's a time when you have to move on. One can't be a mod-el forever, either.

"I found a job, starting at the bottom, with a film production com-pany that made television commer-cials. I worked my way up and after 10 years, left for a job with a record-ing studio. I then worked with a film editor on feature films.

"A few years ago, mutual friends introduced me to a musician. After we started dating, we discovered we had been working at Playboy at the same time. He had been their mus-ical director for years and wanted to organize a reunion in Chicago. I

Travel agent, Patti Murphy.

helped him pull the event together in October 1995. One of the Bunnies I'd lost touch with and hoped to see was Terri Kimball, who was a Bunny of the Year and a Playmate. When she and I dressed for work in the morning, we'd take turns changing in the ladies' room, both of us too shy to take our clothes off in the dressing room!" ■

Los Angeles Club
1965

Front Row, Left to Right
Audrey Boutee
Pat Molitor
Sharon Moorman
Marianna Case
Judy Hopkins
Robbin Stein
Joan Nemer

Second Row
Nancy Viller
Kathryn Harrow
Vicki Valentino
   (September 1963
   Playmate)
Cindy Ogus
Bi Egnell
Lori Fontaine
Alfreda Masters
Nikki Dau (behind
   Alfreda)
Lois Kramer
Gwen Lipscomb
Tina Gamwell
Gayle Spencer
Anna Marie Mills
Susie Scott

Third Row
Susan Stevenson
Arlene Cody
Arlyne Venditto
Joan Daniels
Bobbi Benson
Julie Zweig
   (in Bunny costume)
Teddy Parks
Rita Perez
Jackie Frevert
Heidi Becker (June 1961
   Playmate)

Elisabetha Kinkel
Tonia Van Deters

Fourth Row
Denise Frank
Barbro Graflind
Judy Carleton
Sherrie Kuzin
Doris Karloff
   (in Bunny costume)
Sharon Rogers
   (January 1964 Playmate
   in Bunny costume)
Donna Lesh
   (in Bunny costume)
Terry Kaufman
Mitzi Scott
Sunny Nelson
Linda Feller
Barbara Wait
Nancy Muller
Patti Murphy

Top Row
Ann Knippel
Dianne Fontell
Linda Kelly (face hidden)
Kay Sampson
Pat Rose (partially hidden)
Jeri Devereaux
Carla Sigerseth
Carol Coggin
Irene Drake
Susan Wright
Eva Spangberg
   (partially hidden)
Danielle Eden
   (partially hidden)
Marianne Stiteler

MARIA ROACH

I think I was the only Bunny in the Los Angeles Club who lived at home with her parents," says Maria Roach, daughter of legendary motion-picture pioneer Hal Roach. The elder Roach, renowned creator of the *Our Gang* series and producer of Laurel and Hardy films, among many early comedy classics, lived to the age of 101. "My father spent a lifetime espousing clean, decent family entertainment in movies and television. My parents were strict, but neither had a problem with me working as a Bunny. In fact, it was my mother who suggested I apply for a job at Playboy.

"In 1968 I was 21 years old, a full-time student in UCLA's film school and working part-time as a dental assistant, making very little money. A friend took a job as a cocktail waitress at a Hollywood strip club called the Pink Pussycat, and I was going to apply for a job there myself. My mother saw an ad for Bunnies in the newspapers, and said, 'Why not try Playboy first—you'll be better protected and make more money.'

"I was shocked that I was hired, especially after Maude, the wardrobe woman, gave me a Bunny costume belonging to Playmate Gwen Wong Wayne to try on. I'm tall, Gwen is petite—and I had nowhere near her voluptuous figure.

"I would have to describe myself at that time as a serious person—reserved, studious, motivated and responsible. Someone who'd had 'etiquette' lessons, wore a rosary around her neck and attended Marymount, a Catholic all-girls high school in West Los Angeles. There are certain life experiences that make you who you are: Growing up as the daughter of Hal Roach with my two sisters, living next door to Mia Farrow's family in Beverly Hills and attending Marymount were all life-defining experiences.

"So, too, was working as a Bunny. In its most positive sense, it fed a part of me that had never been nourished before. I developed confidence, poise and learned how to talk to people. In high school I always knew I had a brain, but I never knew I was attractive. My mother did a good job trying to negate that aspect of my personality, so being accepted by the Playboy Club gave me a new level of self-esteem. The whole experience surprised me; it was so different, so exciting and so unlike me. I bought a red wig, then a short curly one, and had a ball role playing. I could be anyone I wanted to be. My life revolved around classes at UCLA during the day and working as a Bunny at night. I kept my school books in the gift shop so I could study when it was quiet at the Club. I turned down an opportunity to be a Jet Bunny because it would have interfered with classes.

Maria Roach and Astronaut Scott Carpenter
on their wedding day, 1970.

"I imagine feminists may find this convoluted, but being a Bunny empowered me. I tapped into a new awareness of myself. I felt a certain amount of power as a woman that I was never in touch with before. Say what you will, I've always thought Hugh Hefner was a feminist, and way ahead of his time. He genuinely cared about women and gave them career opportunities within the Playboy corporation. Sexual harassment was an issue for him long before feminists or the media were focusing on it. No one could touch the Bunnies; if a guy hit on you, all you had to say was, 'I'm very sorry, we are not allowed to socialize with customers.' The management always backed you up, and as a result we all developed 'attitudes.' If a customer was in the least snippy toward me, I'd think, 'Why are you doing this? I have your evening in my hands.' Another result of those years is that I am a serious over-tipper.

"I left Playboy in 1970 when I graduated from UCLA. I was offered an opportunity to go into a management training program with Playboy in Chicago, but opted to take a job as a film production assistant. I then met Scott Carpenter, the astronaut, when he was the host and narrator of a TV pilot I was working on. My father, who had great expectations for me, once said, 'I hope you are not going to ruin your life by marrying and having kids.' But once I married Scott and made a commitment to my family, I temporarily gave up my career aspirations until our two children were in school. With both children now in college, I feel a sense of renewal and vibrancy about forging a new career.

Maria Roach at home in Los Angeles.

"I still sometimes have dreams that I'm working at the Sunset Boulevard Playboy Club—I can't find my tray and my feet hurt—and it's kind of fun to look back on it now. Of all the things I've done in my life, I don't think anything would have turned out as it has without my experience working as a Bunny. It's an experience I treasure." ∎

Julie Cobb

Actress and stage director Julie Cobb.

A t the time I got the job, I was unso-phisticated, insecure and very mod-est. When I left the Los Angeles Playboy Club less than a year later, being a Bunny seemed to me like a character role I had played in a five-month run. It was a perfor-mance and I wore a great costume. And getting that gig did a lot for my self-esteem.

"My parents, actors Lee J. Cobb, and Helen Beverly, divorced. I grew up with my glamorous mother as my role model. I don't think I really had any idea how I looked. I just didn't know myself then.

"Getting the job was good for my ego for five minutes. That little question that I had about myself being an attractive, fem-inine, sexually alluring woman was satisfied.

"However, I worried there would be some stigma attached because, finally, it's a cocktail waitress job. But everybody sort of took it in stride. I remember telling my father, and his concerns seemed to be about me working nights and coming home late. I was living with my boyfriend at the time, and he was supportive, too. Actually, he was more than fine about it because he could say his girlfriend was a Playboy Bunny, and they gave us a copy of the magazine to take home every month.

"The fact is, so many cocktail waitresses back then wore something skimpy, even skimpier than the Bunny costume, but this was the Playboy Club as associated with *Playboy* magazine. That notoriety made all the difference.

"I went through all the training, but I really only served drinks two or three times. I couldn't take it. I had never been around people who drank, and I had no experience as a waitress. I found it very hard work and became so flustered that I spilled things. The

Bunny Mother assigned me to the gift shop, and I also worked as a Door Bunny. I didn't make as much money, but I was able to handle it.

"I was on the TV show *Playboy After Dark* a couple of times as part of the background. I did a *Playboy* photo session, but not nude. I was approached about doing test shots to be a Playmate, but I could not do it. I never even considered whether it would damage or enhance my acting career. I just couldn't get past the personal hurdle of posing nude.

"I was also asked if I wanted to be a stewardess on Hefner's airplane. I didn't want to do that either. The truth is, I wasn't really mature enough to hold down a job for any length of time. The Bunny Mother was sweet, but very firm with me when I would miss work or phone in sick. I quit when I started getting television work as an actress.

"In retrospect, I realize working as a Playboy Bunny represented an important transition for me. I'd quit college, gained weight and had little self-esteem. Working as a Bunny forced me to confront personal issues, physically and emotionally. I kept my costume when I left, but I don't know where it is today. I wish I did. Mine was green satin. It would be fun to look at it again and show my teenage daughter. I wonder what she'd think.

"Today, the Playboy Club is a complete anachronism. Men and women wear white shirts, pants and long aprons to serve drinks and food. Everyone is so very conscious of what is acceptable that I can't even imagine a world in which my daughter would be a Bunny. But looking back, the innocent playfulness and flirtation of being a Bunny conjures up a time for me when there wasn't so much political strife between the sexes. There was glamour and a touch of naughtiness, and it was fun to be on the receiving end of admiring glances."

Julie is the wife of James Cromwell, a 1996 best-supporting actor Oscar nominee for his role as Farmer Hoggett in *Babe*. Julie won a 1994 Dramalogue Award in Los Angeles for her direction of *Twelve Angry Men*, the stage version of the 1957 film that starred her father, Lee J. Cobb. She also contributes a column, "The Path," for *Country Connections* magazine. ∎

BONNIE MAZRIA KATZ

Years after I left Playboy, I joined a UCLA extension class called Women's Voices and wrote 'I Was a Kosher Bunny,' a one-woman piece in which I did the Bunny Dip while serving Snapple to my kids. In 1994, I performed the piece on a cable television program. I chose to write about being a Bunny because it's part of my life's story as a woman—and it was a wonderful experience.

"In 1972, I was studying the-atre at Los Angeles City College when I decided to join friends at-tending San Francisco's American Conservatory Theatre. I packed up my little VW, drove to San Fran-cisco and moved in with my brother. I needed a job working nights, and a girlfriend who was working in the Manhattan Play-boy Club suggested that I get a job as a Bunny.

"It took a stretch of the imag-ination to believe that someone my brothers had called 'a surf-board' would fit the Playboy image. I was tall and so skinny that in high school, I used to eat something called 'Weight-On' to build myself up. I was shocked when the general manager of the San Francisco Playboy Club called to tell me I was hired.

"I was born in Brooklyn, the youngest child in a traditional Jewish family; college, marriage and raising a family were the

Bonnie Katz is completing her B.A. degree. She plans to earn a master's in psychology and practice marriage, family and child counseling. She recently produced the play, *Daughters*, at the Hudson Theatre in Hollywood.

Things to Do. Becoming a Playboy Bunny was not. Although I knew the men in my fam-ily would not approve, I was surprised by my mother's rage. When I called to tell her about the job she was so upset she called me a slut. We didn't talk for weeks. My father and older brother eventually learned where I was working, but they never discussed it with me. Even my sister, who is 10 years older than me, disapproved.

"After two years in San Francisco, I transferred to the new Los Angeles Club in Century City, where I worked as a Bumper Pool Bunny. I got all the shots down from playing every night and, after a while, I could beat any man at pool. On Sunday nights, Bunnies were invited to the Playboy Mansion for dinner and a movie with Hef. I loved throwing on blue jeans and driving up to the gates of the Mansion in my red VW. My name would be on a list, along with those of celebrities and other Bunnies, and I felt like part of the family. The buffet was always wonderful, and it was great fun having butlers serving you chocolate-chip cookies. I made so many close friends among the Bunnies.

"It was also at this time that my life took a spiritual turn toward my Jewish heritage. I became kosher and began studying Hebrew. One of the Club's chefs, a German named Hans, made me special dishes.

"I was saving money to go to Israel and Greece with my sister when one of my Bunny friends introduced me to a man at a Beverly Hills disco, the Candy Store. I had noticed this man on several occasions, but we hadn't met. The night my friend brought him to our table to meet me, I discovered he was an Israeli. He offered to teach me Hebrew. We dated for about two months and I fell in love. Shortly before I was to leave for Israel, I told him jokingly that we should get married. On an impulse, he called an airline and booked tickets to Las Vegas. It was a very nontraditional ceremony! I called the Playboy Club to tell the Bunny Mother I was getting married and wouldn't be coming in to work that night. Afterward, we told our mothers and they set about planning a second wedding, a traditional Jewish one. For 20 years, we've celebrated the two anniversaries.

"Certainly one thing Playboy taught me was not to judge people quickly. There was such a myth about girls who worked as Bunnies I would never tell a man I was dating that I worked at the Club. I didn't like the preconceived ideas people had. In social situations even after I was married, people who discovered that I worked at Playboy began to treat me differently. Conversations would stop because everyone was curious to know what it was like to work as a Bunny. Women felt threatened. Men thought you were easy. In either case, I felt there was a stigma.

"When my older daughter was about 14 and learned that I had been a Bunny, she was appalled. 'Mom, I can't believe you did that!' she said, with visions of *Playboy* magazine in her head and no knowledge of what the experience of being a Bunny was actually like. I explained that while I was a Bunny in the 1970s, I also identified myself as a feminist and supported the causes of the Women's Movement. My sense of integrity and moral values certainly didn't go down the drain when I put on a sexy little costume to work as a Bunny. Now that my daughter is 21 and a film major at NYU, she has a different perspective and put her earlier remarks down to youthful prejudice.

"One day I worked in the VIP Room at a private party for Hadassah, a Jewish women's organization. That was a unique situation for me because those women got such a kick out of having a Jewish Bunny serving them—and none of them gave me a hard time. They just couldn't get over the fact that there were Jewish Bunnies." ∎

The Big Bunny

UP, UP AND AWAY , , ,

Hef with the Jet Bunnies, 1970.

The original Jet Bunnies selected from various Playboy Clubs to be flight attendants aboard the "Big Bunny" were trained in Los Angeles by Continental Airlines hostess supervisor Darlene Fuentes (who also trained stewards for Air Force One, the Presidential jet), with a postgraduate course from Purdue Airlines (the certified carrier operating the DC9-30) in Lafayette, Indiana. Tonia Shipley, from the Kansas City Club, headed the Chicago crew, and Avis Miller, from the Phoenix Club and a 1970 Playmate, headed the Los Angeles-based crew. Among the other original crew members were Britt Elders, Kathy Jovanovic, Shawn Ferguson, Rosemary Melendez and Marsha Morris.

Britt Elders

Former Atlanta Bunny Britt Elders, who moved to Chicago when she was selected to be one of the original Jet Bunnies, says, "I will always think of Hef on board the DC-9 with a Pepsi in one hand and Monopoly dice in the other hand.

"On one of our trips to Europe, Hef wanted apple pie, and I had to carefully explain to the European catering staff how to make an American-style apple pie. While his guests dined on chateaubriand and lobster with fine wines, Hef preferred simpler fare. He liked my meat loaf and fried chicken, with canned Green Giant-brand baby peas, so much that he asked me to send my recipes to the chef at the Playboy Mansion.

"Hef was always extraordinarily thoughtful toward the flight crew. After we flew Hef and his guests to a skiing holiday in Colorado, the Jet Bunnies stayed behind to finish chores aboard the aircraft, while several limousines ferried his party to the slopes. It came as a complete surprise to us when, a half-hour later, another limousine pulled up to the Big Bunny and we discovered Hef had arranged for us to ski in Aspen."

Britt Elders now owns J & B Acres, Hunters & Jumpers, an equestrian school in suburban Chicago. ∎

Equestrian trainer and dog breeder Britt Elders at J & B Acres with two of her Doberman pinschers.

Hef's Meatloaf

2 pounds ground sirloin

1 envelope McCormick meat loaf seasoning

1 cup crumbled saltines

Mush together. Form loaf in pan.

Bake 1 hour at 325°.

Serve with Green Giant baby Le Seur peas,

mashed potatoes and gravy made with Campbell's

tomato soup and meat juices.

Hef's Fried Chicken

Combine in an air-sickness bag:

1 handful of flour

Lawry's seasoning salt

Dash garlic powder

Dash dried parsley

Shake chicken pieces in bag

with flour mixture.

Fry in electric skillet until done.

Hef's Grilled Cheese Sandwich

2 slices white bread, buttered on

both sides.

3 slices American cheese

Grill in electric skillet until

golden brown.

Jet Bunnies Britt Elders, Tonia Shipley, Kathy Jovanovic
and Shawn Ferguson boarding the Big Bunny, 1970.

KATHARINA JOVANOVIC LEVENTHAL

"W alter Holmes, who designed the marvelous Jet Bunny uniforms, designed my wedding gown," says Kathy Leventhal, now vice president of Chicago's Ronsley Events, which she and husband Michael run.

"I felt so privileged to be one of ten chosen out of nearly a thousand Bunnies to work as a Jet Bunny. It was like a paid vacation. The three-week tour of Europe and Africa with Barbi and 15 of Hef's closest friends aboard the Big Bunny was the first time all of the Jet Bunnies traveled together internationally. But whatever was planned throughout the trip—visiting the Serengeti Plain in East Africa, a camel party on the beach in Morocco, cruising on a yacht in Greece, a tram ride in Munich to the

top of the Zugspitz, sightseeing in Rome and London—the Jet Bunnies were treated as members of the entourage. Wherever we landed, the press was there to greet us with flashbulbs popping."

Kathy, who worked as a Bunny for 10 years, says, "My former life meshed very well with my life to-day, where I still work *behind* the scenes to help create memorable occasions. When Princess Diana visited Chicago, our firm handled the events, including a gala for 1,600 people. But my husband Michael and I also *attend* these gala events and are a part of the social fabric of our city." ■

Jet Bunnies Britt Elders,
Kathy Jovanovic and Tonia Shipley
(back to front) in black and white
nylon ciré costumes designed
by Walter Holmes.

238

Top left: The Living Room
area of the Big Bunny.

Bottom left: Hefner's private
quarters with the famous
elliptical bed upholstered in
black Himalayan goat leather
and covered with a spread of
Tasmanian opossum pelts.

Below right: Hefner talking
with Jet Bunnies on a flight
from Chicago to California.

Big Bunny Baby Lift

*T*he Baby Lift began in April 1975 with a telephone call from Yul Brynner to Hugh Hefner on behalf of the Friends of Children and a planeload of Vietnamese orphans," former San Francisco Bunny Mother Frankie Helms recalls. The 41 infants, some of them survivors of an ill-fated earlier flight that had crashed, were destined for adoption by American and European families. An airplane was needed to transport the babies from San Francisco to New York's LaGuardia Airport, with stops in Denver and Chicago.

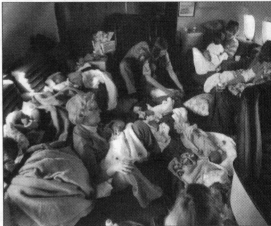

The Brynners, who were adopting one of the babies airlifted through the concerted efforts of the Catholic Relief Services and the Friends of Children, "asked Hef to make the Big Bunny available for the Baby Lift—and, of course, he did," Frankie recalls. "I got a call at home close to midnight asking me to be at the airport to help out—there were only 11 of us on board, each with four babies to tend. I would just finish changing one, and it would be time to do the next. Several of the infants were ill from the rich baby formula they weren't used to, and a few were badly scarred from burns they'd suffered from the plane crash. One of my little charges could only be comforted if I held him and let him put his hand in my mouth. He was so frightened. By the time we reached New York and the waiting arms, I could barely let him go."

Baby lift, 1975. Janice Raymond (standing, Jet Bunny/Playmate, December 1974) and Bunny Mother, Frankie Helms (center, holding a baby) tend Vietnamese orphans aboard the Big Bunny.

Francesca Helms, known as Frankie, was one of the most beloved of all the Bunny Mothers, and the self-described adviser, zipper-upper, confidante and friend to a generation of Bunnies, beginning with the opening of the St. Louis Club in 1962. During her 15-year career with Playboy, Frankie was also Bunny Mother in the Phoenix, Miami, Jamaica, Atlanta and San Francisco clubs. Today she is a concierge at the Luxor hotel in Las Vegas.

GWEN WONG WAYNE

During my 10-year Playboy odyssey, I was a Bunny, a Playmate and a Jet Bunny on the DC-9 Big Bunny. During this period I also managed to graduate from college with a degree in art.

"My aunt, Sienna Wong, had been a Bunny in Miami and New York and she encouraged me to apply for a job at the new Playboy Club opening in Los Angeles January 1, 1965. I was 22, married and had two children, my first born in Ohio when I was 17.

"I don't drink and it took me a while to remember not to put a cherry in a martini or an olive in a Manhattan. Obviously I figured it out because I was later asked to become a Training Bunny. Doing promotions on behalf of Playboy over the years helped me deal with my self-consciousness. As a Playmate and a Jet Bunny I frequently did press interviews and made personal appearances around the country.

"When I first became a Bunny, I was asked if I wanted to be a Playmate and I declined. Several years later when my marriage was ending, I changed my mind. I wanted money in the bank in case I needed it for my children. Mario Casilli took my centerfold photographs. It was a terrible ordeal for poor Mario because I was so shy. He'd say, 'Here, Gwen, have a glass of wine,' thinking that maybe then I would take my blouse off! Even without the drink I somehow worked up the nerve and appeared in the April 1967 issue of Playboy.

"I look back now on that time during the Vietnam war when I used to get thousands of letters from soldiers on the front lines and send a note with a picture to as many of them as I could. After all, it was 1967 and my centerfold in *Playboy* made me a wartime pinup girl. I'm glad I saved so many of their letters because they are even more touching to read all these years later. I didn't realize at the time how much of their true emotion about the war and going into combat they expressed in their letters to me. Those soldiers were so young and if they needed a 'sweetheart' to pour out their feelings to, I'm glad it was sometimes me.

"I never felt demeaned or diminished because I was a Bunny or a Playmate. It was my choice. Today, so many people talk about being a victim and look for someone to blame, not taking responsibility for their own lives. When I did promotions, I knew I was representing myself as well as other women who were Bunnies and Playmates, so I always tried to convey that I had an intellect, that my personal life didn't revolve exclusively around Playboy.

Gwen Wong Wayne in her art studio with one of her original body sculptures.

"Soon after I did the centerfold, Hef bought the stretch DC-9 and I was asked to become one of the Jet Bunnies. It was a great experience. In the beginning we mostly flew the Los Angeles-Chicago route, with a few visits to Jamaica. Then I heard about the three-month tour of Europe and Africa that Hef was planning and I really wanted to go. It was probably the longest time Hef had been away from his home base at one time. Six Jet Bunnies, three each from Chicago and Los Angeles, were assigned—and I was one of them.

"We had FAA training in Miami through Continental Airlines. The Big Bunny would not have been allowed to leave the airfield if we hadn't been fully qualified flight attendants. Hef couldn't swim and he used to joke, 'Whichever one of you saves me will be taken care of for life!'

"We did all of the work stewardesses normally do and we also prepared gourmet meals. Chateaubriand, roast duckling, lobster, peanut butter-and-jelly sandwiches—whatever anyone on board wanted, we would provide. There were always lots of Twinkies and Pepsi on board for Hef, and our 'house' wine was a Lafitte Rothschild Bordeaux. Deep-frying chicken for Hef was scary and I prayed we wouldn't hit an air pocket. The head stewardess, Avis Miller, who was also a former Playmate, and Hef's valet, Jodie, were always on board to see that things were done properly.

"We were well-paid and, of course, limousines were always waiting for us upon arrival—along with the local photographers and press. The Jet Bunnies did a great deal of promotional work wherever they went.

"The Bunny Mother notified us of flights. Between them I worked as a Bunny in the Club. I was also doing Playmate promotions around the country and attending college. I knew I wouldn't be a Bunny forever and that I needed to prepare myself for a career.

"It was a hectic life. I would work nights at the Club, come home and get to bed by 2:30 a.m., rise four hours later and make it to class by 7:20—wondering if I'd ever make it through day after day. By taking courses year-round, I completed the four-year program in three years. As soon as I graduated in 1975 I left Playboy and went to work in an architectural firm as an interior designer. I sat at a drawing board all day working nine-to-five on my first job. I was then in my early 30s. The change in my lifestyle was literally from night to day.

"In 1977, I became an apprentice in set design at CBS for a year and then left to open my own design firm. I was wild about food and took culinary courses with all the fine chefs, eventually becoming an assistant pastry chef at Trump's. On my first day, I told Chef Michael Roberts that I was willing to do anything. He took me at my word and I was put to work removing the stems from forty boxes of strawberries. I loved it.

"These days I'm married, the mother of two grown children—and a grandmother. I work as an artist doing body casting and sculptural portraiture in my Los Angeles-based studio. I think of myself as a 'plaster surgeon.' When I first conceived the idea, I got in touch with the curator of the Hollywood Wax Museum to show me the fundamentals and then I experimented. Over the years, I've gained knowledge from many people who have shared their techniques. I do both traditional bronzes and contemporary faux bronzes that I paint." ∎

London

London

BUNNIES FOR BRITAIN

Queen Elizabeth II meets Bunny
Louise Palmer at Ascot, 1966.

O n Saturday, June 25, 1966, 32 Bunnies greeted Hugh Hefner's arrival aboard the Big Bunny at London's Heathrow Airport for the opening later that week of the first European Playboy Club. "Swinging London," the apt term coined by *Time* magazine that captured the essence of the trendy English youth culture, was in full swing.

The London Club, 18th in the chain, occupied a new seven-story Walter Gropius-designed building in Park Lane overlooking Hyde Park. Located between the Dorchester and Hilton Hotels, Playboy had all the familiar rooms (Penthouse, Playroom, VIP

Room, Playmate Bar, Living Room and Cartoon Corner) but also sported a discotheque and, more importantly, casinos with 27 gaming tables (roulette, blackjack and punto banco) throughout the Club. The Bunny Croupier had entered the Playboy lexicon.

Following a now well-established pattern, when Playboy applied for a liquor license, the guardians of public morality voiced objections to the scantily clad waitresses—and this in a town awash with leggy young women wearing micro-minis. (With the later passage of the new Gaming Law in 1970, the Gaming Board required Bunny Croupiers to wear "modesty bibs" to conform to the requirement that casinos not offer any "inducement to gamble.")

Fifteen hundred guests attended the black-tie charity opening of the London Playboy Club on June 28, including Ringo Starr, Rex Harrison, Ursula Andress and *Time* magazine's Henry Luce III. Twenty-thousand Keyholders had paid a pre-opening membership fee of £5 for the privilege of visiting the Club any time of their choosing 24 hours a day, seven days a week.

Six British Bunnies, personally selected by Victor Lownes and Tony Roma, were sent to Chicago for training. Their airline bags proclaimed "Bunnies From Britain." The first Bunny from Britain was Dolly Read.

Dolly Read Martin

In 1963 I'd come to London from Bristol, England, to find work as an actress. I was 17. What I found were the beginnings of what became known around the world as 'Swinging London.' I dated pop singer Adam Faith and did a Hammer movie, *Kiss of the Vampire*. I was on-screen for five minutes and got eaten by bats.

"In 1965, Playboy was looking for six British Bunnies to train in America for six months before returning to open the London Club. My friend Valerie and I had been sent by my acting agent to audition for Victor Lownes. He decided I was too plump. He said, 'You're my idea of a Bunny, but not Hugh Hefner's.' But he liked me because I had a funny take on life and made him laugh.

"At the time, I was staying with Valerie in her London flat. Victor called her for a Saturday night date. She had plans, but I didn't, so he invited me to a lavish dinner at the Dorchester Hotel hosted by the Crown Prince of Saudi Arabia. During dinner, Victor told me he was leaving for Chicago the following Monday and asked if I would like to join him. It was my dream to visit America, and I said Yes! I knew only the 'movie' America—gangsters and cowboys—and I longed to go. But I had no visa, only my British passport. Victor told me to be at his flat Monday morning, packed and ready to leave, and he would take care of everything.

"I showed up on his doorstep with a suit-case at 9 a.m. Victor was in bed dictating letters to his secretary. My immediate thought was that he'd only been bluffing, but off we went to the American Embassy, where Victor claimed I was his fiancée and he wanted to take me to America to meet his son.

"We left London that day.

"I was just shy of my 20th birthday when I arrived in Chicago to stay at the Playboy Mansion. Victor and I stayed in the Blue Room. It was all quite amazing for a middle-class English girl from Bristol. The parties, celebrities and the Sunday night movies—I had never been in anyone's home where first-run movies were screened. Hugh Hefner would appear

Dolly Read Martin at home in Los Angeles.

with his pipe and a beautiful, slender blonde he was dating. His girlfriend took me on a tour of his Mansion, showing me the motorized circular bed that went 'round and 'round.

"Within the week, I discovered Victor was cheating on me, sneaking down to the swimming pool with another girl in the middle of the night. But he was so charming, he could get away with anything. When I accompanied Victor to the opening of the Boston Club, we flew up from New York in a small chartered craft. It was snowing heavily. By the time we reached Boston we were in a fierce storm. The airport was closed. When Victor heard that we had been refused landing permission, he demanded that the pilot tell air traffic control that we were running out of fuel. We were allowed to land, and made it to the Boston Club in time for the opening.

"One salutary aspect of the trip is that Victor learned I was Hefner's idea of a Bunny, after all. I became the first of the six British Bunnies hired. Within months Hefner had also selected me to be the May 1966 Playmate.

"The six British Bunnies stayed at the Mansion in the Bunny Dorm. We took train-ing and rotated a month each working as Door Bunny, Camera Bunny and Cocktail

Bunny in the various Showrooms. I never dreamed how hard the work would be. We were young, eager girls who were soon worn out by the pressure and sheer long hours. Publicity and promotional work took up our days, and we worked as Bunnies at night. It was exhausting. Much of the glamour faded for me when I became run-down and ill toward the end of my stint in the Chicago Club.

"Victor was in London, but I would call him frequently. Invariably a girlfriend would answer the telephone. Finally I told him I never wanted to see him again. But when I returned for the opening of the London Club, he surprised me at the airport with my parents in tow and luncheon reservations for all of us. He was so crafty! I do have a soft spot for him.

"The London Club opened on July 1, 1966. There were celebrities galore, including Julie Christie, Ringo Starr, Michael Caine and Hugh O'Brian. With all the publicity, thousands of women—and a few men dressed up as women— had applied to be Bunnies. The job was considered glamorous work, but money was the big lure. In 1965, London shop girls and secretaries were earning less than $50 a week, while I made more than a hundred dollars a week as a Door Bunny. That was considered a fortune. Bunnies working in the Showrooms and Casino could earn even more with tips.

"But I no longer wanted to live in England— and after making a stupid remark about English men that was quoted in the newspapers, it was time for me to leave town! Within a week of the opening, I quit. While I still had my visa, I wanted to return to the States and get on with my acting career. It was through Playboy in Chicago that I got my work permit. I did Playmate promotions and, in 1967, worked about six months as a Bunny in New York. I enjoyed that Club the most, primarily because of the marvelous camaraderie among the people working there. I loved

London Club on Park Lane in fashionable Mayfair, 1965.

going to work. And when I was ill with pneumonia, everyone rallied around bringing me food, taking care of me.

"The following year, I moved to Los Angeles determined to pursue my acting career. I was broke and applied for a job at the International House of Pancakes in West Hollywood. I told the manager I had waitressing experience working at the Playboy Club. 'Oh, no,' he said, 'being a Bunny isn't work. You don't know what work is!' I was so angry because he wouldn't even give me a chance. Not long after that, my agent sent me to audition for a role in *Beyond the Valley of the Dolls*. As I drove along Pico Boulevard in my old Dodge Dart toward 20th Century-Fox Studios, I saw a huge bill-board for *Hello, Dolly!* I thought, 'Now there's a Good Omen.' It was—I got the lead role in the film at a salary of $500 a week.

"At about the same time, I began dating Dick Martin, the most wonderful man in the world, who was doing *Laugh-In* with his partner Dan Rowan. The show was a huge breakthrough success. Dick has the most amazing mind and makes me laugh. We've now been married 29 years.

"I believe in laughter—I think a big belly laugh jiggles your insides and keeps you healthy. Certainly happy. It's funny how you always remember the hard times, though. Whenever I went on the road with Dick and Dan, I always refused to eat in an International House of Pancakes, even if it was the only restaurant in town open." ∎

TIA MAZZA

I was sent by Playboy to open the London Club in July 1966. On my 21st birthday I remember sitting in the Dorchester Hotel drinking champagne and thinking 'This is exactly where I want to be, in London, celebrating my birthday and making plans to leave tomorrow for a weekend in Paris.'

"Playboy had selected 10 Bunnies from various U.S. Clubs to train the English girls. I had applied, and when I was chosen, Tony Roma called to ask, 'Do you still want to go?' Of course I did, but I was so timid in those days. It would be the first time I was away from home and my first trip on an airplane.

"During the six months I worked in the London Club, I took every opportunity to travel. Bonnie, an

Bridal Millinery designed by Tia Mazza at New York's Saks Fifth Avenue. The Philadelphia Museum of Art commissioned Tia to design hats for its Hats of the 20th-Century exhibit.

English Bunny I met at the Club, and I zigzagged through Italy, France and Spain, where we ran out of money. When I was detained upon arrival at Heathrow Airport, I told the immigration officer I was a Bunny and that Victor Lownes would vouch for me. Victor had, of course, become notorious in London. The immigration officer came back with a smile and said 'Mr. Lownes is pleased to be your sponsor.'

"In Europe, everyone and everything I encountered was flamboyant, extreme and part of a jet-set culture that was unfamiliar to me. I would never have believed people had such wealth. In the casinos you could watch gamblers placing bets using gold plaques worth £100,000, about $200,000 then. I never thought I would even know someone with that kind of money, but I was with a friend when he lost over $30,000 on a single roll of dice: After losing, my friend looked at me and asked if I would like dinner now or later. He didn't blink. I'd entered another world.

"I was lucky that I had such strong bonds with my family. I could appreciate my London experience without it turning my head. It was an amazing six-month adventure.

"I married in 1969 but continued to work. Playboy spoiled me: They funded my education and gave me a wide latitude in my work schedule. I would often join my husband, a businessman, on his frequent trips to the Orient and Africa, and spent a good deal of my time in our home in Vermont. Although I had a busy personal life, there was no reason for me to quit working. I worked at Playboy over a period of 20 years, beginning in September 1963. I was one of the few Bunnies rehired when the Club reopened after its renovation, and stayed on to work in customer service until the Club closed permanently on August 6, 1983. I wanted to be close to my friends at Playboy, and there was always something going on there that I wanted to be a part of.

"While I was at Playboy, I took advantage of their tuition assistance program. I began designing hats when I took a course at the Fashion Institute of Technology. One day someone in class said, 'You know, you could sell those hats.' I went to Barneys and showed the buyer my hats. I was trembling so much that the woman said, 'Tia, calm down, we're taking everything.' They did—and then ordered more. That was the beginning of my millinery career." ∎

Left: London Club Casino, 1966.

Below:VIP Room, London, 1966.

Tokyo

Tokyo

BUNNIES ON THE GINZA

Bunny Yuriko, Tokyo, 1980.

The first Japanese Playboy Club opened in Tokyo December 9, 1976," Judi Bradford recalls. "Several months prior to the opening two Japanese women in their mid-20s were sent to the Los Angeles Playboy Club, where I was the Bunny Mother, and I trained them. They spoke English moderately well and adapted quickly. But when I went as an adviser to open the Club in Tokyo, I faced complete culture shock.

"The first thing that struck me in Tokyo is how much of the advertising featured blond, western-looking models. Once I saw those billboards and posters, I understood why the Japanese

Bunny Director Harriet Bassler opened 15 Playboy Clubs, including the franchise Clubs in Japan.

"Shortly before the doors opened for our first press night in Tokyo, we discovered all the Japanese Bunnies, in costume, tidying and vacuuming the men's rooms. We had to tell them it wasn't necessary to pitch in and clean bathrooms.

"I was instructed to bring only light-haired, full-figured Bunnies from America. Blonde and buxom; those were the requirements. Japanese men felt perfectly comfortable coming on to the blond American girls, but not the Japanese Bunnies. The manager of the Osaka Club spoke no English, but he could sing the lyrics to every single Frank Sinatra song.

"The Club's Japanese owners handpicked all the Japanese Bunnies—which was just as well. The girls I would have chosen were not the ones they chose. I looked for taller girls with some shape to their bodies, who had outgoing personalities and showed some warmth with people. They chose smaller, quieter girls. The Japanese girls were far more shy about undressing in front of one another and having their costumes fitted.

"Another striking difference is that lot of women came to the American Playboy Clubs, while most of the customers in the Japanese Clubs were men.

"The Japanese owners in Nagoya would have preferred to have had geishas on hand, along with the Bunnies."

franchise owner, who also opened a Baskin-Robbins ice cream store in Tokyo, insisted that we bring only tall, blond, bosomy American Bunnies with us for the Club's opening. I'm African-American; as the Bunny Mother in the Los Angeles Club, I hired across all racial and ethnic lines.

"The Japanese clubs were run entirely by Japanese, and employed Japanese Bunnies. I worked with the women through an interpreter, although a few of the women spoke English. Not surprisingly, Japanese men did not readily understand the concept of Bunnies. Social clubs in Japan are patronized mostly by men, and hostesses are available to mingle and drink with the customers. In Japanese clubs, a man could bring his own whisky into the bar and, if a customer wanted more intimate companionship with the hostesses

serving him, it could be arranged. Imagine trying to institute our 'Don't touch the Bunnies' rule.

"While we had to appreciate and adapt to their culture, it was at times difficult. To a Westerner's eye, Japanese women functioned as second-class citizens. For example, after the Japanese Bunnies put on their makeup and costumes, they would clean the bathrooms and do various other chores before going on the floor to serve drinks. They just assumed these menial labors were expected of them. Living accommodations were so expensive in Tokyo that several of the Bunnies used the public baths because they did-n't have facilities where they lived."

Barbara Mack

The third Playboy Club in Japan opened August 16, 1979, occupying one floor in a high-rise office building in Nagoya. I was one of the New York Bunnies who accompanied Bunny Director Harriet Bassler to oversee the training of approximately 25 Japanese Bunnies.

"We were window dressing. The Japanese franchise holders specified that they wanted only American Bunnies who were tall and blond. We were not granted work visas; we were allowed only to observe and consult with the Japanese franchise holders who ran the Club. I was not permitted to wear the Bunny costume. When I was on duty in the Club, I wore the official promotion outfit, a white miniskirt and a black turtleneck with the Bunny logo.

"The big surprise were the geisha girls who moved in on the Bunnies on opening night. Harriet Bassler was appalled when she saw the geishas in action. In complete violation of Playboy protocol, the geishas mingled with Keyholders, passing along drink orders to the Japanese Bunnies as though they were busboys. When a Bunny returned with a tray full of drinks, the geisha would take over serving the customer. Clearly the franchise holders were trying to get around the strict Bunny rules and satisfy their clientele who expected more interaction with the girls. Harriet reported the franchise Club's policy violation to Playboy in Chicago and the following night the geishas were gone. Who knows if they brought the geishas back three months later when we left.

"It was clear that the Japanese perceived Bunnies as performing a similar role to geishas, but considered geishas the superior article. Meanwhile, the Americans looked aghast at the geishas, who sat with their arms around Keyholders, drinking and partying. The Japanese Bunnies were just plain miffed at being treated as errand girls."

Today, Barbara, a real-estate agent, lives in Florida with her son. ∎

Will the Last Bunny Out the Door Please Turn Out the Lights?

"Bunnies for the '80s."

*T*he last remaining Playboy Club in America closed its doors July 31, 1988, in Lansing, Michigan, its memorabilia auctioned off for charity.

Located in the Hilton Inn, the Lansing Club was the last of five Midwestern franchise clubs that the new 32-year-old president of Playboy Enterprises, Christie Hefner, had opened in the 1980s in an attempt to revive the company's Club division. In the end, a reason given by a Hilton Inn official for closing the Lansing Playboy Club was that "it sometimes discourages group meeting planners from selecting the Lansing Hotel." The franchised Playboy Clubs in

Des Moines, Iowa, and Omaha, Nebraska, had closed their doors that spring. The only Playboy Clubs remaining in the world were five franchise clubs in Japan.

Two years earlier, on June 30, 1986, the last three Playboy-owned clubs in New York, Los Angeles and Chicago (the flagship club that had opened February 29, 1960) had closed. Hugh Hefner, declaring Bunnies "passé," personally presided over the closing of the Los Angeles Club in Century City. The Playboy clubs, blamed for corporate losses of $3.5 million in the first three months of 1986, had numbered 22 during the empire's heyday in the 1970s.

The New York Playboy Club at 5 E. 59th St., which had opened in December 1962, closed for 17 months in September 1974 for a complete renovation. The refurbished Club reopened in February 1976 and closed for good seven years later in August 1983. The building was sold for $11 million.

Two years later, on November 6, 1983, Playboy's Empire Club, an updated reincarnation, opened in a new location, the Lexington Hotel on 48th Street. "The Playboy-for-the-'80s" version featured 55 Bunnies wearing a wide range of newly styled costumes with motifs ranging from Carmen Miranda to Michael Jackson, Cupid and Statue of Liberty-inspired outfits that only nominally retained the classic Bunny corset look. Most costumes came with hats rather than Bunny ears, and few sported the old-style collars, cuffs and bow ties.

Ellie Parrino

Ellie Parrino, owner of Miss Ellie's Homesick Bar and Grill in New York's Upper West Side, says, "I wanted to be a princess, but there were no princess jobs. I had platinum blonde hair and wore four pair of eyelashes, so I wasn't exactly typing-pool material. On the train going home one day in 1965, the subway doors opened at the stop on Fifth Avenue at 59th Street. I suddenly realized that's where the Playboy Club had opened. I jumped off the train and the next thing I knew, I was on the seventh floor seeing about a Bunny job.

"I went to work for Playboy a few months after I got married, and soon discovered that I was pregnant. So I never worked as a Table Bunny, but I did work in the gift shop and then got a job working the switchboard. I left Playboy four different times, and always came back to a different job. After I had another child, I worked in catering, then as a room director and a Bunny Mother. When the Playboy Club on 59th and Fifth closed for good in 1983, I stayed on for several months helping to pack things up. I was the last person to walk out the door as the interior of the building was being demolished. I still have dreams about Playboy. It was home to me, and I had the keys to the front door, to the whole kingdom. I think if the Club hadn't closed, I swear I'd still be there."

The most startling addition was the 20 Rabbits—male "Bunnies," if you will—who joined the staff to attract female Keyholders. "We wanted to open a club that would be forward-looking, a club for the '80s and '90s," Christie Hefner said. New memberships sold two-to-one to women. To reflect this gender trend among new Keyholders, three women were appointed to the five-person panel selecting the 75 Bunnies and Rabbits out of the 5,500 job applicants.

"This club comes after the Women's Liberation Movement and the Sexual Revolution," Hefner said at the time. To have a successful club that could work into the 1990s, female customers and male Rabbits were deemed mandatory ingredients. Playboy's Empire Club, the $4 million enterprise that was launched as a prototype for revitalizing the company's remaining Clubs throughout the country, stayed in business only seven months.

Despite the "updating," the Club fell victim to Playboy's old-style image—for both new and veteran Keyholders. The new-style Bunnies were deemed "camp" by the yuppie club-goers, too young even to appreciate their nostalgic value. As discreet as the Playboy name and emblem were at the entrance, it could have been any club anywhere. Meanwhile, there were 70,000 Keyholders from "the good old days" who were turned off by loud music, new Spanish tapas-style grazing food, burlesque-show costumes and scantily dressed MALES serving cocktails. The hybrid did not work.

The embodiment of the magazine's much-vaunted philosophy and life-style, the Playboy Clubs helped spark the Sexual Revolution of the 1960s, but they also sputtered as the revolution rocketed past outmoded images and concepts. Bunnies, daring and unconventional in their day, became as much icons of the past as Roaring '20s Flappers. Even former Bunnies, who loved their jobs, wished the party had ended a decade sooner.

NEW YORK

Judy Bruno Bennett

I was a Bunny for 12 years—sooooo long that I never saw *Saturday Night Live* until the reruns came on. There were things that were happening in the world that I never knew about because my life revolved around Playboy.

"When the Club reopened after renovation in 1975, I went back because I thought it was going to be the way it was—the same fun, the same girls, the same good money. But a lot of the Bunnies that I'd known so well were not rehired. The customers were no longer gentlemen. The Bunny Mother was a different kind of person, without the necessary knowledge and discipline to stay on top of things. The management running the Club was no longer top-notch. Everything fell apart, and Playboy lost its prestige.

"To keep up with the times, the Penthouse was turned into a disco with taped music. For a while Lainie Kazan was brought in to book entertainment in the Playroom, and it came to be known as Lainie's Room. She hired jazz musicians like Joe Pass, Sheila Jordan, Damita Jo, Billy Eckstine and Joe Williams—great talent. But there were not a lot of customers who wanted to hear jazz in the age of disco. The era of glamorous Bunnies and a lively nightclub scene were over.

"The Bunnies themselves were a different breed. Times were changing, and women weren't wearing a lot of makeup. It was the hippie era, and women weren't into glamour. The classic Bunny costume was revamped for the Showrooms. They had us wearing psy-

chedelic costumes with stockings and garters that looked like something that belonged on 42nd Street. It was a joke. And we still had to wear a tail and ears with it!

"After 1975, there were still a lot of girls who were going to college and working to start other careers, but there were also others who just liked to hang out. There were a lot of drugs around in the '70s. Some girls would come down on the floor totally strung out. I don't know how they got away with it, but the Bunny Mother looked the other way. I saw a girl just go really nuts one night in 1981 and I thought, 'Wow, there's something very wrong here.' By that time, we knew the Club was on its way out and would close.

Judy Bruno Bennett.

"Even though I was there during the declining years, I have some great memories. I studied voice while I was at the Club, and in 1980 I was hired to sing in the Playmate Bar for a month. It was a great opportunity. I still do a jazz workshop with Barry Harris in New York.

"I met my husband one night when I was working as a Camera Bunny. The camera wasn't working, and he stopped to help me with it. He was a drummer with the Art Weiss Trio. We weren't supposed to date, but he and I went out to breakfast anyway. We kept our relationship a secret until I left Playboy in 1982.

"The Club at 5 E. 59th St. closed for the last time in 1983 and then reopened briefly, with both male and female Bunnies, at the Hotel Lexington. It wasn't a nightclub. It was a disco on 49th Street in the heart of Hooker Heaven near the Waldorf-Astoria Hotel. I stopped in once to look around, and it was very disappointing.

"More than a decade after the Club finally closed, there's an amazing mystique about Bunnies, just as there is about Ziegfeld Girls. We were waitresses and they were chorus dancers, but there'll always be that aura of glamour and sexuality attached to Bunnies and showgirls.

"If Playboy Clubs still existed today and my daughter wanted to become a Bunny, I would tell her, 'Go for it.' She has a good head, and she could handle it just as I once did. I was not wild and crazy, either. I just had a good time." ∎

CHICAGO
Jacqueline Williams

Jacqueline Williams, an intoxicating ethnic blend of African-American, Jewish and Native American raised in Chicago's South Side, worked as a Bunny for 10 years, beginning in 1974 when she was 21 years old.

"I told my father I was going to apply for a job at Playboy and he gave me the saddest look that I can only translate as, 'Oh, my poor child is going to have her feelings hurt.' I'm 5'8" and in those days, I weighed about 100 pounds. I looked like a Biafran child, but I was hired anyway. The Bunny Mother insisted I do something with my pulled-back hair, which she thought looked too severe. The Bunny Image in the 1970s required big hair, false eyelashes and vivid red lips. I went out and bought a fall and did 'big hair' for about six months—and looked horrid! One day I showed up without the wig, put the Bunny ears on my slicked-back hair and went out on the floor. From that point on, I wore my hair back and looked like me.

"When I started at the Club it was like being at a big party, but it was also a growing experience that was often very amusing. One white girl kept staring at my face because she couldn't believe a black girl could have freckles on her nose. Two different cultures coming face to face and discovering, 'My God, *they* have freckles too.'

"At the time I was hired in 1974, there were 101 Bunnies in the Chicago Club; 10 of them black, two Hispanic, a few Asian, but mostly Caucasian blondes. Most of the black girls had very ethnic features: dark skin, wide nose, the butt, the Afro. And then along came me; not a dog, but not Queen Nefertiti either. I was just very different and became the black girl with the look everyone wanted. Shortly after I was hired, I became a candidate in the 1974 Bunny of the Year contest; I lost, but won the contest in 1982. During that time, not many black girls with complexions as dark as mine were being photographed for magazines, but Jean Louis Ginibre, the editor of *Oui* magazine, loved my look. I did a lot of work for *Oui*, and shot a pictorial for Playboy in Mexico. But when I was photographed for a

Jacqueline Williams in Epicure, the
Neiman Marcus gourmet shop.

Playboy centerfold, I was told my pictures looked too high-fashion, like a nude ad for *Vogue*, rather than the girl-next-door. Nevertheless, I was *Playboy*'s promotion girl in the 1970s, and probably their most-photographed black girl. It was a grand time for me; as a Bunny and a model, I was making more than $50,000 a year.

"People always thought the Playmates were Bunnies—some were—and we were always being asked which issue of *Playboy* we had appeared in. But because of the costume and the mystique of the Bunny Image, Bunnies were always at an advantage over Playmates whenever they appeared together at any function. When I was asked to work as a Bunny greeting guests at a cocktail reception in Amsterdam for the launch of a new magazine, everyone paid more attention to the Bunnies than to the centerfolds.

"During my last five years with Playboy, I was a Training Bunny and a union steward, often troubleshooting in various other Clubs that were opening or running retraining ses-

Gwen Wade

Gwen Wade, one of the original Chicago Bunnies hired in 1960, says, "They finally 'retired' me in 1970, after ten years. I think I must have been the oldest Bunny in existence! But by 1970, the money wasn't there anymore. Business was bad. If six girls were working a Showroom, three were sent home after the first show. The novelty wore off because the Clubs overexpanded. There was a profound difference in the caliber of customer.

"One day I was walking down State Street and passed some garbage men emptying bins. One of them started calling out to me. I thought he was a crazy until I heard him say, 'Bunny Gwen, stop, you waited on us last night!' He told me that he and two friends had chipped in to buy a membership and they all took turns using the key. I didn't mind that they were members, but it was an indication of what was happening with the clientele.

"I had time to prepare myself to do something else and went to beauty school. After I left Playboy I went into partnership with another Bunny and opened a beauty shop. I stay in touch with a number of former Bunnies and we still get together."

sions. At first I thought the 'Bunny Dip' and our stylized table service was the corniest thing I'd ever seen until I compared the level of our service with that in other restaurants. Bunnies weren't just pretty girls; they were well-trained restaurant personnel, always attentive to the customer. We were instilled with a sense of pride in doing our job well and didn't feel demeaned by service. The Bunny Perch was all about remaining on the floor to serve customers, not just displaying yourself. If a woman across the room pulled out a cigarette, it was my pleasure to walk over and light it for her. The language we used was appealing: 'May I refresh your cocktail?' Not 'How 'bout another?'

"Whoever came up with the idea of Bunny Image was probably a genius. I realized during the time I helped negotiate what would turn out to be the final Bunny contract that while Bunny Image was an important union issue, the term was never really defined. A Bunny couldn't claim she was fired because she was too fat or too old—only that she no longer had the Bunny Image. I was so proud of the contract we negotiated because we determined reasonable guidelines for severance pay based on longevity of Bunny Image. But I could also see the handwriting on the wall. Business had dropped off; times were changing.

"Shortly after negotiating that contract, I went to Miami with the Director of Bunnies 'to hire and train new girls,' even though we suspected that Club would be closing in a month or so. After the 'Bunny Hunt,' as these hiring sessions were called, we took the new recruits for dinner. One of the 18-year-olds couldn't believe that I had worked as a Bunny for 10 years, and I heard the Director of Bunnies say, 'Well, I think there's a point when it's time to hang up your ears.' I've never been naive, but I was surprised to hear her say that.

"When I returned to Chicago, I told several of the Bunnies, 'My advice is take your severance money and run.' But I was amazed by their reaction: Some of those girls preferred to be terminated for almost any infraction and leave with nothing rather than be dismissed for Bunny Image. There was something about losing Bunny Image that totally blew them away and ate at their self-esteem.

"I was 30 years old when I left Playboy in 1984. I had stayed 10 years because I'd had a tremendously productive, good time. I had been a union steward and worked closely with management so I knew the Club would be going through a major change, but I don't think even I foresaw the closing of all the Clubs. I left on a strange note: During my last week, the woman who had been Director of Bunnies was actually fired before any of us were terminated, but she had laid the way for the aftermath. I took my severance pay, about $15,000, and went to culinary school.

"In 1985 Rich Melman, the hot restaurateur who had started Ed Debevic's and a lot of other theme restaurants, was hired as a consultant to turn the Playboy Clubs around. I was going to New York on a visit and was invited to a preview of the new Club that was opening in the Hotel Lexington. Everyone was very excited about it, but I walked in and felt like I was in the Hard Rock Café. Hef's pajamas were hanging on the wall. Bunnies were wearing Carmen Miranda and Michael Jackson outfits. Male Bunnies with bare chests, but wearing collars and cuffs, were serving drinks. I returned to Chicago and said, 'I give you six months. Maybe. What most clubs in New York budget for light and sound, you've spent on refurbishment and costumes.' Nobody was happy with my comments, but in six months, the Club was closed. And that's when the doors began to slam closed on all the Playboy Clubs.

"I still have three of my Bunny costumes: a yellow one, my silver Bunny of the Year costume, and the black costume I fought so long and hard to get—because black girls were seldom allowed to wear black costumes.

"I keep in touch with about 30 former Bunnies, many of whom stop in to see me at Epicure, the Neiman Marcus gourmet shop where I work, and once a year I have a brunch for almost 50 former Bunnies." ■

LOS ANGELES

PAT LACEY

I grew up in South Central Los Angeles, a black ghetto at the time but not at all the gang-ridden neighborhood it is today. My parents were hard-working. They were not in a position to pay for my college education, but that wasn't a big deal. I worked to pay for my own education.

"As a teenager, I tagged along with my older sister and her girlfriends one night as they cruised Sunset Strip, the happening street in the early 1960s. As we passed a construction site near the corner of Alta Loma Road, I saw huge white Bunny heads on a fence. I was so excited, hanging out the back window looking at those Playboy Club signs. I knew then that I wanted to be a Bunny.

"In the meantime I went to college, with the idea of going into some branch of law enforcement, and took a part-time job as a pharmacist's assistant in a drugstore that was near the Playboy Club. The pharmacist, who was a Keyholder, urged me to apply for a Bunny job after the Club opened New Year's Eve in 1964. When I turned 21 the following March, I did.

"Three hundred girls showed up for the Bunny Hunt. Alice Nichols, the Bunny Mother, and Joni Mattis, who was assisting her, made little notations on each of our information cards as we left, telling us they would be getting in touch over the weekend. I waited, but didn't get a call.

"On Monday morning, I called Joni and said I'd been out of town all weekend—had they tried to reach me? Joni asked me to

Pat Lacey in the Bunny dressing room, Los Angeles Club, 1967.

describe myself and I told her I was African-American and had worn a pink dress. 'Oh, we've been trying to find you,' she said. 'Get on down here!'

"From my first day, I took pride in being professional about the job. I was taught how to look someone in the eye, handle myself with dignity and make an impression. I was exposed to a wide range of people. I learned something from everyone around me, including the Bunnies who came from every sort of ethnic and social background. I earned very good money. And for those Bunnies going to school, Playboy paid 80 percent of the tuition fees. It was a safe haven.

"I did promotional work for Playboy and appeared on *Playboy After Dark*. I also became close to Barbi Benton, Hef's girlfriend at the time. I think she put in a good word for me, and Hef chose me to be one of the Jet Bunnies.

As women's roles began to change, we caused Playboy's policies to evolve with the times. In 1968, in the days of Angela Davis and the militant Black Panther Movement, I

Pat Lacey, Director of Ring Girls at The Great Western Forum, also works in Playboy's Los Angeles publicity office.

was one of four Bunnies who showed up for work wearing an Afro. I didn't know what the reaction would be but, very shortly, Afros were just another hairdo, and perfectly acceptable.

"I always found Hef supportive. I realize that some of the early rules reflected his desire to preserve a mystique surrounding Bunnies. For example, Bunnies couldn't reveal their last names, wear any personal jewelry, meet husbands or boyfriends in the vicinity of the Club or date a Keyholder. Over time, all of those rules were eliminated. The biggest policy change came in 1967, when the Clubs welcomed women as Keyholders.

"I worked as a Bunny for 13 years. I married and left briefly in 1978 to give birth to my son. One day, the Club's general manager asked me if I wanted to start work as a Day manager. I worked in that capacity for a while and was then hired to be the Bunny Mother.

"Christie Hefner, the new president of Playboy Enterprises in 1982, did everything she could to rejuvenate the Clubs, including designing new costumes and hiring male Bunnies [Rabbits]. But the concept was old. It was time to close. We had about four months' warning of the closure. As the Bunny Mother, it became increasingly difficult for me to keep a good staff in place because everyone was looking for new jobs. It was exhausting work. There were so many directives coming out of Chicago, including the one to keep Bunny costumes under lock and key so they wouldn't disappear as souvenirs.

"At the party on the final night, I couldn't help thinking about the first time I walked into the Playboy Club and saw all those gorgeous women in Bunny costumes—and realized I was one, too. I worked at the Los Angeles Playboy Club for 21 years, until it closed June 30, 1986." ■

Yes, Gloria, There Is Life After Bunnydom

EPILOGUE

"Can we just keep it between us — I mean about having been Playboy Bunnies together?"

William Hamilton, from The New Society

On a warm summer evening in June 1986, my husband and I went to see a movie in Century City Plaza, a commercial and entertainment center in west Los Angeles. A magazine photographer, an old friend and colleague of my husband's, spotted us in line waiting to buy tickets. He was in a hurry and had cameras hanging on his shoulders, but stopped to say hello.

"The Playboy Club's closing tonight," he told us. "You want me to get you in?" How could I say no?

We stepped out of line and followed our friend. We crossed the plaza and rode an escalator to an upper tier of shops and restaurants. High-beam searchlights fanned the sky, drawing a crowd around the door to the Club. I was surprised to find myself genuinely excited and already wondering if I would see anyone I knew.

I had not been inside a Playboy Club since June 1966, my last night on the job in New York almost exactly 20 years earlier. In fact, I hadn't even known there was a Los Angeles Playboy Club in Century City.

I stood at the bar in my cotton dress, scanning the crowd for familiar faces, but my eyes were on the Bunnies. Their costumes were similar to the ones I had worn, but many were in patterns and multicolored prints I'd never seen before. I watched Bunnies saunter up to tables with trays full of drinks, smiling and dipping, making it look easy. I was mesmerized watching them at the service bar as they called in their drink orders and dredged the fruit containers for cocktail garnishes. (I remembered we had called it "garbage.") Lots of chardonnay drinkers, I noticed. I tried to recall if I'd ever served even a single glass of wine during the entire time I was a Bunny. In the early '60s people drank whiskey with their steaks, and we carried trays laden with gimlets, Manhattans, rusty nails and white Russians.

So much had changed for me—and the world around me—in the 20 years since I had worked as a Bunny. Yet, as I mentally ran through the call-in order from Scotch to cordials, I felt that, in a sense, no time at all had passed. I could probably pick up a tray and pitch in right now, I thought, and wouldn't it be fun to zip myself into a Bunny costume again— silly thoughts for a woman in her 40s. I looked around, mindful that this was the Last Night, the last time I would have a chance to glimpse this brief scene from my past, and savored my memories.

■ ■ ■ ■

I said "wow" and "holy cow" quite a lot in those days—and so did a lot of other wide-eyed, eager young women like me who arrived in New York fresh out of school with dreams of pursuing a career. At the Playboy Club, I met people from so many different backgrounds, people I could never have met in college or anywhere else in such numbers and variety. I won't ever forget the knish I ate at Coney Island my third day in New York, or my first bowl of *vichyssoise* (that tasted suspiciously like my mother's potato soup) in a French café near Bloomingdale's. That period of my life was a time for me to disconnect/reconnect: to leave the small-town girl behind, split from my past (as warm and nurturing as it had been) and take charge of my life. Nothing was ever the same for me again.

More than that, it felt as if I had stood on that very spot in time when everything about our society seemingly changed in an instant. I recall those easy, early liberating days of panty hose and The Pill. Incredibly, women still wore hats and gloves, but no longer considered wearing a girdle *de rigueur*. How can one explain to girls of today that lithe, Twiggy-thin young women once wore girdles routinely, not to contain any excess flesh, but because they needed the garters to hold up their stockings? Imagine the thrilling day when one replaced Playtex with panty hose; that moment happened for me when I pulled on my very first pair of sheer black Danskins at the Playboy Club. Wow, these weren't the thick dance tights I wore for mime classes at the Academy. Holy cow, I can wear these in flesh tones with a dress. This was at least a year before panty hose actually took the country by storm.

The Pill and its alternative companion, the IUD, were other items I learned about in the Bunny dressing room. Again, how can one explain that in a roomful of very pretty, nubile young women between the ages of 18 and 21, many (most?) were still virgins? Including me. By choice. We had necked and petted our way through most of our teenage years, managing to stay intact because one careless mistake most often meant not just an unwanted pregnancy, but an unwanted marriage. Abortion was illegal, costly and dangerous. The combination of those circumstances provided us with very clear-cut choices; I was among that number not about to foolishly squander my future, or subject myself to the horror and anguish of kitchen-table butchery. Then along came The Pill and The IUD. Overnight, our world became a sexual playground. Peter Yates' 1969 film, *John and Mary* about two people (Dustin Hoffman and Mia Farrow), who meet in a singles' bar, make love and wake up in the morning not knowing each other's names, is practically a documentary of that time.

I also remember staring at my very first Playboy payroll check. Again, wow, holy cow. I had already pocketed my daily tip money in cash. But at the end of my second week, I was holding a check in my hands that represented my hourly wages and signed tips, less the cost of a pair of Danskin tights, and it was more money than I knew my Dad earned in a week. Holy cow. On the one hand, embarrassed and feeling a pang of nonspecific guilt, I knew this was a piece of news I would not share with my parents. On the other hand, my 19-year-old sensibilities seized the brand-new idea that I not only could take care of myself, but also do it in style. I could pay my way through school, and afford theatre tickets and long-distance calls home on the holidays. I could afford to splurge $16 on a haircut, shampoo and set at Vidal Sassoon's beauty salon, Charles of the Ritz. When I sat down to dinner with "Bunny Marie" in the employees' lounge at the Playboy Club one February evening in 1963, and learned that she had already graduated from college and traveled to Europe, I was not in the least envious. It was entirely within my realm of newly perceived possibilities to graduate from the Academy, plan a trip to Europe and live the glamorous, eventful life I imagined she led as one of the older Night Bunnies.

At the same time, Gloria (Bunny Marie) Steinem was gathering her notes for her *Show* magazine article, the *Saturday Evening Post* was preparing a piece on the Playboy Club, in which Bunnies were described as "half geisha and half-double malted, in a swimsuit that shows what swimsuits show. To Club members, a wiggling, giggling invitation to 'let's pretend' sin; to Playboy promotion writers, 'a beautiful, personable, fun-loving girl who is working in the most exciting and glamorous setting in the world of show business.' " To the women who worked as Bunnies, I would like to add: "ambitious, resourceful and precocious precursors to the Sexual and Feminist Revolutions."

As I write this, more than 30 years since I "retired my satin ears," and more than 10 years after the last Playboy Club closed, passions and phobias about Bunnies still abound. While pretty girls have served food and drink to paying customers for centuries, the "serving wenches" who became Playboy Bunnies must hold the record for being both the most celebrated and most maligned waitresses in history.

In 1960, the Playboy Club reinvented the job description and the glorified waitress, no experience required, became an institution: the Playboy Bunny. The Bunny Image was that of a young, fresh-faced girl with a woman's body, innocent and alluring at the same time. She was chosen for her brains, beauty and personality, and was expected to have aspirations beyond any employment category the club could offer. Potential Bunnies were recruited through newspaper ads targeting college girls and aspiring models and actresses, not want ads for "restaurant help." Every nightclub in town had food, drink and entertainment, but customers went to the Playboy Club to see the Bunnies. The gorgeous girls in the (hardly by today's standards) scanty satin costumes with the perky Bunny ears and puffy tail were the primary lure attracting customers to the Clubs around the world for 25 years.

Again, I feel that I stood in that very spot of time when, in a blink, I saw the possiblilites for a future in which a young woman could aspire to anything and not have to be relegated to the limitations others defined for her. Imagine my frustration, then, to find that, even today, many carry around the image of the women I worked with as so haplessly downtrodden under the Playboy Club yoke that they couldn't possibly have known exactly what they were doing, that they were not capable of making shrewd and conscious choices on their own. Thus, thanks in part to Gloria Steinem's "women-as-victim" mode, Bunnies are frozen in amber, forever young and dumb, the archetypical female sexual objects forced into positions of servitude to men. My point of view: We willingly exploited our sexuality and, as Bunnies, also exploited our intelligence, wit, upper arm strength, youthful exuberance and full range of survival instincts. We saw an opportunity and grabbed it.

At the same time that I was working my way through school as a Playboy Bunny, my brother back in Minnesota, who is a year younger than I am, found part-time jobs packing takeout in a Chinese restaurant and bagging groceries in a supermarket, earning a minimum wage that exploited *his* youth and inexperience. It's true neither of his jobs required him to wear a brief satin costume with matching pumps, but then I would hardly consider that any more demeaning than humping bags of groceries to an icy parking lot throughout a long, frigid Minnesota winter. Frankly, I would rather have worked as a Bunny serving cocktails than filling cartons with chop suey, too. The argument is often made that women had fewer good job opportunities at that time. To get ahead, we had to be resourceful. On the other hand, my brother wonders ruefully just what options young guys of that time had to earn the kind of money I could as a Playboy Bunny.

It would be nice if Gloria Steinem could be gracious enough to admit that she perhaps sold some of these women short in 1963—even as she takes well-earned credit for implanting some of the feminist concepts that made their later successes and achievements possible.

But had my path not crossed with hers again several years ago, I'm sure it would never have occurred to me to look into Life After Bunnydom, or track down the women I worked with 30 years ago in the New York Playboy Club. Almost all of the women I got in touch with wanted to know up front whether or not I had positive feelings about having worked as a Playboy Bunny. Many of the women, particularly those who didn't know me personally, were initially cautious about being interviewed; they made it clear they did not want to talk with me if I felt critical of the women who had worked as Bunnies.

"Be honest about it, Kay," Marcia Donen Roma said. "Just tell it like it really was."

I have attempted to do so, and in the course of writing about our Bunny years, I have had the enormous personal satisfaction and enjoyment of renewing friendships with a great many exceptional women. Among them, Lauren Hutton, who had begun this whole journey with me the day in 1963 when we were both hired as Bunnies. We met again, after many years, on Wilshire Boulevard in Beverly Hills. "My God, it's Lady Kathryn!" she laughed upon seeing me. I'd forgotten that had been my nickname at the Club, bestowed on me, very possibly, by Lauren herself. We fell to talking as though no time at all had passed. The supermodel, still at the top of her profession after the age of 50, was filming four independent features back-to-back, had launched a line of eyeglasses (REM), filmed the documentary *Little Warriors* with her boyfriend, director Luca Babini, had gone wreck diving in Pearl Harbor, was stumping for the Women's Campaign Fund and writing her autobiography. Back in her hotel room, laughing and talking about mutual friends, I helped her stuff the last of her belongings into an already overstuffed bag before her flight back to New York. "God, I'd love to see everyone again. Let's get together."

"We will," I assured her, and gave her telephone numbers of several of our "Bunny" friends.

On my way home, I realized it was Lauren who had best summed up my own feelings about the Bunny years when she had said:

We were young women on the move, out there pushing a new frontier. We were like sisters learning together how to take charge of our own lives. We protected each other. We were a rare bouquet.

Appendix

UNITED STATES	
Chicago	2/29/60
Miami	5/10/61
New Orleans	10/5/61
*St. Louis	10/16/62
New York	12/8/62
*Phoenix	12/19/62
Detroit	12/28/63
Kansas City	6/13/64
Cincinnati	9/16/64
Los Angeles	1/1/65
Boston	2/26/65
Atlanta	3/6/65
San Francisco	11/13/65
Denver	12/9/67
Baltimore	7/11/77
Dallas	7/27/77
*Buffalo	4/24/81
*St. Petersburg	5/8/81
*San Diego	12/17/81
*Lansing	9/17/82
*Columbus	12/7/82
Omaha	5/18/84
Des Moines	12/3/84

* Franchise Club

PHILIPPINES	
*Manila	1/ - /64

UNITED KINGDOM	
London	7/1/66
Clermont	3/6/72
Manchester	12/13/73
Portsmouth	12/ - /72
Victoria Casino	3/ - /80

RESORT HOTELS	
Jamaica	1/4/65
Montreal	7/15/67
Lake Geneva	5/6/68
Chicago Towers	11/1/70
Miami Plaza	12/22/70
Great Gorge	12/22/71
Bahamas	4/11/78
Atlantic City	4/14/81

JAPAN	
*Tokyo	12/9/76
*Osaka	2/1/78
*Nagoya	7/16/79
*Sapporo	4/25/80

SPECIAL ADDENDUM FOR THE BUNNY MANUAL FOR THE NEW YORK PLAYBOY CLUB TO
BECOME EFFECTIVE UPON THE INSTITUTION OF CABARET ENTERTAINMENT IN THE CLUB

1. Bunnies are expressly forbidden to provide any personal
   information, date or _mingle_ with any cabaret performers at
   the Club.

2. Bunnies are expressly forbidden to _mingle_ or fraternize with
   patrons within the Club at any time and we have instructed
   Willmark Service Systems to report any instances of mingling,
   before, during or after the cabaret entertainment or at
   any other time.

3. All service is to be suspended during cabaret entertainment
   and Bunnies are to leave the room and to wait in the service
   bar area until performances are concluded.

4. The prohibitions against mingling indicated above relate to
   cabaret entertainment are for purposes of emphasis and are
   not to be construed as permitting mingling at any other time.

5. Mingling at the New York Playboy Club _at any time_ will result
   in immediate dismissal.

6. Bunnies are forbidden to dance with patrons of the Club under
   any circumstances. For the purpose of definition, dancing
   by Bunnies is to be construed as mingling.

7. Under no circumstances are Bunnies to be photographed with
   patrons of the Club. Bunnies photographed with patrons are
   to be regarded as mingling.

Arnold J. Morton

**PLAYBOY
CLUB
BUNNY
MANUAL**

ON THE FLOOR

"Bunny Dip".......When a Bunny sets napkins or drinks on
the far end of a table, she does not
awkwardly reach across the table -- she
does the "Bunny Dip." This keeps her
tray away from the patrons and enables
her to give graceful, stylized service.
The "Bunny Dip" is performed by arch-
ing the back as much as possible, then
bending the knees to whatever degree is
necessary. Raise the left heel as you bend
the knees.

"Bunny Stance"..... When in view of patrons, a Bunny should
stand in a slightly exaggerated model's
stance -- legs together, back arched,
hips tucked well under.

"Busing a table".... To take away all dirty glasses and to put
the table in order for the next party.

"Perching".........To sit, or "perch," on the back of a chair,
sofa or on a railing while waiting to be of
service. Never "perch" too close to where
a patron is seated.

ABBREVIATIONS USED ON CHECKS

☐ .... On the rocks   T ....Lemon twist

L .... Lime wedge   X..........Extra dry
      (squeeze of lime)

MERIT - DEMERIT SCHEDULE

Section 520.21 - Appendix "A"

I.   GENERAL

A Bunny who accrues 100 merits is awarded the sum of $25.00.

A Bunny who accrues 100 demerits is dismissed from the Playboy Club.

Merits cancel demerits at the rate of one merit cancelling one demerit.

A Bunny's demerits are automatically cancelled on the date of her yearly anniversary of employment with the Playboy Club.

A Bunny who transfers to another Playboy Club carries her merits and/or demerits with her.

II.   MERITS

Merits can be gained for the following helpful considerations done at the request of the Playboy Club:

1. Bunny of the Week---------------------------------25 merits

   That Bunny who has done the most through her personality, attitude and cooperation to enhance the reputation of the Playboy Club during the preceding week in the eyes of the Room Directors and Bartenders with whom she has worked. No Bunny can become "Bunny of the Week" if she has received demerits during that week.

2. Bunny of the Week Votes----------------------1 merit per vote

   The "Bunny of the Week" receives 25 merits, but all other Bunnies who received votes are granted the number of merits equal to the actual number of votes received. Bar check errors of any kind, although in many cases demeritable, will not be grounds for loss of Bunny of the Week votes and merits.

3. Bunny Voluntarily Placing Herself on Reserve--------15 merits

   When any given Club is up to strength, Bunnies will be asked to put themselves on reserve rather than be on the actual schedule.

521. 6   # TOOLS OF SERVICE
Your Properly Equipped Serving Tray

A) Pens

B) Playboy Lighter

C) Tax Chart
(under Tip Tray)

D) Tip Tray

E) Playboy matches
(on Tip Tray)

F) Clean Ash Trays
(on Tip Tray)

G) Bar Rag or Sponge
(under Napkins)

H) Napkins

I) Bar Checks
(set on top of equipment)

BUNNY COSTUME ACCESSORIES

FLASHLIGHT

ROSETTE AND NAMEPLATE
worn on right hip

NICKEL WRAPPED
IN DOLLAR BILL
FOR PURCHASE OF
CIGARETTES

PROPER TRAY SET-UP

Make sure that all glasses into which the Bartender pours directly touch the rim of the tray. Note that the glasses into which the Bartender pours the same liquor or drink are arranged so that the glass rims touch.

Top View

Front View

CALLING IN YOUR DRINK ORDER

(Commit to Memory)

PROPER SEQUENCE FOR DRINK ORDERS:

①	Scotch Whisky	⑨	Brandy (including cognac brandies)
②	Canadian Whiskey	⑩	Cordials & Liqueurs
③	Bourbon & Blended Whiskey	⑪	Mixed Drinks
④	Rye Whiskey	⑫	Blended Drinks
⑤	Irish Whiskey	⑬	Creamed Drinks
⑥	Gin	⑭	Beer & Ale
⑦	Vodka	⑮	Wine
⑧	Rum	⑯	Mugged Drinks
		⑰	Irish Coffee

- -

When you have an order that involves different types of liquor and specific name brands of liquor, always "call in" the type of liquor first and the name brand last. For example, if you were given the following order:

①	Scotch & Soda	⑥	Martini
②	Bourbon & Water	⑦	Heineken's Beer
③	Bourbon & Coke	⑧	Old Forester & Water
④	Cutty Sark & Water	⑨	Tom Collins
⑤	7-7	⑩	Pink Lady

The proper ordering sequence would be:

①	Scotch	⑥	7 Crown
②	Cutty Sark	⑦	Martini
③ ④ } 2 bourbon		⑧	Tom Collins
		⑨	Pink Lady
⑤	Old Forester	⑩	Heineken's

Note that you have ordered the ① Scotch first, then the name brand Scotch -- ② Cutty Sark, then ③ & ④ bourbon (since there are two orders of bourbon, say "two bourbon"), then the brand name of bourbon and blend -- ⑤ Old Forester and ⑥ Seagram's 7 Crown, then the mixed drink -- ⑦ martini, then the blended drink -- ⑧ Tom Collins, then the creamed drink -- ⑨ Pink Lady and last, the beer -- ⑩ Heineken's.

521.3   THE PROPER GARNISH TO STAGE YOUR DRINKS

Always place garnish on a Playboy pick except if it is lemon twist or lime wedge
(squeeze).

Bloody Mary.......... lime wedge

Brandy Alexander...... sprinkle of nutmeg

Champagne Cocktail.... lemon twist (sugar cube with bitters)

Collins .... cherry, orange(or pineapple) slice, tall straws

Cuba Libre........... lime wedge

Daiquiri, frozen .... cherry on top, cocktail straws

Flamingo............. cherry, orange(or pineapple) slice, tall straws

Fruit Punch.......... cherry, orange(or pineapple) slice, lime circle, tall straws
    (non-alcoholic)
Gibson .... onion

Gimlet .... lime circle

Manhattan............. cherry
    Perfect Manhattan.... lemon twist
    Dry Manhattan....... lemon twist
Marguerita............ rim glass with salt

Martini .... olive
    Dry Martini........ lemon twist
Mist or Frappé........ shaved ice, cocktail straws (Mist gets a twist)

Old Fashioned......... cherry, orange(or pineapple) slice, lemon twist

Planter's Punch........ cherry, orange(or pineapple) slice, tall straws

Rabbit Punch.......... cherry, orange(or pineapple) slice, lime circle

Rob Roy.............. lemon twist
    Perfect Rob Roy..... lemon twist
    Dry Rob Roy........ lemon twist
Señor Playboy......... lime wedge

Sidecar.............. rim glass with lime and frost with sugar

Slings............... cherry, orange(or pineapple) slice, tall straws

Soft Drinks........... (only when served to ladies) cherry, orange(or pineapple)
                      slice, tall straws
Sours................ cherry, orange(or pineapple) slice

Tonic Drinks......... lime wedge

GLASSES

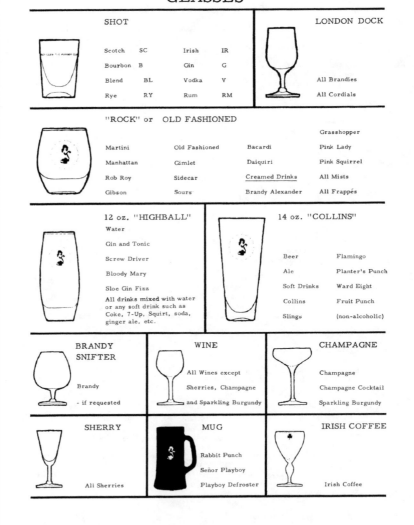

SHOT				LONDON DOCK
Scotch	SC	Irish	IR	
Bourbon	B	Gin	G	
Blend	BL	Vodka	V	All Brandies
Rye	RY	Rum	RM	All Cordials

"ROCK" or OLD FASHIONED

			Grasshopper
Martini	Old Fashioned	Bacardi	Pink Lady
Manhattan	Gimlet	Daiquiri	Pink Squirrel
Rob Roy	Sidecar	Creamed Drinks	All Mists
Gibson	Sours	Brandy Alexander	All Frappés

12 oz. "HIGHBALL"

Water

Gin and Tonic

Screw Driver

Bloody Mary

Sloe Gin Fizz

All drinks mixed with water or any soft drink such as Coke, 7-Up, Squirt, soda, ginger ale, etc.

14 oz. "COLLINS"

Beer	Flamingo
Ale	Planter's Punch
Soft Drinks	Ward Eight
Collins	Fruit Punch
Slings	(non-alcoholic)

BRANDY SNIFTER

Brandy

- if requested

WINE

All Wines except Sherries, Champagne and Sparkling Burgundy

CHAMPAGNE

Champagne

Champagne Cocktail

Sparkling Burgundy

SHERRY

All Sherries

MUG

Rabbit Punch

Señor Playboy

Playboy Defroster

IRISH COFFEE

Irish Coffee

Index

Frontispiece and illustrations: LeRoy Neiman, pages 47, 93, 103, 113

Cartoon, William Hamilton, page 271

Elliott Erwitt, Magnum Photos Inc, pages 18, 120, 140

Ben Martin, pages 32, 35, 61, 63, 67, 72, 73, 76, 77, 83, 85, 87, 89, 91, 98, 99, 101, 109, 132, 136, 143, 166, 169, 171, 175, 178, 179, 181, 187, 192, 196, 212, 225, 229, 232, 236, 242, 249, 252, 254, 264, 266

Courtesy Joyce Nizzari, page 52

Jim Frank, *Chicago Sun-Times,* page 79

AP/Wide World Photos, pages 122, 134, 164

New York Daily News, page 126, 129

Norman Currie, Corbis-Bettman, page 130

Courtesy Barbara Bosson, page 139

Fred W. McDarrah, page 141

Guy Gross, 142

Tanya Burnett, page 146

LaSpada/DeCaro, page 146

Mary Ann Halpin, page 149, 153

Beverly M. Sawyer, page 152

Courtesy Chialing Young, 154, 155, 156

Carl Iri, page 163

Sheldon Gottsman, *NY Journal-American,* page 166

Greg Gorman, 184

Courtesy Anna Lederer, page 185

Juliann Lucas, page 190

Bill Dobbins, page 191

Courtesy Denise McAdams, page 193

Courtesy Jacklyn Zeman, page 198

Courtesy Tia Mazza, page 199

Courtesy Mary Chipman, page 201

Courtesy Cheryl McArthur, page 204, 205

Courtesy Liz Doyle, page 209

Mario Casilli/ABC, Inc. © 1998; page 218

Courtesy Julie Cobb, 230

Courtesy Bonnie Katz, page 231

Kathryn Leigh Scott is an actress, author and publisher who lives with her husband Geoff Miller in Los Angeles and London. Few book projects have given Ms. Scott the enormous personal satisfaction and enjoyment as has *The Bunny Years*, not least because it has enabled her to renew friendships with so many exceptional women.

Printed in the United States
By Bookmasters